LIBRARY maSHUPS

Exploring new ways to deliver library data

EDITED BY
NICOLE C. ENGARD

facet publishing

© Nicole C. Engard 2009

Published by Facet Publishing,
7 Ridgmount Street, London WC1E 7AE
www.facetpublishing.co.uk

Facet Publishing is wholly owned by CILIP: the Chartered Institute
of Library and Information Professionals.

First published in the USA by Information Today, Inc., 2009
This UK edition 2009

British Library Cataloguing in Publication Data
A catalogue record for this book is available from the
British Library.

ISBN 978-1-85604-703-6

Printed and bound in the United States of America.

To Brian for his patience, support, and love,
to my father for sharing his creative drive, and
to my mother for giving me her strength

Contents

Acknowledgments

I would like to thank many people for their help in making this guide a reality. First, I must thank Rachel Singer Gordon for asking me to write a book for the last 3 years and supporting me while I was working on it. Second, I have to thank Kathy Coon, my mentor, for urging me to write my first library technology article. Without that push I wouldn't be here today.

I'd also like to thank the many authors who contributed to this title, to create a wide-reaching overview of mashups for libraries. Without all of your contributions, this book wouldn't exist. Last, I thank my husband, Brian, and my children (shelties Coda and Beau) for their understanding while I spent more time with my computer than with them over the past year.

Acknowledgements

About the Website

mashups.web2learning.net

Each chapter in this book references websites with definitions and examples of mashups. Although links to each of these can be found in Appendix A, the web is not static, and links may move or disappear; even during the editing of this book, several have changed.

For that reason, I will be maintaining mashups.web2learning.net, a website that will retain an up-to-date list of links for you to reference whenever you'd like. This website will also save you the trouble of having to type cumbersome links by hand; just visit mashups. web2learning.net and choose either the *Links* page or the chapter the link appeared in from the table of contents, and you will be able to click through to visit the site.

Should you notice any broken links on the site or in the book, please feel free to email me updates at nengard@gmail.com.

Disclaimer

Neither the publisher nor the author make any claim as to the results that may be obtained through the use of this webpage or of any of the Internet resources it references or links to. Neither publisher nor author will be held liable for any results, or lack thereof, obtained by the use of this page or any of its links; for any third-party charges; or for any hardware, software, or other problems that may occur as the result of using it. This webpage is subject to change or discontinuation without notice at the discretion of the publisher and author.

Foreword

The book you hold in your hands is about possibilities and inspiration. As I read through the chapters of *Library Mashups*, I was struck by the language used by the various authors. The majority of chapters include the term "easy" or "easily," a reflection of one of the major strengths of applying Web 2.0 principles to libraries.

In fact, reading through the book, it becomes clear how libraries are using these new tools to implement traditional library values in a way that hasn't been possible online until now. We're used to applying words like free, value, robust, enrich, and opportunities to physical library services, but we've been less able to apply these terms to our online services. In fact, our catalogs (often our most valuable online asset) are usually described in the opposite terms—cumbersome, silo, difficult, arcane, and closed.

What a welcome change it is to read a book that includes an entire section on library catalogs and uses such positive and optimistic words as "any," "all," "social," and "open." And not just "open source," but "open access" and "open data," all of which support the mission of libraries: open and unfettered access to ideas and information. The chapters you'll find here highlight ways libraries can repurpose third-party data and tools to enrich their own services, as well as how to free their own resources to live outside the confines of their own websites.

A secondary theme to this book can be summed up in two specific word sets: easy/quick and just do/simply. None of these words tend to be used when discussing maintenance of library websites, and yet the authors in this text continually note how easy it is to get started mashing up data, particularly in the first section. Every reader will find something of value in these case studies, whether you're a "newbie" beginner or a veteran programmer. The ideas expressed and made concrete are not just "we could do this." Every author includes specific examples showing what can be done here and now, not someday, and for a variety of content types, not just catalogs or web pages. The inclusion of working examples for a coin collection, digital image archive, video archive, and even a campus map show how librarians can add great value using these new tools.

Even more impressive is the constant attention to and discussion of larger issues such as ownership of data, copyright, and accurate metadata. So many resources that explain mashups cover only the technical aspects of using a third-party, likely commercial, service. In this work, however, it's clear that these libraries carefully considered all of the ramifications of using the tools they chose and implemented specific procedures to maintain copies of the data within their own domains in case something suddenly happened to the external provider. This type of forethought is sure to be valuable in the future, and too many resources on this topic fail to even mention this issue, let alone provide plans for dealing with it. This book is a unique and valuable resource for this quality alone.

While some in our profession have questioned the value of Web 2.0, and its corollary Library 2.0, this book illustrates not only what is different from the past but also how libraries can continue adding new value in the future. Creatively utilizing these new tools has empowered libraries to experiment and create new resources, as well as enhance traditional ones. Pay attention as you read to the sense of empowerment that permeates the authors' writings, and you'll realize that the changes we're seeing online are not a harbinger of doom for libraries. Rather, they are a promise for our future. As most of the authors note, they were able to accomplish great things with limited resources, little to no budget, and relatively few staff (sometimes just one person). While resources vary greatly from library to library, there is surely something here that will inspire you and make you think differently about some service your library currently offers.

Dream big, and set your content free.

—Jenny Levine
The Shifted Librarian

Introduction

Nicole C. Engard

I designed my first website in 1997. I use the word *designed* lightly, as it was full of gaudy background images—and at least one animated graphic on each page! I was so proud of that site, as I'm sure many of us were when we created our first. However, times have changed, and the tools have gotten so much better.

That first website was a hint into my future: It was a collection of all of my bookmarks organized into categories for easy browsing. (Sound like a future librarian to you?) I created a resource that my friends and family used when they needed to find information online. After years of maintaining this website with only simple HTML, I became frustrated by the lack of an easy way to keep things up-to-date and abandoned it.

It took more than 10 years, but the day is finally here when I can re-create that website (without the flashy images and gaudy background, of course) and easily maintain a collection of useful links with my friends, family, and colleagues. That website is the companion to this book, found at mashups.web2learning.net. It was created using a simple mashup of my Delicious bookmarks (www.delicious. com/librarymashups) and a WordPress (www.wordpress.org) blog—a method I learned from reading a chapter in this book.

Mashups (as many of the contributors to this title will tell you) are web applications that use content from more than one source to create a single new service, displayed in a single graphical interface. This means that I can bookmark all of the links found in this book and share them with you on my WordPress-powered website with minimal effort. In fact, I just had to check a few boxes on a form and then copy and paste a snippet of code.

The following chapters will share similar methods and tips that will help you graduate your library website from its static form to a dynamic, easy-to-maintain tool that your patrons will return to over and over. Libraries and library-related groups around the world share their mashup experiences in hopes of showing you that updating your website does not have to be a full-time job—and does not have to be a chore you dread.

Although the Delicious mashup I used for my website was practically effortless, it is important to note that not all mashups are that simple. Some of the authors in this book go to great lengths to detail exactly how mashups work and the technology behind them. While this information is both important and useful, don't let it scare you off from trying to use mashups in your own library. In many cases, web applications (like Delicious) will provide graphical interfaces to make mashing up data as simple as filling in a form.

The first section of this book, "What Are Mashups?," introduces mashup terminology and provides general reference sources to continue your mashup education. While reading these chapters, and the rest of the book, remember to turn to Appendix B for a glossary of terms, which will help when you come across a term that you don't know or remember.

In the second section of this book, "Mashing Up Library Websites," the authors show you how to use mashups to improve your static library website. These chapters outline how sites you may currently be using for fun and personal organization can be turned into powerful tools for delivering information to your patrons and showing the human side of your library.

In the third section, "Mashing Up Catalog Data," things get a bit technical as the authors show us how to pull valuable information out of our integrated library systems in order to remix it and improve its visibility to our patrons. As we all know, getting information out of most library catalogs (with the exception of open source offerings) is nearly, if not actually, impossible—but these authors don't let that discourage them, and neither should you.

In the fourth section, "Maps, Pictures, and Video ... Oh My!" we see how libraries are using some of the most popular types of mashups. By using tools such as Google Maps (maps.google.com), Flickr (www.flickr.com), and blip.tv (blip.tv), these libraries are able to create entirely new tools for their patrons, improving patrons' online experiences and providing superior service.

Last but not least, the fifth section, "Adding Value to Your Services," gives you additional mashup ideas for making your library's online presence that much more valuable to patrons. Ideas like adding data from LibraryThing (www.librarything.com) to your library site and pushing your local repository data out to other campus resources show you that the power of mashups can be harnessed by anyone with a will to make a change.

The goal of this guide is to teach you the basics of what mashups are and how they have been used in libraries worldwide. It is my hope that after reading this book, you will be inspired to make at least one change to your library site. This can be as simple as copying and pasting a bit of code into your site or adding a collection of ever-changing links. Take what you learn from these authors and add a dash of your own imagination; you'll be surprised what can evolve.

Part I

What Are Mashups?

CHAPTER 1

What Is a Mashup?

Darlene Fichter
University of Saskatchewan Library

A mashup is a web application that uses content from more than one source to create a single new service displayed in a single graphical interface. For example, you could combine the addresses and photographs of your library branches with a Google map to create a map mashup (Figure 1.1). The term *mashup* originally comes from pop music, where people seamlessly combine music from one song with the vocal track from another—thereby mashing them together to create something new.

Mashups have recently exploded on the web, for two main reasons. First, many of the major internet companies, such as Yahoo! (www.yahoo.com), Google (www.google.com), and Amazon (www.amazon.com), have opened up their data to be used with other data sources without a lengthy licensing negotiation. In just a minute or two, you can set up and use the data resources they make available. The other reason for this rapid growth is the advent of new tools that make creating mashups easy for anyone, regardless of their technical know-how.

Popular Mashups

The most popular type of mashup is a map mashup. Map mashups make up 36 percent of the mashups tracked by ProgrammableWeb (www.programmableweb.com), the most comprehensive listing of mashups. Figure 1.2 shows the distribution of mashups by type.

Other types of popular mashups mix video and photos. For example, the Viral Video Chart (viralvideochart.unrulymedia.com) site tracks

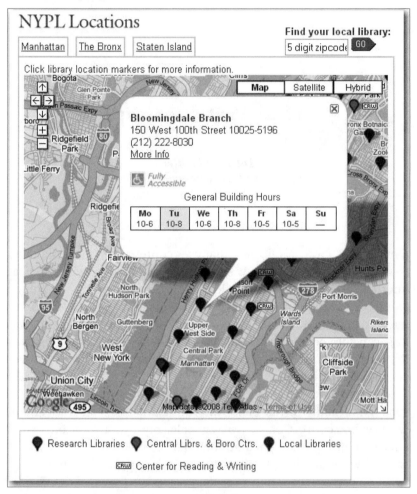

Figure 1.1   Google Maps mashup of New York Public Library branches

YouTube (www.youtube.com), MySpace (www.myspace.com), and Google Video (video.google.com) in order to identify the most talked about new clips, overall and by category (Figure 1.3).

There are many wonderful mashup services built using photos. Here are three examples to spark your imagination:

1. Colr Pickr (krazydad.com/colrpickr), developed by Jim Bumgardner, lets you search Flickr (www.flickr.com) photos by color. Flickr is a widely used photo-sharing site (offering both free and professional accounts) that attracts many libraries and librarians. Use Colr Pickr to click on a

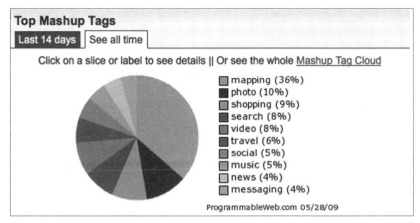

Figure 1.2   Pie chart showing popularity of different types of mashups

VIRAL VIDEO CHART Compiled by Unruly Media

Home   Right Now   Ads   Animals   Brands   Celebs   Funny   Games   Movies   Music   Politics   Soccer   Tech

Top 20 Viral Videos

✉ Send to a Friend   RSS

Top in 24 hours   7 days   30 days   **365 days**

1   Susan Boyle Stuns Crowd with Epic Singing

Break   13564 new posts   157,189,753 views

2   Oren Lavie - Her Morning Elegance

Dailymotion   6481 new posts   9,900,878 views

3   Where the Hell is Matt? (2008), une vidéo de BriKO. where, the, hell, matt, pays

Dailymotion   6123 new posts   22,035,092 views

4   Christian the Lion

Metacafe   4722 new posts   49,204,309 views

5   David After Dentist

YouTube   4409 new posts   24,229,511 views

Figure 1.3   Most talked-about videos for the past 365 days

color in a photo or color wheel, and it will retrieve photos that have a large concentration of that color.

2. There are also mashup tools that use photographs to create books, posters, magazine covers, and so on. Most of us have received photograph booklets comprised of stunning images with short captions. One way to create these photograph books is to use a mashup tool called Bookr (www. pimpampum.net/bookr). Start by searching Flickr to locate images. Then, add these photos to a booklet page and type in your caption. Save your work, and email the book to friends or publish it on your blog or library website.

3. A mashup tool called Ad Generator (theadgenerator.org), created by Alexis Lloyd for his MFA thesis project, is intended to inform, enlighten, and entertain site visitors. The mashup randomly combines slogans and images to explore the relationship among language, manipulation, and images.

Mashups come in all shapes and sizes, from the very simple to the complex. Some mix and mash up search results, others introduce interesting visualizations, and still others aggregate and combine newsfeeds. Libraries have lots of opportunities to use mashups to help liven up their websites, deliver new and interesting services, or entertain website visitors. We'll explore some of these options later in this chapter and throughout this book and hopefully spark some new ideas for mashups at your own library.

Mashup Ecosystem

The mashup ecosystem contains some wonderful ingredients to make a rich and fertile environment; Figure 1.4 identifies the major players in the mashup ecosystem. The fundamental component of the mashup ecosystem is the "open" data providers operating in the internet "cloud." Companies and organizations such as Yahoo!, Google, Technorati (technorati.com), EVDB (eventful.com), Flickr, government departments, academic research units, and think tanks offer up social, economic, and scientific data. The beauty of the internet is that it's easy to open up data sources. No one needs permission. An organization simply makes a data source available, describes how to access it, and announces its availability, normally setting out the

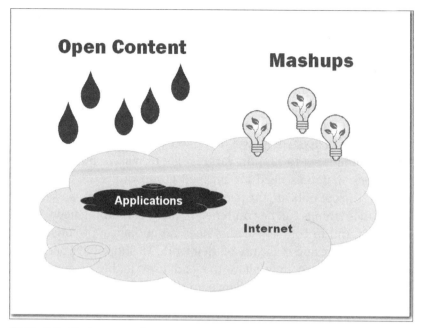

Figure 1.4 Mashup ecosystem

acceptable uses for that data source. Many companies permit free use of their data sources for noncommercial applications; sometimes there are caps on the number of requests per day. Commercial licensing options are also available for some data sources so that corporations can mash up the data source inside the enterprise or use it to build an application for consumers. Most libraries fall into the nonprofit use of data, so it's easy to find data sources to use.

Once the ecosystem is populated with a rich array of data sources, an easy means to access or query the data source is needed so that you can combine the data on your website or in your mashup application. For example, if you would like to add pushpins for library locations to the map of your city or town, you need a mechanism to request a local map zoomed into the appropriate scale to show library locations. Typically, data providers permit access to their information, either as an RSS feed or other XML (eXtensible Markup Language) marked-up format, or via an application programming interface (API). An API spells out how to formulate a query for the data. Usually these queries are written by programmers in languages such as PHP, JavaScript, Perl, Java, .NET, or Python. Programmers are very familiar with APIs and can easily write a few lines of code to collect the data. What if you're not a programmer? No worries—there are lots of web-based applications that let you make use of APIs by pointing, clicking, and pasting a snippet of generated code into your website or blog.

Check out some of the data sources that you can remix into mashups at ProgrammableWeb, Roy Tennant's list of Library Application Program Interfaces (techessence.info/apis), and the JISC Information Environment Service Registry (iesr.ac.uk).

Once the ecosystem is well supplied with raw ingredients, the environment is set to support various "life forms," or new creations. These raw materials need an engaged group of creators and consumers. The creators are the people with a "spark." They can see how two or more things can be combined to make something new, richer, or better. And of course, creators need an audience, or consumers, eager to explore and make use of their work. Mashups have been very successful because they allow the end user to be a creator and because there is an eager audience for these new creations.

Where do libraries fit into this ecosystem? Everywhere. We can be data providers, allowing our customers and mashup developers to remix our data, including acquisition lists, most popular titles, catalog records, event and program information, digital collections, and so forth. Libraries are also mashup creators, mixing open data sources with each other or with in-house data sources. And last but not least, we are consumers. Libraries benefit from mashups for internal use and as information sources for our patrons.

Library-Created Mashup Tour

Let's dive in and take a look at how some libraries are using mashups to create new services and features for their websites.

1. Library Locations

Let's start with a couple of examples of the most popular type of mashup, the map mashup. The simplest map mashup can be created by adding a map link to your library locations page. The link calls up Google Maps (maps.google.com) with a pushpin for the location of your library and an overlay window that provides some basic information, such as library hours. For an example of this approach, look at Cambridge Libraries and Galleries' location page (cambridge libraries.ca/library.cfm?subsection=locations).

On the Hillsborough County Public Library Cooperative (HCPLC) website, a Google Maps mashup shows the locations of the libraries and partner agencies (www.hcplc.org/hcplc/liblocales)(Figure 1.5). Another page uses color-coded pushpins to group different kinds of service locations (www.hcplc.org/hcplc/liblocales/locationsallmap. html). One of the nice features of a Google Maps mashup is the "get directions" capability.

2. Sweetening Up the Library Catalog

The University of Texas tries to provide its users with more from the OPAC by using Google Books Preview. Whenever a visitor looks at a page in the catalog, a script runs behind the scenes to check whether the book is available in Google Book Search. If it is, a hyperlink for Preview appears. Clicking this link will open an overlay window for browsing the full text. Figure 1.6 shows the Preview window overlaying the catalog search results for the title *Reworking the Student Departure Puzzle*.

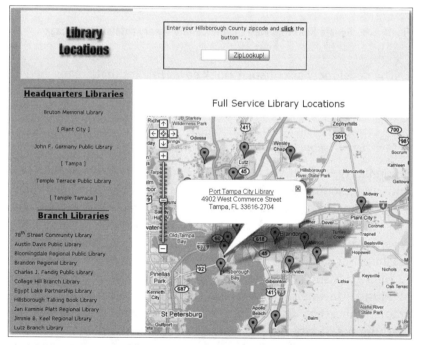

Figure 1.5   Google Maps mashup of Hillsborough County Public Library
Cooperative locations

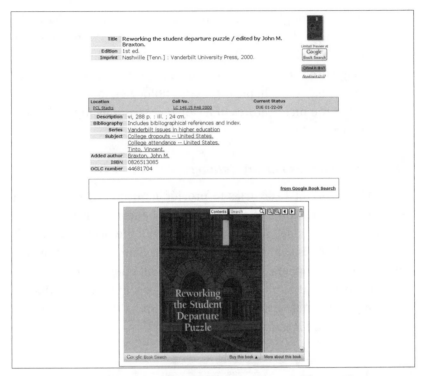

Figure 1.6   Google Books Preview integrated into library catalog result page

The developers also display book cover images that are mashed in using the Amazon API (aws.amazon.com), as well as tags and reviews from LibraryThing (www.librarything.com).

3. Creating Discovery Tools for Collections

A popular type of library mashup that enhances discovery of collections and resources is the book cover carousel. Just like the "new book" or "recommended book" shelves in libraries, library websites can offer a dynamic display of book covers by combining book lists and book covers. We'll take a look at one of these later, in the user-created mashups section.

Figure 1.7 shows an ideal use of a map mashup for discovery. McMaster University Library had print indexes to its aerial photographs collection. By putting these online with a Google Maps mashup, the library allowed researchers to see the photos available for a particular location and/or a particular year. It's incredibly fast and easy to browse what's available.

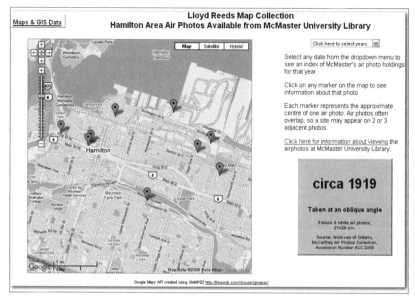

Figure 1.7   Google Maps mashup of Hamilton area air photos circa 1919

User-Created Library Mashup Tour

Next let's see how some libraries have become data providers and how some library users are mixing up that data to provide interesting, exciting, and occasionally wacky mashups.

1. Finding Short Books

Let's start with a bit of a wacky mashup—the LazyLibrary (www.lazy library.com). Every school and public librarian has heard a request from reluctant or time-pressed readers for a short book about "topic X." According to the LazyLibrary website, "this mashup pulls in book data from Amazon and filters out anything with more than 200 pages. Add to that an exceptional user interface and you have one solid serv-ice for anyone looking to get more out of reading less" (Figure 1.8).

2. Visualizing Your Bookshelf

Edward Vielmetti, also known as Superpatron (vielmetti.typepad. com/superpatron), was an early pioneer in showing how library users can remix library data streams. He took an RSS feed from the Ann Arbor District Library's catalog (www.aadl.org/catalog) and created a

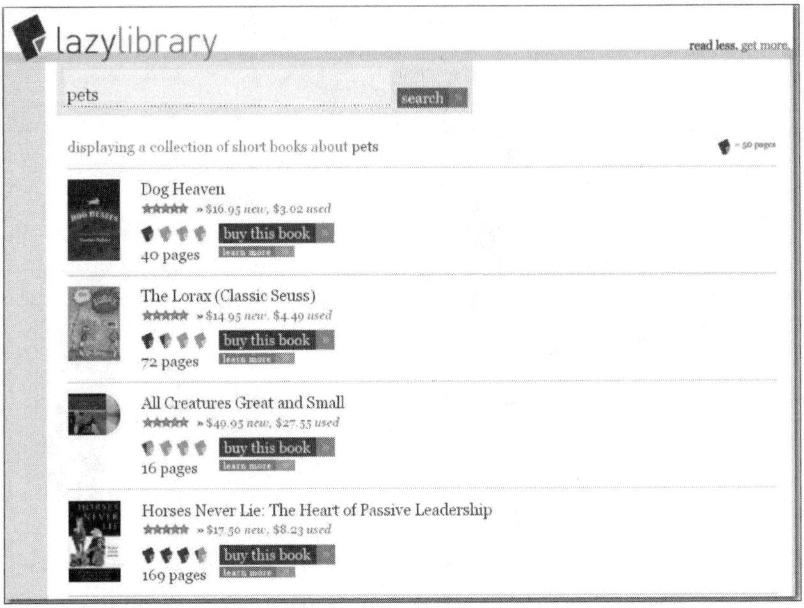

Figure 1.8   "Short Books" about pets from LazyLibrary

Figure 1.9   Wall of Knitting Book Covers created from the RSS feed from the Ann
             Arbor District Library

wall of book covers showing new nonfiction books, new children's books, and new knitting books (Figure 1.9).

The book covers were from Syndetic Solutions, and the RSS feed was generated by a catalog search. Vielmetti did this as a proof-of-concept exercise, and his work inspired Kate, an avid knitter who blogs at *Four Obsessions: Reading, Writing, Cooking and Crafting* (4obsessions.blogspot.com), to post the new knitting books and their covers on her blog (Figure 1.10). She also added the RSS feed to her reader to get the jump on requesting new items. Kate has another area on her blog where she displays covers of books she's checked out of the library.

Figure 1.10 Four Obsessions' display of knitting book covers

3. The Portable Library

Jesse Andrews is a self-proclaimed book lover and developer of Book Burro (www.bookburro.org), a client-side mashup. Book Burro is an extension for the Firefox and Flock web browsers. With Book Burro, any time you are surfing and encounter a page with book information, a small panel will overlay the page with options to click for more information, such as library holdings and online bookstore prices. Figure 1.11 shows the activation of the small panel and the search options.

Figure 1.11   Pale yellow Book Burro overlay on Amazon book page

Library Mashups: The Good, the Bad, and the Ugly

Hopefully this brief tour of library-related mashups has given you a peek at the diversity, creativity, and utility of library mashups. Throughout the rest of this book, other library-related mashups will be explored and described in detail. By creating and remixing publicly available data, libraries can offer richer and more dynamic services to library patrons and empower them to develop some wonderful services.

Mashups are not perfect, however. There are some downsides and some caveats to creating and using mashups. Some of the first ones that pop to mind are privacy, rights management, reliability, and provenance.

First and foremost, when creating a mashup, respect copyright and rights management terms. Not all data sources available via an API or XML data stream can be remixed, and it's critical that copyright and the uses allowed by the copyright holder be respected.

Second, privacy is definitely a factor for any provider, particularly for libraries that are vigilant in protecting the privacy of our users and their borrowing habits. The issue of privacy extends beyond just one data provider, however. For anyone involved with releasing survey data and maintaining user confidentiality, the risk of disclosure of an individual's identity is not new. It is a bit of a new realm, however, for some of the web companies that are releasing data and finding themselves caught on the wrong foot. Two well-known examples of privacy violation are the AOL release search query data and Google Street View (maps.google.com/help/maps/streetview) sightings.[1]

Let's look at an example of how mashing up from multiple data sources can have surprising and downright unpleasant consequences. Tom Owad was one of the first people to show some of the "Big Brother" effects of open data and mashups. He searched a common name on Amazon and captured a sample of 250,000 people with that name who had wish lists. (Wish lists can list your first and last name, city, and state, if you choose to do so.) Next, he winnowed the list down to people who requested certain "controversial" books, such as George Orwell's *1984*. Once he had that result set, he used the Yahoo! People Search (people.yahoo.com) and was able to find the exact street address and phone number for some of these people. With Google Maps, he was able to pull up a satellite view of their homes. He sent one of them a copy of *1984* as a gift in the mail and blogged about his discoveries. You can read about the steps he took in more detail on his site, Applefritter (www.applefritter.com/banned books).

Before you leap to the conclusion that the internet has to return to a set of balkanized websites to preserve privacy, pause for a moment and consider how we might find a balance between being totally open and totally closed. Sharing data streams and combining them via mashups and web services is in its infancy online, but not so in the world of academic research, statistical agencies, and organizations that have for decades created public-use microdata files that are anonymized to allow reuse. A bit of thoughtful planning can minimize the risk of disclosure. The media coverage of the missteps by high-profile companies has helped sensitize us and raise awareness about disclosure risks with data providers.

Fortunately, libraries already have a high level of awareness of the risks of disclosure, and we simply need to apply what we know when opening up library data sources. For example, we may be able to randomly show books returned during the past 24 hours, but we probably don't want to show this information in real time because doing so would create the possibility of someone identifying an individual borrower by watching the library's circulation desk and website at the same time. The lesson to learn from the Amazon wish list example is the need to release library data carefully for remixing, keeping in mind that it will be combined with other data sources.

One major drawback of mashups is their long-term reliability. The mashup ecosystem is still only a few hundred days old; it's in its infancy. Although a company or organization may provide a data stream via an API today, will it continue to do so in 6 months—or 6 years? When you build a mashup on open data, in many cases you are relying on the kindness of strangers and the future health of the organization offering the service. You need to consider carefully who is offering the resource and that entity's capacity and commitment to supporting it over time. You also need to consider plan B—what if the data stream goes away? Is there another source you can use? The bottom line is: How much should you invest in building a discovery tool or mashup site? This will really depend on the source of the data, the benefits, and the resources involved. Another important factor is scale. If there is a cap on the number of queries per day, the mashup may work fine at the outset, but what if it really takes off? Some providers, such as Google Maps, offer a licensing arrangement for high-volume or commercial applications.

Last but not least, in terms of major considerations when thinking about creating or using a mashup, is the provenance and authority of the mashup resource. The casual viewer often cannot easily discern who provided what piece of data in a mashup, making it difficult to assess credibility and authority. Some mashup developers state the sources of their data streams; others do not. Even if they do state their source, have they manipulated the data—either deliberately, or inadvertently through a miscalculation?

Conclusion

Each month more organizations are opening up data sources, and the mashup ecosystem becomes richer. Mashup code libraries and hosted mashup sites targeting nonprogrammers, such as Microsoft Popfly (www.popfly.com) and Yahoo! Pipes (pipes.yahoo.com), add more features and services. Put on your creative thinking cap and start dreaming about new services and features that would delight, entertain, inform, and promote libraries. Think about ways to allow your library users to remix library data. There are many exciting opportunities for libraries and users to create interesting mashups.

Endnote

1. In August 2006, AOL released search data logs for more than half a million anonymized users from a 3-month period for academic researchers to analyze. Although the logs were anonymized, the search queries themselves included private information. Within just a few days, there was an outcry about the privacy breach; AOL took down the data set and apologized. In 2007, Google launched its new service—Street View—with street-level photographs of North American cities in which you could clearly see faces of people caught on camera. Some of these included benign but unsettling photographs, such as a crisp photograph of Mary Kalin-Casey's cat sunning itself inside her living room. Other photographs were not so benign, including burglars breaking into apartments, nude sunbathers, and arrests.

CHAPTER 2

Behind the Scenes: Some Technical Details on Mashups

Bonaria Biancu
Università degli Studi di Milano-Bicocca

API: The Secret of the Mashup

According to the description on ProgrammableWeb (www.program mableweb.com), a mashup involves the combination of data from two or more web sources to build new applications and services.[1] To create a mashup, it is therefore essential to be able to gather structured information from websites (or to extract the available content and convert it to a structured format). The most effective and desirable access mechanism to a web service is its application programming interface (API). APIs are a set of functions, procedures, or classes for accessing a web service. They reveal the underlying logic on which a service is built, its key resources, and the functions amenable to be performed from outside the site. In other words, they allow a computer program to access and manipulate data on a web service the same way that a website interface lets the human user surf and dive into its content.

Each site chooses how to expose its content to the outside, so there may be great differences between API providers—or even within the same provider for its different services. Naturally, publicly documenting APIs and offering them free of charge makes them easier for programmers to use.

Why do websites choose to provide a public API, exposing their valuable information for free online? The more obvious reasons include driving people to their site and name recognition, but allowing users to intensively manipulate the contents of a website or to invoke its services from within a third-party client is also an excellent way to test the application: When hundreds (or even thousands) of people begin to develop web services on top of a site, the site is put to the test, and any bug in the code is likely to be discovered and fixed.

Those seeking API information are likely to look in the "developer" section of a website, in the site map, or in the help or FAQ pages, while those offering APIs should also make sure that their tools are listed on sites that gather information about APIs (discussed later in this chapter).

A very important aspect to take into consideration when using an API is its license or terms of service (TOS), which are the conditions set out by the API provider. There may be limitations on the type of use that developers should make of an API. In most cases, public APIs are free for noncommercial use, while for commercial use the provider may charge a fee or block access entirely. Additionally, there are often limits applied to the rate and bandwidth usage of the client's requests.

It is also worth noting that APIs evolve over time and may change, so users should check the documentation online from time to time. Another issue to pay attention to is the copyright status of the data being used in the mashup: Items published online may not be legally available for reuse by others, or your application might be asked to meet specific requirements to obtain permissions for republication or reuse. For these reasons, pay careful attention to the license under which information has been published and the conditions under which it may be used by third parties. Whenever a specific license is lacking, apply the laws in force in your country.

In addition to the application logic that allows developers to know what resources are made available and what operations can be performed on them, an important aspect of an API is its communication protocols: How, from a technical point of view, does one invoke the programming interface for the information exchange to take place? What are the syntax requirements for the API requests? Also, what format will the provider use to package information to be sent back to the client making the request? What transport channels must or may be used for the most rapid and secure content exchange? To better understand and answer these questions, we need to take a quick glance at the world of web services and its main features.

Web Services Architectures

The World Wide Web Consortium, known as W3C, defines a web service as "a software system designed to support interoperable machine-to-machine interaction over a network" (www.w3.org/TR/ws-arch/ #whatis). A web service is a technology that enables information and communication exchange between different applications. Understanding how they work is clearly a fundamental requirement for correct use of programming interfaces and the creation of effective mashups.

Web services are based on a conceptual model that has a *service provider*, an application that makes certain information available or that provides the capability to perform certain operations, and a *service consumer*, which will make use of the information or the services. The service consumer (the website in which the mashup takes place) issues a request to a service provider (the website that provides the API). If this request is issued correctly, the service provider sends back a response formatted according to the service's rules.

In practice, the transport protocol and the language most commonly used are HTTP and XML (eXtensible Markup Language). If your program will acquire information, data, or services from a website through its API, you need to know the particular communication requirements for that site and how to format the request according to those requirements. You will then send your request over HTTP choosing one of its methods.

Frameworks in the web service architecture may be different, depending on the technology and protocols employed. The most widely used are REpresentational State Transfer (REST) and SOAP (which originally stood for simple object access protocol, a definition that is no longer used), which lay the foundations of resource-oriented and service-oriented architecture, respectively.

REST is the simplest, and thus by far the most used, protocol in the creation of mashups. As we shall see in the section titled "An Example With Yahoo! Answers," REST consists of a simple-to-implement interface based on a resource-oriented architecture. REST assumes a service user that requests information (or triggers operations) from a specific application. The request employs a URL (Uniform Resource Identifier) containing the API parameters and is transmitted using one of the methods (e.g., GET) over HTTP. Note that REST architecture requires operations to be invoked by the HTTP method, not from within the URL sent over the network, provided that the URL carries only the scoping information (that is, the requested resources). This means that, in a pure REST style, if you simply ask for information from a web service, you should use the GET HTTP method, but if you ask the service to perform any operation on its resources, your request should use a different method, either POST, PUT, or DELETE.[2]

When the query is sent over the network, the service provider sends back a response with the information formatted in a language (typically in XML, although other response formats, such as JSON [JavaScript Object Notation], are being increasingly adopted). The client can then use the response as an input for other operations or can render it graphically in a webpage. As you can see, the REST web service's request-response logic is the same as that used on the web when a human user navigates through various online venues. The only differences are that on one hand the transactions are activated through the API calls rather than URLs sent via browser and, on the other hand, the response format is intended for computer—rather than human—consumption.

SOAP is another web service style that has developed alongside REST; it relies on international standards and protocols and has been adopted primarily in the enterprise world. SOAP uses HTTP as the transport protocol for exchanging information, but it requires that both the requests sent by the service consumer and the answers returned by the service provider be wrapped in an XML envelope. The provider itself describes the web service through specific XML schemas that are then published online so that the consumer application can conform to it.

Most Web 2.0 sites use REST interfaces for their APIs. This makes sense when you consider that one of the goals of Web 2.0 is to lower the technical barriers that in the past have prevented the average user from active participation in online information production. It is easy to issue a request by adding parameters to a URL and sending it to a server from a browser or an HTML form. It is even easier if the URL takes the GET method. Building a rich and compelling mashup is possible with little or no knowledge of programming, thanks to REST.

SOAP is definitely more complex to implement, and according to REST fans (the so-called RESTafarians), it fails to promote the ease of use and effectiveness inherent in the World Wide Web concept. It is, however, important to understand the basics of the SOAP architectural style, both because many sites use only SOAP and because SOAP is more standardized and refined than REST. You might also find SOAP to be a requirement for business-oriented development projects.

Where to Find APIs Online

As you first approach the world of mashups, it is very useful to have access to the experience of other users, as well as to learn which websites are most open to information reuse. A helpful resource to consider for this type of training is ProgrammableWeb. This site has the most comprehensive list of mashups; it also collects news from the web, trends from the industry landscape, technical information, guides, and references. On ProgrammableWeb, mashups can be browsed by category, popularity, date, and tags. Every mashup has an associated description of its functionalities, along with the APIs used, tags, author information, and links to related mashups. In addition, ProgrammableWeb users can vote on the mashups, add them to their favorites list, and follow up on new applications using the same API via RSS feeds.

As Raymond Yee explains in his excellent book *Pro Web 2.0 Mashups* (blog.mashupguide.net), a useful way to develop creative mashup ideas is by studying the applications already created by other users. Ask yourself questions like:

- What is being combined?

- Why are these elements being combined?

- Where is the remixing or the recombination happening?

- How are various elements being combined (that is, first in the interface but also behind the scenes in the technical machinery)?

- How can the mashup be extended?[3]

These questions and their answers provide a useful grid with which to analyze any mashup found on ProgrammableWeb and help you thoroughly understand the dynamics and problems involved in a mashup.

You can also learn quite a bit by studying the message conveyed by the components that enable the mashup, in particular the APIs—the real workhorses of mashups. On this site, each API has an associated analytical fact sheet that gives a general description, tags, latest news, a list of mashups that use it, which protocols are implemented (web service styles such as REST and SOAP, and data formats), functionalities (for example, different types of methods to be invoked), security models (authentication, SSL, etc.), support (offered both from the vendor and from the community worldwide), and the signup requirements and licensing TOS. Often there are also guides on how to use the API, including feedback from those who have used it.

The information provided on ProgrammableWeb and in its how-to documents is very valuable, giving an idea of the range of sites that allow you to exploit their services. Moreover, beginning mashup developers will appreciate the simplicity of the site's contents and the ability to search the database for code libraries and development tools.

ProgrammableWeb is a general directory; although it describes several thousand mashups, very few are library-oriented. However, thanks to the efforts of the Library 2.0 movement and to the release of information management software that is more modular and standards-compliant, library-related mashups and public APIs are beginning to gain a certain public attention. The Library Software Manifesto (techessence.info/manifesto) calls for free access to APIs for libraries that have purchased a library system. It is often only because of such public access interfaces that all the data—bibliographic or not—stored in library databases can be exploited beyond the set of uses provided by vendors (here we talk of legal and permitted uses!). Although libraries, as organizations that deal primarily with information, may seem to be logical players in the world of data and web services, in the past there has not been much awareness about the importance of open APIs or the potential they could have for libraries' goals. For example, there are few APIs for online catalogs, apart from the queries allowed by the Z39.50 protocol. It is difficult, or even impossible, to create a mashup like John Blyberg's SOPAC (www.thesocialopac.net; see Chapter 12) without having an API that supports it. Often librarians do not know whether the software in use in the library has an API, and vendors do not volunteer this type of information.

This makes the effort of the Mashed Library social network (mashedlibrary.ning.com) that much more important. This group collected a list of library-oriented APIs and web services that were then incorporated into a permanent list on TechEssence.info (techessence.info/apis). Many of the APIs listed interact with OPACs (Online Public Access Catalogs); others relate to the software for digital resource management made available by some of the major players in the information technology scene, such as OCLC consortium, Amazon (www.amazon.com), the library-related product vendor Talis, and the social cataloging service LibraryThing (www.librarything.com). I should also mention the JISC Information Environment Service Registry (iesr.ac.uk), a machine-readable registry of electronic resources, including APIs, with access information and documentation, and the SRU (Search and Retrieve URL) web service, developed by the Library of Congress as an evolution of the Z39.50 protocol.

It is time to foster bottom-up initiatives in the library and information science arena and to harness librarians' creativity to make more flexible and up-to-date use of library software. It is time to extensively exploit integrated library systems in a more user-oriented manner, shaping the ways different sources of digital content expose their data to make information suitable to be used by third-party applications such as a blog, a web calendar, or an RSS feed. This way, users themselves will be able to create applications that neither vendors nor librarians might ever imagine.

If, after reading this book, you want to get your hands dirty with mashup development, you can take either the ProgrammableWeb or the TechEssence list as a starting point for discovering API magic.

Mashups Without APIs

So far we have described APIs and their styles of communication, but what happens if a site does not have structured interfaces through which other services can retrieve the needed information? Although many sites are equipped with APIs, not all make them publicly available to third-party applications; in some cases you can use the API only by paying a fee, while in others, APIs are kept secret by companies or organizations because they are considered strategic for the commercial success of a product or service. There are also websites that do not offer any programming interfaces with which to interact. In these cases it is more difficult to utilize the data; nonetheless, you may still have a chance to create a mashup by tapping into the sources provided.

Useful Mashup Resources

- cURL, curl.haxx.se
- Google Code, APIs, and developer tools, code.google.com/more
- MashupCamp, www.mashupcamp.com
- Poster Add-on, addons.mozilla.org/en-US/firefox/addon/2691
- ProgrammableWeb Mashup feed, www.mashupfeed.com
- W3 Schools SOAP Tutorial, www.w3schools.com/soap
- Raymond Yee, *Pro Web 2.0 Mashups: Remixing Data and Web Services* (Berkeley, CA: Apress, 2008)
- Sam Ruby and Leonard Richardson, *RESTful Web Services* (Farnham, UK: O'Reilly, 2007)

Raymond Yee suggests that you first study the specific URL language used by the site. This is useful even if a public API is present, but it becomes crucial in a case where there is no API and you have to discover on your own the underlying information architecture adopted by a site. The way in which web addresses are built may provide clues about whether and how information is structured into URL-identifiable resources, or perhaps even categorized, tagged, or organized in some way so that a computer program may operate with it.

One reliable source of consistently formatted data that allows for reuse in web services is a site's feed. Feeds are nothing more than small chunks of information formatted in XML or in one of its dialects (such as RSS or ATOM) and are normally used by websites to disseminate updated content that users can read by means of aggregators or feed readers. In fact, feeds can be seen as a basic RESTful web service, given that an XML-formatted response is invoked by a URL request over HTTP.

Utilizing the file that underlies the typical orange icon indicating the presence of a feed, developers can parse the information and use it as input for another application or render it directly in a webpage.

The presence of content import-export features or the use of web development techniques like Ajax (Asynchronous JavaScript and XML; a programming language comprised of JavaScript and XML that is used for creating dynamic web applications) are other hints that the site has data that is able to be processed by an external program.

If a site does not provide an intelligible URL language, feeds, or other gateways to access its data, then you must rely solely on its web interface using the technique known as *screen scraping*. Through this mechanism, information intended exclusively for human consumption is extracted from the webpage and sent as input to a computer program. The screen scraper program then acts on the content presentation layer of the webpages and uses its HTML tags as hooks to identify the desired information resources.

Naturally, these hacking techniques produce results that are often fleeting and unreliable. If a site doesn't allow for an API, there may be solid reasons—including legal ones—that it does not make its data available for third-party use. You must analyze carefully whether screen scraping can be used in a particular situation, even if it represents the only opportunity you have to obtain some piece of information.

An Example With Yahoo! Answers

Let's move from theory to practice and see how a real web service requests data from an online source and processes it to make it usable in a mashup. Given that mashups generally combine data from two or more information resources, for each source in your mashup you will need to understand its particular inputs and outputs, as we illustrate here with Yahoo! Answers (answers.yahoo.com).

There are many websites that make their APIs available to users: search engines such as Google (www.google.com), which provides the opportunity to query its index; media-sharing sites such as Flickr (www.flickr.com) and YouTube (www.youtube.com), from which you can pull pictures and movies; aggregators such as Technorati (www.technorati.com) and Feedreader (www.feedreader.com), from which to get user-generated content and feeds; and many others. Yahoo! (www.yahoo.com) itself offers a wide variety of APIs and web services that interact with its search engine as well as with many others of its online services, such as maps, music, financial information, social bookmarking services, and so on. In the Yahoo! Developer

Network (YDN; developer.yahoo.com), you can find all of the necessary information about the application interfaces and other related technologies, along with guides and video-tutorials, web design libraries, a mashup gallery, reports on hacking initiatives, and support from both the company's team and the developer community. The service chosen as an example for this chapter is Yahoo! Answers.

In its own words, Yahoo! Answers is "an online community where anyone can ask and answer questions on any topic. Yahoo! Answers connects people to the information they're seeking with those who know it." Consulting the YDN Answers section (developer.yahoo. com/answers), we discover that APIs allowing access to questions and answers posted by Yahoo! Answers' users are available for public use. The API uses a REST interface, so we know this means we need to do the following:

- Build a URL with parameters specified by the API.

- Send it using one of the required HTTP methods.

If you want to use the Yahoo! Answers API, you have to request an Application ID (developer.yahoo.com/wsregapp). This procedure is often required by sites hosting open APIs because this way the API provider (that is, the service provider) can track the number and types of the requests and the bandwidth each application makes use of, in addition to the characteristics of the client requesting the content.

There are four types of queries provided by the API: *question Search, getByCategory, getQuestion,* and *getByUser.* These reply with, respectively, questions that match your query's argument, questions from a certain category, details of all the answers given to a question, and Yahoo! Answers questions from a specific user. The API page also has a form so that you can immediately try your queries and verify the answers returned by the service provider. The only HTTP method available to the API is GET; therefore, you can only read information from the site, not upload, edit, or delete data on the server.

The first of the queries, *questionSearch,* "finds open, resolved, or up-for-vote questions that include your search terms." To access searches, you must build a request that retrieves questions using the parameters provided by the API.

The target URL to which the request must be sent is

```
http://answers.yahooapis.com/AnswersService
/V1/questionSearch
```

where *http://answers.yahooapis.com/* is the API hostname, and *AnswersService* is the service. The acronym *V1*, located just after it, refers to the API version number, and *questionSearch* represents the query type we have chosen.

Here are some of the query arguments that you can employ for this kind of request:

- *query* – search terms (required)

- *category_id* – search only in the specified category ID or IDs (IDs may be seen in the request URLs when you browse Yahoo! Answers categories)

- *region* – filter based on country (e.g., us: United States; uk: United Kingdom; it: Italy)

- *sort* – sorting order of result set

    - relevance – by relevance (default)

    - date_desc – by date (newest first)

    - date_asc – by date (oldest first; omit for default "relevance")

    - *appid* – by the application ID (required)

    - *output* – definition of the output for the call (accepted values are "xml," "json," "php," and "rss"; omit for default "xml.")[4]

For example, if you would like to get questions asked by users in the U.S. regarding solar energy in the *Green Living* subcategory and have the results sorted by date, with the most recent questions first, you send

```
GET
http://answers.yahooapis.com/AnswersService
/V1/questionSearch?
appid=MyYahooAppId&query=solar%20energy&cat-
egory_id=2115500307&region=us&sort=date_desc5
```

Note that you must substitute *MyYahooAppId* with your application ID and that arguments and that values must be URL-encoded.[6]

The number *2115500307* in *category_id* is the identifier for the Environment/Green Living category as shown in the URL of the corresponding Yahoo! Answers page. By default the maximum number of results is 10, and the default response format is XML. Because we have not specified either of those parameters, the defaults will be used.

You can test this URL by pasting it in the location bar of your browser.[7] The result is an XML-formatted response containing the requested information, plus a set of further parameters, such as the *id* and the *nick name* of the user who asked the question, the number of answers provided for each question and—if they exist—the preferred ones among them. The XML code may be parsed and sent as input for a third-party application or rendered in an HTML page for displaying the results in your preferred style. For example, a consortium of libraries on a geographical scale could cooperate in reference services, developing a mashup that draws within a unique interface questions about a certain topic from the online reference service's users and from the local Yahoo! ones.

It is also possible to get a feed-style response choosing RSS as the output format (*&output=rss*). In this case the URL resulting from the API call is an RSS feed address that can be used by a feed reader to get notified over time when new questions meeting your criteria appear on Yahoo! Answers.

The JSON output format returns a serialized JavaScript, a less complex format than the XML that is provided by default. JSON can be used in combination with the callback function provided among the API parameters to solve the cross-site security issues like the Same Origin Policy that you are likely to encounter if you write your application in a client-side scripting language such as JavaScript. Last, remember that this web service limits you to 5,000 queries per IP (Internet Protocol) address per day and that you are asked to agree to the Yahoo! API Terms of Use (info.yahoo.com/legal/us/yahoo/api/api-2140.html) and TOS (info.yahoo.com/legal/us/yahoo/utos/utos-173.html). In addition, websites and applications using this Yahoo! web service must display the attribution "Powered by Yahoo! Answers."

Mashup Editors

A significant advantage of the current level of attention to mashups is the fact that there are more and more tools and services being developed that make building a mashup increasingly simple, even for the average internet user. Some of these entirely eliminate the need for programming, hiding such technical details behind the interface. Some big web companies have begun working on editors for mashups, that is, applications that allow you to combine information instantiating simple commands in a visual user interface. As Nicole C. Engard explains in Chapter 7, Yahoo! Pipes (pipes.yahoo.com) has revolutionized the mashup editor.

Microsoft, too, is taking part in the mashup trend and has enhanced its offerings with a web editor for mashups called Popfly (www.popfly.com). This program, which requires the use of the Silverlight (silverlight.net) plug-in, allows the creation of mashups "without writing a line of code," thanks to a graphic editor in which you can drag and drop 3-dimensional components (the *blocks*) from a sidebar containing offerings of *Images and videos, News and RSS, Social networks,* and others, plus a basic *Tools* set. The latter provides the operations that can be applied to the other modules, such as Merge, Sort, or List the content. Sophisticated users can switch to the advanced view that displays the JavaScript code that lies behind each module, which they can then edit directly. It is also possible to customize your application with HTML and to test the running mashup in the debug console.

Thanks to the interconnection of the Popfly editor with Web 2.0 social sites, you can easily create mashups like slideshows of your favorite pictures and podcast and video players. Popfly also offers a space for hosting both webpages and applications developed with the mashup editor.

Among other visual mashup editors that deserve a mention are openkapow (openkapow.com), Intel Mash Maker (mashmaker.intel. com/web/index.php), and Dapper (www.dapper.net), as well as more business-oriented tools like the JackBe Presto Platform (www.jack be.com/products) and Serena software (www.serena.com/mashups).

In general, however, for those who are taking their first steps on the mashup path and have limited development skills, it is better to start with one of the first editors described here (Yahoo! Pipes or Microsoft Popfly). These are fully documented and have many examples and quite a few pre-built modules that one can exploit. They also have active online communities that can provide support for beginners and advanced users alike.

Endnotes

1. I would like to thank Karen Coyle and Raymond Yee for their generous feedback and support in writing this chapter.
2. The differences among pure REST and styles such as REST-RPC are well explained in *RESTful Web Services* (see Sidebar titled "Useful Mashup Resources"). Although most web services claim to be RESTful, they often expose data in a hybrid manner (for instance, they put API methods inside the URL rather than utilizing HTTP protocol). See also Duncan Cragg's blog posts: STREST (Service-Trampled REST) Will Break Web 2.0 (duncan-cragg.org/blog/post/strest-service-trampled-rest-will-break-web-20), and The REST Dialogues (duncan-cragg.org/blog/tag/dialogue).
3. Raymond Yee, *Pro Web 2.0 Mashups: Remixing Data and Web Services* (Berkeley, CA : Apress, 2008), 3.
4. The arguments and their explanations are quoted from *questionSearch* page (developer.yahoo.com/answers/V1/questionSearch.html).
5. See YDN to get information about how to build REST URLs (developer.yahoo.com/search/rest.html).
6. URL encoding (or percent encoding) is a technique used to convert special characters in a URL to a valid format. One example of this is the space between words in terms like *solar energy*, which will be encoded to *%20*. For more information, see the Wikipedia page (en.wikipedia.org/wiki/Percent-encoding) and a list of encoded characters (www.w3schools.com/TAGS/ref_urlencode.asp).
7. You can call the API from within a web service written in a server-side programming language such as Perl and PHP or from an Ajax client. You can also try the API functionalities by sending the request through a command-line program like cURL (Client URL Library) or through the Firefox Poster add-on. YDN offers a Software Development Kit (developer.yahoo.com/download/download.html) with code libraries available for public use, to implement web services in diverse programming languages.

Additional References

Arkin, Assan. "Scraping with style: scrAPI toolkit for Ruby." blog.labnotes.org/2006/07/11/scraping-with-style-scrapi-toolkit-for-ruby (accessed January 11, 2009).

Bloch, Joshua. "How to Design a Good API and Why It Matters." www.slideshare.net/guestbe92f4/how-to-design-a-good-a-p-i-and-why-it-matters-g-o-o-g-l-e (accessed January 11, 2009).

Campbell, Ryan. "How to Add an API to Your Web Service." ParticleTree. particletree.com/features/how-to-add-an-api-to-your-web-service (accessed January 11, 2009).

Fox, Pamela. "Web 2.0 & Mashups: How People Can Tap into the 'Grid' for Fun & Profit." Open Grid Forum. www.slideshare.net/wuzziwug/web-20-mashups-how-people-can-tap-into-the-grid-for-fun-profit-20924 (accessed January 11, 2009).

Garrett, Jesse J. "Ajax: A New Approach to Web Applications." Adaptive Path. www.adaptivepath.com/ideas/essays/archives/000385.php (accessed January 11, 2009).

Gregorio, Joe. "How to Create a REST Protocol." XML.com. www.xml.com/pub/a/2004/12/01/restful-web.html (accessed January 11, 2009).

He, Hao. "Implementing REST Web Services: Best Practices and Guidelines." XML.com. www.xml.com/pub/a/2004/08/11/rest.html (accessed January 11, 2009).

Heilmann, Christian. *Beginning JavaScript with DOM Scripting and Ajax: From Novice to Professional.* Berkeley, CA: Apress, 2006.

Herren, John. "Mashup University 4. Intro to Mashups." www.slideshare.net/jhherren/mashup-university-4-intro-to-mashups (accessed January 11, 2009).

Levitt, Jason. "JSON and the Dynamic Script Tag: Easy, XML-less Web Services for JavaScript." XML.com. www.xml.com/pub/a/2005/12/21/json-dynamic-script-tag.html (accessed January 11, 2009).

"Mashup the Library: A Workshop on Mashup Technology and the Art of Remixing Library and Information Resources." CARL North Information Technology Program Archives. carl-acrl.org/ig/carlitn/archives.html (accessed January 11, 2009).

OASIS. "SOA Reference Model." www.oasis-open.org/committees/tc_home.php?wg_abbrev=soa-rm (accessed January 11, 2009).

Schnell, Eric. "Mashups and Web Services." In *Library 2.0 and beyond: Innovative technologies and tomorrow's user*, edited by Nancy Courtney, 63–74. Westport, CT: Libraries Unlimited, 2007.

Theurer, Dan. "Web Services + JSON = Dump Your Proxy." Dan Theurer: Web services, technology and random thoughts! www.theurer.cc/blog/2005/12/15/web-services-json-dump-your-proxy (accessed January 11, 2009).

Udell, Jon. "The Beauty of REST." XML.com. www.xml.com/pub/a/2004/03/17/udell.html (accessed January 11, 2009).

Yee, Raymond. "Semantic Search the US Library of Congress." ProgrammableWeb. blog.programmableweb.com/2008/04/29/semantic-search-the-us-library-of-congress accessed January 11, 2009).

Zakas, Nicholas C., Jeremy McPeak, and Joe Fawcett. *Professional Ajax.* 2nd ed. Indianapolis, IN: Wiley, 2007.

CHAPTER 3

Making Your Data
Available to Be Mashed Up

Ross Singer
Talis

Although most library mashups focus on including external data in library services, there is a lot of value to making our own copious amounts of content and metadata available for reuse as well. In fact, it is precisely at the intersection of external and internal content that mashups get interesting.

However, given the scarcity of open application programming interfaces (APIs) to our library systems and the general lack of awareness of the standards used to share information within the library domain, it might not be obvious how to make the content trapped in our websites and web applications available to be reused. Even when these interfaces are available, their complexity (or their proprietary nature) may not be conducive to the development of mashups. Promoting awareness and educating the public in the use of library standards may be more effort than many are willing to tolerate.

In many cases, therefore, the easiest way to make your data available for use (by you and by others) is simply to make it accessible in the HTML pages your library is already producing. While this approach lacks the sophistication of an API that outputs detailed XML (eXtensible Markup Language), it is simple, approachable by implementers who are less technically inclined, and capable of being done with your content right now. Embedding semantics into your webpages can be a simple way to unlock the meaning of the content buried throughout your library's web presence.

Microformats: The Lower Hanging Fruit

There are a variety of ways to place meaning in your garden-variety HTML documents, each with different positives and negatives. Arguably, the initiative with the lowest barrier to entry in this arena would be microformats (also referred to as mFs, or just uFs). The microformats community's mission is to leverage existing and commonly used technologies to better define the semantics included within webpages. The scope of microformats is quite small, their credo being to "pave cowpaths on the web." This means the community will consider only specifications that have well-documented use cases and for content that is commonly used in current web publishing (although the standard for these criteria is not exactly clear). So, although there will most likely never be a microformat to define MARC (MAchine-Readable Cataloging) within HTML, there *are* specifications for a considerable amount of content found within library websites.

The crux of how microformats work is ingeniously simple and clever. The semantics of the page are set within the class attributes in standard HTML tags. The text contained inside those tags is then considered the value of the field that is being defined. This is probably easiest to show by example and then by explanation.

Let us take the Yale University Subject Specialist page (Figure 3.1), a relatively straightforward, table-based directory of phone numbers, email addresses, office locations, etc. Although this layout works fine for human consumption, there is nothing in the HTML (Figure 3.2) to help a machine know what kind of information is being displayed within this page.

From this webpage, a user would have to manually type in all of a librarian's information to add the librarian as a contact. However, by simply adding a few class attributes to the HTML (and cleaning it up a bit, as shown in Figure 3.3), a user can make the page machine-readable.

This in turn makes the content on the page available to be consumed by other applications, stored in address books, sent to mobile phones, etc. In Figure 3.4 you can see how just adding these small changes to the HTML enables the Operator add-on (addons.mozilla.org/en-US/firefox/addon/4106) for Firefox to take the contact information embedded in the HTML and export it to an email application such as Outlook or Yahoo! Mail.

Subject	Contact	Campus Location	Telephone	E-mail	IM Address
Accounting	Judith Carnes	SSL	432-3306	judith.carnes@yale.edu	AIM: somlibrarian Meebo: somlibrarianatyale
African Studies	Dorothy Woodson	SML 317	432-1883	dorothy.woodson@yale.edu	
African-American Studies	Gregory Eow	SML 226	432-1757	gregory.eow@yale.edu	AIM, Google talk, Yahoo: geatyalelib
American Literature (SML)	Todd Gilman	SML 226	432-1761	todd.gilman@yale.edu	AIM, Yahoo, Google Talk: ToddatYaleLib
American Literature Collection (BRBL)	Patricia Willis	BRBL 25	432-2962	patricia.willis@yale.edu	
American Musical Theatre	Richard Warren	ML 115	432-1795	richard.warren@yale.edu	

Figure 3.1   Yale University Subject Specialist page

```
<TR>
<TD bgcolor="#FFFFFF"><font face="Verdana, Arial, Helvetica, sans-serif" size="2">Accounting </TD>
<TD bgcolor="#FFFFFF"><font face="Verdana, Arial, Helvetica, sans-serif" size="2">Judith Carnes</TD>
<TD bgcolor="#FFFFFF"><font face="Verdana, Arial, Helvetica, sans-serif" size="2">SSL </TD>
<TD bgcolor="#FFFFFF"><font face="Verdana, Arial, Helvetica, sans-serif" size="2"> 432-3306 </TD>
<TD bgcolor="#FFFFFF"><font face="Verdana, Arial, Helvetica, sans-serif" size="2">
<a href="mailto:judith.carnes@yale.edu">judith.carnes@yale.edu</a></TD>
<TD bgcolor="#FFFFFF"><font face="Verdana, Arial, Helvetica, sans-serif" size="2">AIM:  somlibrarian
Meebo:        somlibrarianatyale</TD><TR>
```

Figure 3.2   HTML behind the Yale University Subject Specialist page

```
<TR class="vcard">
<TD bgcolor="#FFFFFF"><span class="role">Accounting</span></TD>
<TD bgcolor="#FFFFFF"><span class="fn">Judith Carnes</span></TD>
<TD bgcolor="#FFFFFF">SSL </TD>
<TD bgcolor="#FFFFFF"><abbr class="tel" title="+12034323306">432-3306</abbr></TD>
<TD bgcolor="#FFFFFF">
<a href="mailto:judith.carnes@yale.edu" class="email">judith.carnes@yale.edu</a></TD>
<TD bgcolor="#FFFFFF">
        AIM: <a class="url" href="aim:goim?screename=somlibrarian">somlibrarian</a>
        Meebo:  <a class="url" href="xmpp:somlibrarianatyale@meebo.com">somlibrarianatyale</a>
</TD></TR>
```

Figure 3.3   Yale University Subject Specialist page with added class attributes

Figure 3.4   Edited Yale University Subject Specialist page with the Firefox Operator add-on

Figure 3.5 Contact info added to Apple's Address Book from the Firefox Operator add-on

Figure 3.5 shows how the data similarly exports to Apple's Address Book application.

So what exactly is happening here? In this example, we are using the microformat hCard, which is based on the internet standard for contact information, vCard, commonly seen in peoples' email signature file, attached with a .vcf extension. Because vCards are ubiquitous, the microformats community, rather than build an entirely new metadata format for describing contact information, took the fields defined in vCard and applied them to the common ways people publish the same sorts of information on the web. In this way, the syntax and semantics would be recognizable to the sorts of people who would be building applications to create and consume the data included in the page (rather than their having to learn the ins and outs of a new format), making the chances of adoption much greater.

To take this a step further, the "Campus Location" column (which, in this example, is not a user-friendly acronym) could link to the Library Locations page, which could also be marked up in hCard. So, for our "SSL" (Social Science Libraries) location, this could link to *http://www.library.yale.edu/libraries/locations.html#ssl*. Unfortunately, hCard cannot include data from another page, and there is (currently) no formally defined means to link from one hCard to another (although there are proposals to do so). So at this point, getting a machine from one page to the other, although possible, presents problems.

```
<dl>
        <dt><a name="ssl"></a><A HREF="http://www.library.yale.edu:80/socsci/">Social Science
Libraries &amp; Information Services</A> (SSL)</dt>
        <dd>140 Prospect Street</dd>

        <dd>Circulation: (203) 432-3300    E-mail: <a
href="mailto:sslis@yale.edu">sslis@yale.edu</a></dd>
        <dd>Reference: (203) 432-3301      E-mail: <a
href="mailto:sslref@yale.edu">sslref@yale.edu</a></dd>
        <dd><em>Mail to</em>: Social Science Library, Yale University,</dd>

        <dd>P.O. Box 208263, New Haven, CT 06520-8263</dd>
        <dd>
<a href="http://www.library.yale.edu/socsci/ssl/directions.html">Travel Directions</a>  
  <a href="http://www.library.yale.edu/hours/ssl.html">Hours</a>
    </dd>
</dl>
```

Figure 3.6 HTML for Yale's Individual Libraries page

```
<dl class="vcard" id="ssl">
        <dt><a name="ssl"></a><A class="fn url org" HREF="http://www.library.yale.edu:80/
socsci/">Social Science Libraries &amp; Information Services</A> (SSL)</dt>
        <div class="adr">
        <dd class="street-address">140 Prospect Street</dd>
        <dd>Circulation: <span class="tel">(203) 432-3300</span>    E-mail: <a
class="email" href="mailto:sslis@yale.edu">sslis@yale.edu</a></dd>
        <dd>Reference: <span class="tel">(203) 432-3301</span>      E-mail:
<a class="email" href="mailto:sslref@yale.edu">sslref@yale.edu</a></dd>
        <dd><em>Mail to</em>: Social Science Library, Yale University,</dd>
        <dd><span class="post-office-box">P.O. Box 208263</span>, <span class="locality">New
Haven</span>, <span class="region">CT</span> <span class="postal-code">06520-8263</
span></dd></div>
        <dd>
<a href="http://www.library.yale.edu/socsci/ssl/directions.html">Travel Directions</a>  
  <a href="http://www.library.yale.edu/hours/ssl.html">Hours</a>
</dd>
```

Figure 3.7   Edited HTML for Yale's Individual Libraries page

However, the destination of that link also proves itself to be a prime candidate for semantic markup as it includes the names and addresses of all of Yale's individual libraries. So, again, a little editing of the original HTML markup (shown in Figure 3.6) can provide a much clearer context (Figure 3.7).

The Firefox Operator add-on, seeing the location information embedded in the page, can then present options for mapping (Figure 3.8).

By selecting "Find with Yahoo! Maps," the user is taken to the correct location (Figure 3.9).

By merely adding a few simple attributes, this page goes from being a static bundle of words to a set of easily mappable locations.

Microformats are not limited merely to contact information. There are a handful of "approved" specifications, such as hCalendar

Figure 3.8   Yale's edited Individual Libraries page with the Operator add-on

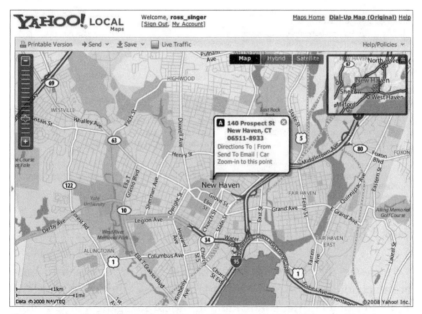

Figure 3.9   Yahoo! Map of Social Science Libraries & Information Services

for calendar markup (to bring data from, say, a library events page into a personal calendar). The draft specifications include two more formats of interest to libraries: hResume (useful for marking up curriculum vitae, for example) and hAtom, a means of embedding the Atom Syndication Protocol into HTML pages. The latter is intriguing from the standpoint that libraries are filled with applications that are veritable black boxes, in which the only customizations available are tweaks to the webpage templates. Through tools like hAtom, it is possible to produce run-of-the-mill syndicated content out of *any* webpage, eliminating the need for expensive add-ons that merely tack an RSS feed onto the library catalog.

As already shown, it is possible to access microformats via a browser extension. Bookmarklets (JavaScript functions saved as bookmarks) are also a popular way to identify and use these specifications. To work with uF marked-up content in a local application, there are microformat parsers written in a wide variety of programming languages. Even Yahoo! Pipes (pipes.yahoo.com) has some filters to locate and use embedded uFs located in webpages to be included in mashups (see Chapter 7 for more on Yahoo! Pipes).

Microformats are easy, useful, and becoming increasingly popular, but they are not perfect. As mentioned earlier, it is not generally possible to authoritatively link pieces of data from one page to another, which, for all of microformats' legitimate attempts to integrate seamlessly into the web, seems to run counter to the spirit of the medium. The namespace of microformats' class names is flat, meaning that words cannot be reused between specifications (unless they have identical semantic meanings). As an example, hCard uses the word *title* to define a person's position within an organization. This means that the word *title* cannot be used to define data such as the name of a book; hAtom ran into this problem (because the title element is an important part of Atom) and resorted to using the class name *entry-title*. Certainly other proposals could follow suit—variations on existing class names, prepending or appending alternative terms to ensure uniqueness—but this gets unwieldy (and unintuitive) at scale.

Interestingly this last point is not a terribly pressing concern for the microformats community because its members have no desire to see a wide proliferation of new specifications, instead limiting the scope to very widely deployed (and therefore limited) design patterns in web publishing. This philosophy has the advantage of making microformats specifications very polished, thought-out, and supportable by a large population, but on the flip side, it is likely that many useful data formats will never be modeled as microformats because their usage will not reach the perceived barrier of "mainstream publishing needs."

RDF in HTML: Upping the Ante

So what if your data does not easily fit into a common publishing paradigm? What about all this other really rich, useful data that appears all throughout the library website? Another option would be to use a couple of other initiatives similar in purpose to microformats but much different in scope. RDFa (Resource Description Framework Attributes) and eRDF (Embedded RDF) are two competing proposals for embedding semantics within HTML using the RDF.

For those not familiar with RDF, it is a means to model information on the web by assigning a URI (Uniform Resource Identifier) to a resource and describing the relationships between that resource and other resources via a structure known as *triples*. A triple quite simply maps to the mental picture of a subject, predicate, and object phrase, in which the subject is the URI of the resource in question, the predicate is an attribute defined in a controlled RDF vocabulary, and the object is either another URI (therefore establishing the relationship between two unique resources) or what is called a *literal* (such as a string or number that defines the actual value of a property associated with a given resource). The combination of these associations produces what is referred to as a graph. The relationships contained within the graph can be produced from as many or as few RDF schemas as necessary to fully describe the resource.

Given that both eRDF and RDFa are able to use any existing RDF vocabulary, as well as the fact that it is possible (and commonplace) to create your own, the flexibility of these technologies make them well-suited to embedding more complicated semantics within your webpages. The downside is a higher barrier for entry—and not only for novices to get up to speed with RDF: A more complicated data model means that more thought needs to be put into how to integrate it intuitively into an existing web presence.

From a conceptual perspective, both technologies take a very similar approach to microformats by using regular HTML tags and attributes to define the semantics of the content. In execution, though, they have their differences, and both approaches have plusses and minuses.

RDFa was conceived first (although not by much) and has the advantage of being endorsed by the World Wide Web Consortium (W3C). The primary defining characteristic of RDFa is the addition of nonstandard attributes to HTML tags to help define the RDF triples. Again, an example will help illustrate the concept. Figure 3.10 shows part of an HTML page that is describing a visiting author and book signing.

Figure 3.11 adds RDFa, allowing much more information to be packed into this announcement.

```
<br />
Friday, September 12 at 12:00 p.m.</span></div>
<div style="margin: 0in 0in 0pt"><span style="font-size: small">The New York Times and #1
Essence bestselling author <br />
<strong>Mary Monroe </strong>visits and signs her new novel, <i>She Had It Coming</i>.
<br />
Central Library, 1st Floor<br />
<br />
```

Figure 3.10   HTML for author visit and book signing

```
<br />
Friday, September 12 at 12:00 p.m.</span></div>
<div xmlns:dc="http://purl.org/dc/elements/1.1/" xmlns:dcterms="http://purl.org/dc/terms/"
about="urn:ISBN:0758212194" ><span rel="dcterms:isPartOf" resource="http://dbpedia.org/
resource/New_York_Times_Best_Seller_list">The New York Times</span> and #1 <span
rel="dcterms:isPartOf" resource="http://www.essence.com/essence/books/">Essence</span>
bestselling author <br />
<strong property="dc:creator">Mary Monroe </strong>visits and signs her new novel,
<i property="dc:title">She Had It Coming</i>.<br />
Central Library, 1st Floor<br />
</div>
```

Figure 3.11   HTML for author visit and book signing with added RDFa

With the added descriptive context, the content contained in this paragraph can be used to mash up with reader reviews, similar best sellers, or current library status.

The downside here is that, given that the original page is marked up with XHTML 1.0 Transitional, the inclusion of RDFa attributes within the HTML tags does not technically validate. This may be a nonstarter for organizations that require valid markup to meet accessibility requirements. That being said, the inclusion of these attributes has shown no effect on rendering in browsers (and, in this case, the webpage in question does not actually validate prior to modification), so this issue is mostly a local value judgment.

The same event marked up using eRDF (Figure 3.12) would look a little different.

Although the end result is more or less the same, there are some differences in the syntax. Unlike RDFa, eRDF stays completely within the existing structure of HTML, so embedding the semantics stays valid even in HTML 4.0 pages.

This has a downside, though. Because relationships to other resources are based on <a> tags, the association to the *New York Times* best seller list DBpedia (dbpedia.org) page in the RDFa example (which is actually an RDF representation of the Wikipedia entry

```
<html>
 <head profile="http://purl.org/NET/erdf/profile">
  <link rel="schema.dc" href="http://purl.org/dc/elements/1.1/"/>
  <link rel="schema.dcterms" href="http://purl.org/dc/terms/"/>
  ...
 </head>
 <body>
  ...
<br />
Friday, September 12 at 12:00 p.m.</span></div>
<div id="urn:ISBN:0758212194" class="-dcterms-BibliographicResource"><a rel="dcterms-isPartOf"
href="http://www.nytimes.com/pages/books/bestseller/">The New York Times</a> and #1 <a
rel="dcterms-isPartOf" href="http://www.essence.com/essence/books/">Essence</a> bestselling
author <br />
<strong class="dc-creator">Mary Monroe </strong>visits and signs her new novel, <i class="dc-
title">She Had It Coming</i>.<br />
Central Library, 1st Floor<br />
</div>
  ...
 </body>
</html>
```

Figure 3.12   HTML for author visit and book signing with added eRDF

on the subject) needs to be changed to a link to the actual list for human friendliness. This is unfortunate, since an RDFa-aware application would be able to "follow its nose" to the DBpedia entry and gain more information about the *New York Times* best seller list—although that would not be possible when linking directly to the list itself. In the case of RDFa, the "resource" attribute allows you to provide a link to the DBpedia URI. This allows an RDF parser to pull the data from the DBpedia RDF representation for information about the *New York Times* best seller list. However, eRDF doesn't seem to have such a facility. So, since you're stuck with using a/href, you have to make the same assertion using Wikipedia as the object—but an RDF-aware application can't get any information from there.

The other downside of eRDF is that the HTML <head> information must be modified to define the namespaces of the RDF vocabularies used in the page. In organizations that use content management systems (CMSs), or in even simpler environments that use simple, static HTML pages derived from Dreamweaver templates, it is not feasible to expect that content creators are universally able to edit the contents of the <head> tag. There are workarounds to this limitation, certainly, such as including all the possible schema definitions within the page templates. Again, however, even this approach may not work in a black box system in which only parts of the templates are available for modification.

So while the RDF in HTML initiatives is much more robust (and, without a doubt, more complicated) than microformats for embedding various kinds of semantic information within webpages, the two styles are not mutually exclusive. Indeed, using the same example, Figure 3.13 takes our original RDFa and then also includes the hCalendar specification from microformats.

```
<div class="vevent">
<abbr class="dtstart" title="2008-09-12T12:00:00Z">Friday, September 12 at 12:00 p.m.</abbr>
<div xmlns:dc="http://purl.org/dc/elements/1.1/" xmlns:dcterms="http://purl.org/dc/terms/"
about="urn:ISBN:0758212194" ><span rel="dcterms:isPartOf" resource="http://dbpedia.org/
resource/New_York_Times_Best_Seller_list">The New York Times</span> and #1 <span
rel="dcterms:isPartOf" resource="http://www.essence.com/essence/books/">Essence</span>
bestselling author <br />
<span class="summary"><strong property="dc:creator">Mary Monroe </strong>visits and signs
her new novel, <i property="dc:title">She Had It Coming</i>.</span><br />
<span class="location">Central Library, 1st Floor</span><br />
</div>
</div>
```

Figure 3.13 HTML for author visit and book signing with RDFa and hCalendar
specification

The addition of semantics for the start time, event title, and location allows interested visitors to add this event to their personal calendar. So, with some very simple changes, a lot of context has been added to the content, which can be reused in a wide variety of ways.

Dealing With the Library's Edge Cases

Library technologists have not been oblivious to the developments going on in the world of semantic markup (or as the microformats community calls it, POSH, or plain old semantic HTML). Two initiatives in particular have been influenced by POSH methodology: COinS (Context Objects in Spans) and unAPI, a specification to enable cut and paste of metadata on the web.

COinS was developed as a way to incorporate citation information inside HTML pages to send to a user's OpenURL link resolver without prior knowledge of the user's institutional affiliation (and therefore of the user's link resolver location). Because the OpenURL resolver chain (from citation to appropriate copy) required a lot of pre-coordinated overhead (registering an institutional link resolver with a citation database, defining the IP [Internet Protocol]) ranges or accounts that are affiliated with a given institution, etc.), the benefits of the OpenURL architecture simply could not scale down for practical inclusion in a bibliography on a personal webpage or a completely neutral and free site such as Wikipedia (www.wikipedia.org). If the organizational affiliation was detached from the metadata, browser plug-ins (such as OCLC's OpenURL Referrer add-on [openly.oclc. org/openurlref] or LibX [www.libx.org]) could detect the citation information in the page and direct the user to an appropriate copy of the resource.

COinS are identified by the use of the class value Z3988 (which refers to Z39.88, the National Information Standards Organization [NISO] standard for OpenURL 1.0). The title attribute is used to store the bibliographic information (known in OpenURL parlance as the context object), which an application can read, append to an OpenURL resolver host base URL (Uniform Resource Locator), and create a link (Figure 3.14).

```
<span class="Z3988"
title="ctx_ver=Z39.88-2004&amp;rfr_id=canarydatabase.org:canarydb&amp;rft_val_fmt=info:ofi/
fmt:kev:mtx:journal&amp;rft_id=info:pmid/11097805&amp;url_ctx_fmt=ori:fmt:kev:mtx:ctx">Heavy
metals contamination and body condition of wintering guillemots (Uria aalge) at the Belgian coast
from 1993 to 1998.</span>
```

Figure 3.14   Citation marked up with COinS

UnAPI came after the development of COinS and differs from the other POSH formats in requiring some sort of web application component to serve the actual metadata (rather than embedding the data itself in the page). UnAPI defines the location of the unAPI server in the HTML <head> tag (Figure 3.15) and uses an approach similar to COinS' to let the server know what resource is being requested.

An application would then take the value of the unAPI-id and request what formats are available. In this example, the URL would be *http://canarydatabase.org/unapi?id=http://canarydatabase.org/*

```
<html>
 <head>
  <link rel="unapi-server" type="application/xml" title="unAPI" href="http://canarydatabase.org/
unapi" />
   ...
 </head>
 <body>
  ...
 <abbr class='unapi-id' title='http://canarydatabase.org/record/109'> </abbr>
  ...
 </body>
</html>
```

Figure 3.15   Page with unAPI markup

record/109. The server returns an XML document (Figure 3.16) with the metadata formats available for the resource.

```
<formats id="http://canarydatabase.org/record/109">
  <format name="endnote" type="text/plain"/>
  <format name="bibtex" type="text/plain"/>
  <format name="ris" type="text/plain"/>
  <format name="mods" type="application/xml"/>
</formats>
```

Figure 3.16   XML document with metadata available for requested resource

The application could then ask the unAPI server for the resource in a specific format (*http://canarydatabase.org/unapi?id=http://canary database.org/record/109&format=bibtex*) and get the metadata to use elsewhere.

Although neither COinS nor unAPI shares the mainstream appeal of microformats, they are both very simple, leverage existing library standards and technologies, and offer an effective way to make more robust data available.

Pulling Out the Stops: Linked Data

Although POSH approaches to contextualizing data in HTML are effective and have a fairly low barrier to entry, they also require shoe-horning metadata into a human interface, which may have usability and design implications. Another approach to making your data available is known as linked data, which effectively makes other representations of the resources defined at a URL available as RDF for machines to consume and navigate. This design uses the basic architecture of the web to achieve its functionality. By utilizing content negotiation (which happens during every HTTP request, anyway), an application can ask for the manner in which the website will return its content. For instance, it could request HTML for a human using a web browser, and for a machine it can return RDF, XML, JSON (JavaScript Object Notation), or other machine-readable formats.

Figure 3.17 shows the response from the website lcsh.info, an experimental (and now defunct)[1] project to turn Library of Congress subject authorities into the Simple Knowledge Organization System

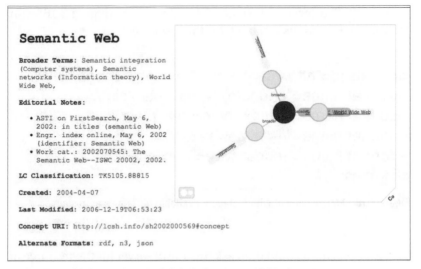

Figure 3.17 Response from lcsh.info in human-readable format

as seen in a web browser. The same URL can be requested to return the RDF format N3, as shown in Figure 3.18.

With this design, the same URLs can be used for human- and machine-readable interfaces, with the optimal data being displayed

```
ross-singers-computer:~ rosssinger$ curl --header "Accept: text/n3"  http://lcsh
.info/sh2002000569

@prefix _6: <http://lcsh.info/sh2002000569#>.
@prefix _7: <http://lcsh.info/sh95000541#>.
@prefix _8: <http://lcsh.info/sh2004000479#>.
@prefix _9: <http://lcsh.info/sh92004914#>.
@prefix dcterms: <http://purl.org/dc/terms/>.
@prefix rdf: <http://www.w3.org/1999/02/22-rdf-syntax-ns#>.
@prefix skos: <http://www.w3.org/2004/02/skos/core#>.

_6:concept a skos:Concept;
    dcterms:LCC "TK5105.88815";
    dcterms:created "2004-04-07"^^<http://www.w3.org/2001/XMLSchema#date>;
    dcterms:modified "2006-12-19T06:53:23"^^<http://www.w3.org/2001/XMLSchema#d
ateTime>;
    skos:broader _8:concept,
        _9:concept,
        _7:concept;
    skos:editorialNote "ASTI on FirstSearch, May 6, 2002: in titles (semantic W
eb)"@en,
        "Engr. index online, May 6, 2002 (identifier: Semantic Web)"@en,
        "Work cat.: 2002070545: The Semantic Web--ISWC 20002, 2002."@en;
    skos:inScheme <http://lcsh.info/>;
    skos:prefLabel "Semantic Web"@en.
```

Figure 3.18 Response from lcsh.info in machine-readable format

for each. Other machines can then also refer to the identifiers exposed, allowing rich contextual associations between resources and across websites and services. For example, the National Library of Sweden's OPAC (Online Public Access Catalog), named LIBRIS, is also a linked data application and uses the subject headings from lcsh.info and DBpedia[2]. An RDF-aware application can follow these references and find more resources about the same subject, with the confidence that all references to these subject URIs are talking about the same thing.

Of course, this method requires much more of an architectural commitment, which may not be available to all libraries. The underlying data would need to be structured in a way that makes it available in this capacity, which simply is not the case for most applications employed currently. However, Drupal (www.drupal.org), the open source CMS, is in the process of exposing all of its contents as linked open data and RDF, which would effectively democratize the linked data movement by bringing it to common, commodity software.

All Approaches Welcome

At the end of the day, *any* semantics available in library data is better than none. By taking any of the previously mentioned methods of adding context to content (or a combination of several), webpages become their own data sources, their content useful to other applications and uses. The exact approach taken will be dependent on the technological environment, local needs, expertise, and personal preference of the content creators, but the benefits will be available to anybody willing to take advantage of them.

Mashing up the library does not have to be a one-way street of incorporating external data into our services. External data enriched with the context of local library information is an even better way to make our websites useful and relevant.

Endnotes

1. The Library of Congress has since released an official version based on lcsh.info at id.loc.gov.
2. With the release of the official Authorities and Vocabularies service from the Library of Congress, LIBRIS also used subject headings from id.loc.gov.

CHAPTER 4

Mashing Up With Librarian Knowledge

Thomas Brevik
Royal Norwegian Naval Academy

Externalizing human knowledge is one of mankind's oldest activities. It has taken the form of oral stories, cave paintings, words printed on pages, audiovisual media—and today, the digital format. This last format is in many ways the most challenging for those whose profession involves collecting, ordering, and disseminating knowledge in any form. But at the same time, the possibilities inherent in externalizing knowledge have increased by many orders of magnitude. This new format also allows for mixing knowledge with other sources of information to generate even higher levels of useful knowledge.

One new challenge is the increasing expectation, if not demand, that bodies of knowledge previously restricted to professions such as medicine and law must be accessible and available to the general public. Patients come to the doctor armed with a greater knowledge of their condition than ever before and are rapidly becoming partners in treatment discussions. This was unheard of in the age of print, but today we see a new public attitude toward professional knowledge. This demand for externalized professional knowledge may feel to librarians like a threat or a devaluation of the profession, but it can also be viewed as a great opportunity.

The opportunity to externalize our professional knowledge also provides the chance to be relevant to new generations of information seekers. By putting as much of our knowledge as possible out on the web (and keeping it updated!), we give the public a chance to profit by our sharing. We also enhance our own body of knowledge by opening it up to input from both inside and outside the profession, and by making this knowledge mashable, we contribute to new and surprising combinations of knowledge. In my opinion this comes close to the core of librarianship as a profession.

The development of mashable bodies of knowledge creates a unique opportunity for libraries. If we lead—and we have the necessary concepts, body of professional knowledge, and professional ethos to do so—others can benefit from our trailblazing. Medical and legal professionals are already forging ahead, but usually in closed or fragmented environments or formats and with nonmashable bodies of externalized knowledge. By embracing openness, setting an example, and developing methods, standards, and tools, librarians can both enhance their professional role and contribute to a more open universe of knowledge and knowledge sharing.

But this window of opportunity is rapidly closing. Already we see Google (www.google.com) entering the arena with Knol (knol.google. com), and other attractive methods of externalizing knowledge will appear. Librarians can supply an alternative, not by "out-knoling" Google, but by using and promoting open and useful tools and resources that highlight our commitment to sharing our own professional knowledge and the fact that we have the knowledge and professional direction to help others do the same.

In Norway we have two very good examples of externalized librarian knowledge. Ønskebok.no (www.onskebok.no; see Figure 4.1) is the Norwegian equivalent of the British whichbook.net (www.which book.net; see Figure 4.2), which uses our professional ability to analyze literature to create a combination of personal reader comments; analysis along user-oriented scales such as more or less sex, bleak or less bleak, and optimistic or pessimistic; and finally a passage from the book in question. Together these elements form a pretty good digital version of a good book talk. This database is not searchable in the traditional meaning of the word but focuses on findability. Users find book suggestions by sliding scales that show their reading preferences and make choices on aspects like the sexual orientation of the main character, the location, and the type of plot. The wonderful thing about whichbook and ønskebok is that the data can best, if not only, be generated by librarians who undergo training in addition to their professional education and experience. The corps of librarian readers is a growing body of professionals who can use their knowledge to contribute to an increasingly useful database of information that will last far longer than any one professional career.

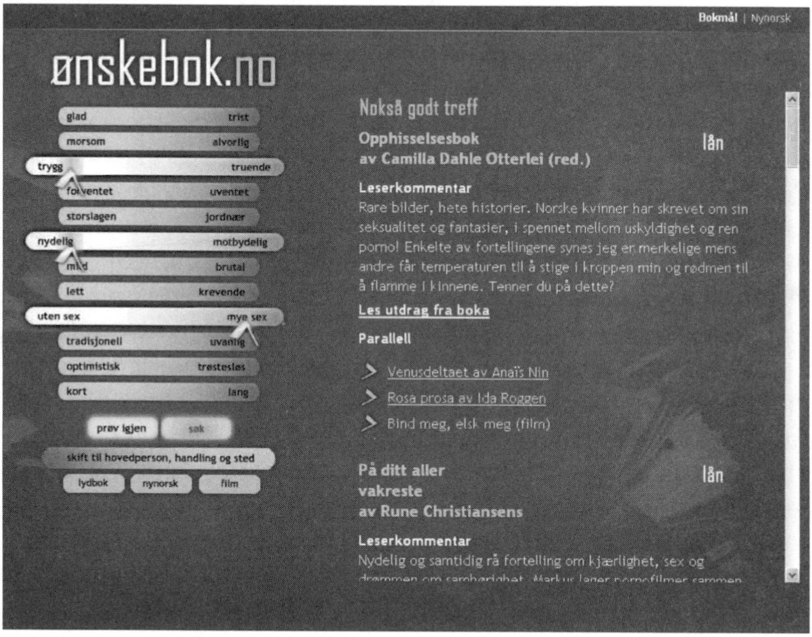

Figure 4.1 ønskebok.no

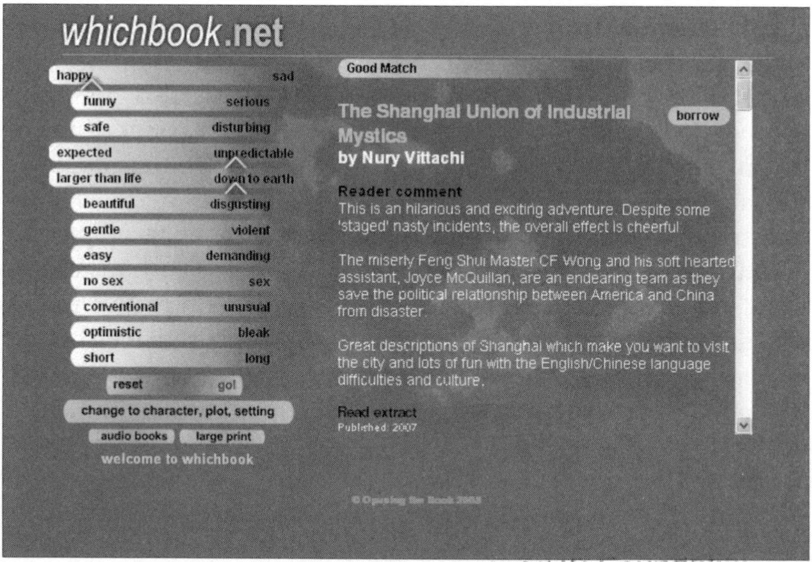

Figure 4.2 whichbook.net

This data is mashed up with all public library catalogs in Norway. When users look for a good read on ønskebok.no, they are immediately informed whether their library has the book available and, if not, where they can get it. I expect future possibilities for connecting the data in ønskebok.no to other bodies of knowledge, like information on authors in Wikipedia (www.wikipedia.org) and geographical locations in map services like Google Earth (earth.google.com). Although whichbook.net is not yet open source, it is one of the best examples I can find of an original and user-oriented approach to externalizing a unique part of our professional knowledge.

The second example of externalized librarian knowledge is the wiki that the Norwegian national online reference service Biblioteksvar (biblioteksvar.no; English version, biblioteksvar.no/en) has built (library answer; see Figure 4.3). It contains reference questions and answers and reference resources. This is not a new idea; many libraries have done this before in many forms. Again, it is a way of transferring knowledge from one librarian to another, as we have done before with books, journal articles, etc., but with the added bonus that in this format the information can be updated and added to. Mistakes are corrected as they are discovered. New sources are added and old sources removed when appropriate. All this from a cooperative environment in which librarians from around the country all contribute to the reference service. The librarians add their little bits of knowledge and get the benefit of access to a great knowledge database in return. The wiki also contains professional training and advice, such as how to conduct a reference interview. This data has not yet been mashed up, but I suspect that the day when we will all benefit from connecting the wiki to our catalogs, map services, or other mashable information is not far away.

Externalizing our professional knowledge cannot be accomplished with one large, centrally funded and administered project. To accomplish something this big demands an effort from those involved in libraries around the world. It is not enough to publish a blog or edit an entry in Wikipedia, although this is a small contribution. Libraries will have to identify the right tools, or even invent the tools if they do not exist, as is the case with whichbook.net. Then we must involve all library workers, not only librarians, in the input.

Externalizing the core of our professional knowledge is probably the greatest challenge our profession has faced because it breaks with a more than 2,000-year-old tradition of keeping certain types of

biblioteksvar.no   SøkWiki: [   ] [Go]

Lenker
Emneportaler og
søkemotorer
Gratis leksikon
Taktanalyse
Sex og samliv
Krisetelefoner
Spørretjenester
Lovlig nedlastning av mp3

Skole
Særemne
Religion
Naturfag

Kjekt å vite
Brukermanual
Opphavsrett
Hurtigtaster
Digitale referanseverktøy
Treningsklinger
Sette over sms/e-post
Lagre URL-er
Om fagbibliotekene
Biblioteksvar i media

Om det å svare
Referanseintervju
Spørsmål og svar

Wikihjelp
Skrivehjelp
Sandkasse

(Rediger menyen)

Referanseintervju   Siste endringer · Utskriftsvisning · Sidehistorie · Rediger side

Referanseintervju

Det er viktig å komme i dialog med brukerne og utnytte styrken som ligger i chat som kommunikasjonsform. Vi har mulighet til å utdype spørsmål, kommentere og få tilbakemeldinger i chatten, ikke ulikt referanseintervjuet som finner sted i biblioteket. Særlig i chat er dette intervjuet viktig, i og med at vi ikke kan se våre brukere.

Standardmeldinger

Meldingene er ment som en hjelp i dialogen, til å få sent over meldinger raskt uten å skrive dem ned. De gir også en pekepinn på at henvendelser bør besvares nokså formelt og ikke gå over til en sosial chat.

Samtalen

Åpningsmeldingen "Hei, hva kan jeg hjelpe deg med?" innbyr til samtale og vi må bli flinkere til å følge opp spørsmålene til brukerne. I mange chatter blir referanseintervjuet unngått ved at man direkte sender en melding om at bibliotekvakten skal foreta et søk. Det oppmuntres derfor til at man går aktivt inn i dialogen, som jo er chatformens store fordel, og gjør et referanseintervju før man setter igang med søkingen.

Referanseintervjuet

- Målet for tjenesten er å svare brukeren i chatten.
- Brukerne må ikke sendes bort fra tjenesten med uforrettet sak.
- Er spørsmålet vanskelig ber man om e-postadressen og sender svaret over senere.

Åpne spørsmål

- Still åpne spørsmål eller gjenta forespørselen med andre ord slik at du er sikker på hva brukeren mener
- Utdyp spørsmålet
- Spør gjerne hva det skal brukes til, slik at svaret sammenfaller med brukerens forventninger
- Gå i dialog med brukeren
- Vær åpen og direkte

Figure 4.3   biblioteksvar.no

knowledge to ourselves. When it is out on the web, searchable and accessible, we are more exposed and can be held accountable for our professional practices and decisions by people outside our profession. Who wants to be scrutinized by everybody?

The thing is, though: What is the alternative? Accountability might be forced on us by the public in other ways, ways we will have less control over, and that will have less benefit for both ourselves and the public. A forced accountability might actually be detrimental to our mission of openness and accessibility by imposing the use of inappropriate tools or closed formats.

Second, there is the openness issue. Will we make our information available in formats that lend themselves to mashing up? Our history of holding on to catalog silos and our acceptance of closed databases do not make our dedication to openness and accessibility obvious to anybody outside the profession. It was not that many years ago that many European libraries still had large parts of their collections in closed stacks. So even if we now embrace openness in word, we still have to prove in deed that we are in fact on the right side of one of the most controversial issues of our age.

What are we waiting for? Our knees to stop shaking, maybe? It is a daunting idea to pull so much of what we value as our core competencies out of our heads and professional hearts into the open. Are we afraid? I know I am. There is something that scares me more than this, though, and that is the idea of sitting abandoned and left behind by larger social forces and developments that scream out for librarians to participate.

Part II

Mashing Up Library Websites

CHAPTER 5

Information in Context

Brian Herzog
Chelmsford Public Library

This chapter is titled "Information in Context" for two reasons. First, information alone is not always helpful; the right answer at the wrong time is often just as unhelpful as the wrong answer. Second, to be truly useful, not only does information need to be accurate and relevant, but also the person seeking it needs to be able to recognize it as pertinent to his or her need and to know intuitively how to put it to use to solve a problem.

Library websites are prime locations for thinking about information in context. Patrons come to us for information, so our websites should be able to guide them to the resource they need—ideally, without navigation assistance from library staff. This saves patrons time in finding an answer to their question (24 hours a day) and allows library staff to focus on working with the most difficult questions or with patrons who need assistance in other areas.

Library websites are generally chock full of useful resources, but the way these are presented is often not intuitive, leaving patrons unable to navigate on their own or identify the resource applicable to their need. This problem can stem from an overuse of library jargon, a lack of time or web coding skills, or ignorance of a better way of promoting a program or resource.

The solution (to some) of these problems is the second reason for this chapter's title. The technologies underlying Web 2.0 make it easier for anyone to increase the functionality, interactivity, relevancy, usefulness, and all-around interestingness of a website. Information (in the form of text, links, photographs, videos, etc.) can be uploaded and hosted on web servers that might be different from the one where the library's website is hosted, then easily brought back and displayed on the library website through RSS feeds or embedded objects (more on those later). Most of these external hosting services are specifically designed for this purpose. They take care of the technical aspects of storing and formatting the information, which allows librarians to do what we do best: Organize information and present it to patrons in a useful and meaningful way.

The end goal of any library resource (print, electronic, or the physical layout of the library itself) is to be useful to the patron. Developing webpages using these principles and technologies allows library websites to be more useful to patrons because content that was previously difficult or time-consuming to manage can now be included with ease. Integrating external information into our websites makes them a destination rich with meaningful resources instead of just a list of links to other places.

Information Out of Context

To illustrate the difference between implementing a resource in a way that might be confusing and implementing it in a way that is inherently useful, here is an example that I often see on library websites. Many libraries provide a subscription-based product called BookLetters (www.bookletters.com) to their patrons. (I'm using this just as an example, not to imply endorsement.) Among other things, BookLetters provides various lists of books (best sellers, award winners, etc.), allowing libraries to "wrap" these lists so that they look like library webpages, even though the information actually resides on the BookLetters web server.

This in itself is a good example of integrating useful information into your library website—or at least making it look as if it's part of your library website. But what I want to focus on here is *how* it's integrated. Many librarians know what BookLetters refers to, but my guess is that the majority of patrons do not. So even if the BookLetters content itself is integrated well into the website, the patron needs to be guided to this content in a meaningful way.

Figure 5.1 shows a mock-up of two versions of a library website. On the left, the BookLetters logo is included to guide the patron to this content. However, this approach requires patrons to know what BookLetters is and why it could help them, or it requires them to just be curious and find it by chance. Using this approach does make sense

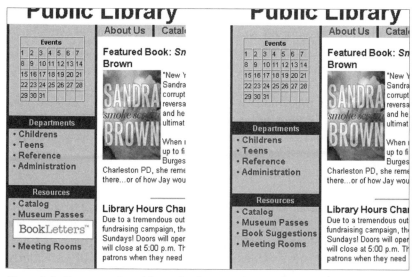

Figure 5.1   Two examples of how a book suggestion service can be integrated into a library website; one uses the company's logo, and the other uses a text link that should be self-explanatory.

from the website maintainer's point of view—this is, after all, the link to the BookLetters content—but it might make no sense at all to an uninitiated patron. On the right side, the same website has been reworked to better integrate this content into the website's look and navigation. "Book Suggestions" is probably more meaningful to patrons, which increases their likelihood of finding the information when they need it.

Giving patrons some context for this link helps guide them to the content. A text link such as "Book Suggestions" might not be as visually appealing as a corporate logo, but it is more descriptive of the content and fits in with the rest of the website. What's also nice is that, even though this content is on another web server, wrapping it in the look of the library website means that patrons using it will probably not even know that they have left their library's website. In their mind, the library is providing them with valuable information, because this content has been embedded within the library's site.

Embedding Content

BookLetters is a subscription service specifically designed to fit into library websites. However, many other Web 2.0 sites, both free and subscription-based, can also be integrated into library websites; the possibilities are limited only by your creativity. Once you have worked out what kind of content you would like to include, actually getting that content to appear is easy.

Most popular Web 2.0 sites, such as YouTube (www.youtube.com), offer an "embed this video" or "get our widget" feature to make it easy to embed any content uploaded to their servers into your website. This is simple in that, depending on how you manage your website, you don't necessarily need to know anything about file formats, FTPing, or even HTML coding; all you need to know is how to copy and paste.

Listed here are some thoughts on putting Web 2.0 sites and embedded content to good and fun use. Once you have an idea (let's say you have videorecorded kids reviewing their favorite books and want to display these videos on your website), the process is fairly straightforward. Upload the video to your YouTube account and then view the video. Figure 5.2 shows, circled, where to find the embed code you will need to copy and paste into your website to make this video display on your webpage.

Figure 5.2   The content of most Web 2.0 websites, including this YouTube video, provides the code you need to embed that content into your own website. No real technical understanding is needed; you just copy and paste it where you want the content to appear.

Although the code itself looks complicated, no real technical understanding of how it works is needed. All you need to do is highlight and copy the code that appears in the Embed window and then paste it into your site at the spot where you would like the content to appear. The video still "lives" on the YouTube server; it is just being displayed on your website. This lets you organize this information and present it to patrons in a way that is useful and relevant to them, within the context of the library website.

Another popular type of Web 2.0 content is photographs. Just as YouTube is only one option for hosting video, you can choose from among many photo hosting websites. One of the leaders is Flickr (www.flickr.com). Most people who maintain websites are already likely familiar with working with images. Moving away from hosting your own images to uploading photos to your Flickr account lets you take advantage of the other features Flickr offers, including interactive, social features.

Like videos, single photos can be embedded into a webpage (just as if they were stored on your own web server). One convenient feature of Flickr is that it automatically resizes your photos for you and provides properly formatted code to embed them into your website. Flickr has built-in ways to organize your photos, called *sets* and *collections*, and you can use tags as keywords for further organization. Sets, tags, and collections can be used to display groups of photographs on your website, and Flickr also provides users with the code for embedding a *badge* (a series of photographs) or a slideshow. By combining tags and sets, you can control what is displayed within your own site and where it will show up.

Most Web 2.0 sites also provide an RSS feed, which can be used to stream content from one website to another. You can subscribe to an RSS feed to get the latest information from a particular source (which is why an RSS feed of *your own* website is a nice thing to offer your patrons). Feeds, however, can also be used as another method of embedding rich and valuable content into your library's site.

Before you can display an RSS feed on your website, the feed needs to be converted into code that can be embedded. Although many options are available, one simple tool is Feed to JavaScript (Feed2JS; www.feed2js.org). Paste the URL (Uniform Resource Locator) for any feed into a box on the Feed2JS website, and Feed2JS gives you the code to embed on your website; it provides both basic and advanced formatting options, so you can control the way the content looks.

Another somewhat new feature libraries can embed in their web-sites is the entire text of a book. Thanks to the Google Book Search (books.google.com), the full text of digitized books in the public domain can be placed, in their entirety, right into a library's website. Embedding an entire book can provide easy access for class assignments, book groups, local history, or featured topics or to supplement the library's print collection for out-of-print titles. Instructions found online (googlesystem.blogspot.com/2008/09/embeddable-google-books.html) provide an example, but the following is all that is needed is to embed the code:

```
<script type="text/javascript"
src="http://books.google.com/books/
previewlib.js"></script>
<script type="text/javascript">
GBS_insertEmbeddedViewer('GkCpLIk7aisC,'600
,500);
</script>
```

Just replace *"GkCpLIk7aisC"* with the book ID from your chosen title. (The book ID can be found in the URL when you view that book on Google.)

Once you start looking for them, you'll find lots of websites offering ways to embed their content on your website. Table 5.1 offers a few ideas for using embedded content to enrich your own site.

Library Subject Guides Using Delicious

Another type of embedded content ideally suited to libraries is available from Delicious (delicious.com) and allows you to create subject guides. Delicious is a social bookmarking website that allows users to create a list of favorite, or bookmarked, websites. Delicious also allows users to describe and tag these websites, which means libraries can create their own structured vocabulary and descriptions for useful websites.

Libraries have been maintaining subject guides on their websites for as long as there have been library websites. By using the Web 2.0 technology on the Delicious website, librarians can easily update their online subject guides whenever they stumble across a useful website, without having to open their local copy of a webpage, edit that page to include the link to the new resource, save it, and FTP the

Table 5.1   Ideas for embedding content types

Videos	Photographs	Feeds	Some Links for Other Ideas
• Book reviews • Library tour or a tour of historical sites around your community • Overview of library resources and facilities • Teen movie-making club • Staff introductions (I know, it'll never happen) • Training on using library resources	• Library tour • Photos of patrons • Photos of a library or town events • Staff introductions • Highlights of a collection, such as historical photographs • Displays of other peoples' photos of your library or community via a Flickr pool or a badge and tags	• Promotion of your library blog on other library webpages • Display of blog posts with certain tags on related webpages • Display of community news (especially headlines from your local paper) • Promotion of community connections by displaying feeds from patrons' blogs, photo streams, or other local sources	• Local weather forecasts (www.weather.com) • Polls and quizzes, to see how patrons feel about an issue or just solicit input (www.flexipoll.com) • Online chat, to ask a librarian a question or have a discussion (www.meebome.com) • Games, for a game club, to illustrate an article or collection, or just for fun (www.everyflashgame.com) • Book information, to show new additions or a special collection (www.librarything.com)

new page up to the web server (or send an email asking the webmaster to do all this for them). Delicious allows you to add websites to your account from anywhere and has built-in tools for embedding your Delicious bookmarks in your website. This means that as soon as you add a website to your Delicious account, it is also automatically added to your website's subject guide—with no code tinkering in between. Delicious also offers formatting control so that when your bookmarks are fed into your website, they look just like everything else on your webpage.

The process for creating subject guides incorporating Delicious is simple and flexible, offering different methods for adding websites to your account. The first step is to create a Delicious account (secure.delicious.com/register) with the Delicious web form. Now you need to start bookmarking resources into your account. One

option is to enter the website manually. After logging in, click the Save
New Bookmarks link (highlighted in Figure 5.3), and then enter the
website's URL into the box provided and click Next.

**Figure 5.3   To begin bookmarking websites to your Delicious account, click the
Save New Bookmarks link.**

The next screen, shown in Figure 5.4, displays the website's URL
and title and offers input boxes for notes and tags. You can edit any of
these fields as appropriate for display within your subject guide (the
Notes field will appear as a description of the website). The Tags field
is of particular importance for library subject guides as this is how
each bookmarked website is designated to appear under a particular
subject. You can always go back and change or add tags, but subject
guide maintenance will be easier if you have an idea of the structured
vocabulary you'd like to use right from the beginning. Depending on
your subject guides, your tags can be as broad or as narrow as necessary. Tags can also be combined to produce subject guides, and websites can appear in more than one guide.

Below these fields you will see lists of suggested tags, which other people have used to describe this website. (If no suggested tags appear, then
no one else has tagged this website in Delicious.) In addition to others'
tags, all the tags you have used within your account are also displayed—

Figure 5.4 Editing website information that will appear in your Delicious account

which makes sticking to your own structured vocabulary a little easier. After you have finished editing the fields, click Save, and this website will be bookmarked into your account. Note that this screen also allows you to choose whether to share a bookmarked website. Because we're talking about making online subject guides to aid library patrons, these websites should all be shared.

Delicious also offers ways to streamline the bookmarking process. The most useful of these are toolbar buttons that are installed right in your internet browser (either Mozilla Firefox or Microsoft Internet Explorer). Instructions for installing these buttons are found at delicious.com/help/tools, along with additional information on their use. Once the toolbar buttons are installed in your browser, adding websites to your delicious account is much easier. When you're viewing a website you'd like to add, just click the Delicious Tag button (shown in Figure 5.5). This will launch a new window in which you can edit the URL, title, notes, and tags for that website. Clicking Save on this window will bookmark the website to your account and close the window, returning you to the site you were viewing, all with minimal interruption of your browsing process. These browser buttons

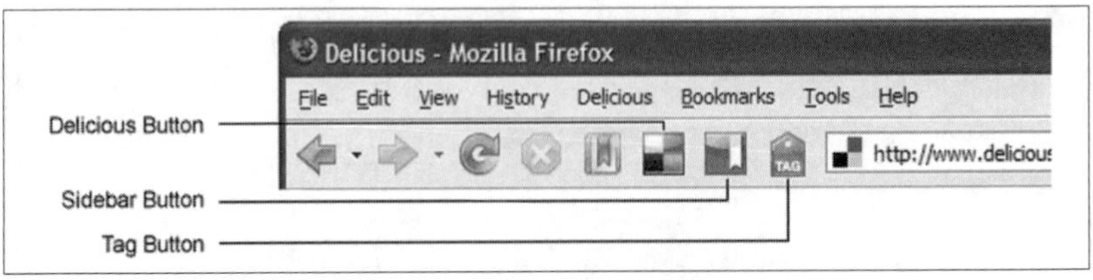

Figure 5.5 Example of Delicious browser buttons in Firefox

can be installed on all computers used by the librarians maintaining online subject guides, helping make this project collaborative; now your librarians can add and tag useful websites whenever they come across them (not needing to jot them down or email them to someone to add to the website later).

As websites are bookmarked into your Delicious account, they are automatically added to your account's RSS feed. To display your bookmarked websites in subject guides on your library's site, your feed needs to be converted to code that can be embedded on your webpage. You can use tools such as Feed2JS to do this, but Delicious has its own built-in feature called Linkrolls, which is easy to use (see Figure 5.6). Access Linkrolls through your account at delicious.com/help/linkrolls.

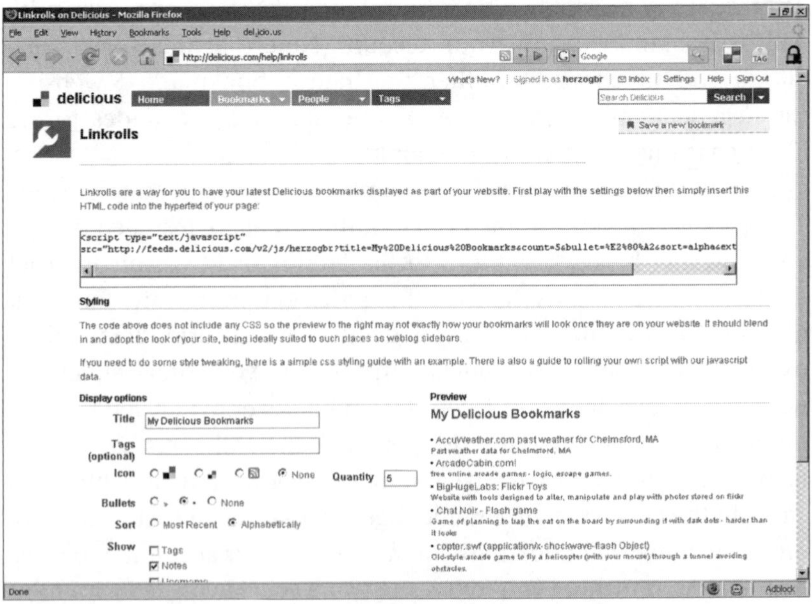

Figure 5.6 Linkrolls setup screen to customize the feeds into your subject guides

This form not only provides you with the code to copy and paste into your own website, but also provides options (at the bottom of the screen) to let you do feed customization and some basic formatting. (For more advanced display formatting, use the CSS [Cascading Style Sheets] styling guide provided by Delicious at delicious.com/help/linkrolls/css.) You can customize many options: what you would like the title text to be (leave blank for no title), whether to display an icon, how many bookmarks to display, how to sort the bookmarks, and how much information to display. As these options are changed, a live preview of how the feed will look is displayed in the Preview section on the right. Also, the code to embed the feed into your website is created in real time in the window above. (Note that websites can be listed either in alphabetical order or with the most recent additions first. Unfortunately, Delicious doesn't offer any kind of weighting system to allow you to display the "best" websites first. This means that as you bookmark more websites, the order in which they display on your webpage will change.)

To make these true subject guides, we need to create multiple feeds to organize the bookmarked websites by topic. This is where a structured vocabulary in your tags field comes into play. Hopefully you have tagged all your bookmarked websites well, with tags such as Local, Government, Sports, and News. To create feeds for specific subjects, enter the tag for that subject into the tag field. Tags can be combined to make even narrower subject guides. For instance, with our example tags, we could make a subject guide from the tag News for all news-related bookmarked websites and a second, narrower, subject guide for just local news by using the News and Local tags: News Local (use a space in between tags to combine them).

Once a feed is set to the options you want, copy the code from the window at the top of the Linkrolls page and paste it into your own webpage. Each of your feeds can be placed into individual subject guides, or you can put multiple feeds into a single subject guide webpage. One example of this is to create a Health subject guide and have individual feeds on the same page for Health Seniors, Health Women, Health Kids, Health Drug Information, Health Alternative Medicine, Health Doctor Locators, and so on (provided you tagged your bookmarked websites with these tags ahead of time). All this will display on a single webpage but categorized logically.

As with most Web 2.0 tools, the possibilities are limited only by your creativity. In addition to regular subject guides, other ideas include showing the 10 most recently bookmarked websites on your homepage, with a feed just for staff-related bookmarks, or even feeding in the bookmarks of all Delicious users who use specific tags, such as your town name, local sports team, or other topics of interest to patrons.

Web 2.0h-No's to Keep in Mind

As useful as Delicious (and other Web 2.0 tools) can be, there are always drawbacks and concerns to keep in mind. First and foremost, because content is hosted on web servers other than your own, your website is subject to the availability and speed of those servers. If they are temporarily unavailable (or go out of business permanently), you lose access to that content—which might leave a hole in your website. For websites or accounts that are subscription-based, you should have contractual recourse. But for the free websites (which are often the most popular), long-term reliability can be gauged only by what you may know about their business atmosphere, their current popularity, or their market penetration. Well-known popular websites such as Flickr and YouTube, owned by Yahoo! and Google, respectively, will probably be around for a while, but there is no guarantee. And even if there is no problem with the content itself, server or network slowdowns can noticeably affect how quickly your webpages with embedded content load.

Be sure to read the terms of use of these websites to know what control you retain over the content you upload and what rights you might forfeit. And when it comes to content, although you can control the content of what you upload to your own accounts, you lose that control when you embed content or feeds from someone else's account. If you embed a perfect video for your library website, and then later the owner of that video deletes it from his or her account, you lose access to it. Keep in mind, also, if you are embedding feeds from news services or other websites, there is a chance that something they contain may be objectionable to your patrons or violate library policy in some way.

Despite these concerns, embedding content into your library's website can be a valuable way to supplement other library resources, provide a framework for content your patrons might not otherwise see, and encourage interaction and involvement. Goodwill and usefulness can be immeasurable, but actual utility must always take precedence over novelty. Don't be afraid to try something just to see how it works or to see whether people will use it (this is usually the best way to learn, and the best way to show other people what is possible). But by that same token, don't embed content in your website just because you can. Library websites, like libraries, are intended to serve our patrons, and they will only use us to the extent that they find us useful. By providing useful information in a meaningful context, the library's website will hopefully be ready and waiting when a patron comes looking to fill an information need.

CHAPTER 6

Mashing Up the Library Website

Lichen Rancourt
Manchester City Library

When I arrived at the Manchester City (NH) Library, its website was, like many others, static. It was informative in the sense that it gave the viewer a brief introduction to the library, but it was not dynamic, contained out-of-date information, and was difficult both to navigate and to maintain. Most sadly, it did not accurately reflect the library as an active and dynamic community center. My challenge was to create an integrated web presence that was still informative but more interesting, fun, and easier to navigate and to use.

Five goals played a role in transforming the site into one that people would want to visit—for reasons other than just garnering straight information. Each involved library staff and patrons in a manner the library had not previously experienced, enabling the website to accurately portray the library and become indispensable to both casual users and more intense patrons. Those goals were as follows:

- It would be easy to maintain.

- It had to accurately represent the library as an active and vital place.

- It would expose the library's resources and make them easier to use.

- It would provide an opportunity for interactivity if the viewer wanted it.

- It would allow for integration of library-generated content into the lives of our users.

73

The trick seemed to be to liberate both existing and desired content, so that it could be repurposed in new ways or mashed up. This would help automate the onerous task of editing code to update the site, allowing the librarians to concentrate instead on generating content, interacting with web users, and promoting library services.

With these goals in mind, I mapped out several different services that would help me begin to create a fun, dynamic, comprehensive, and vital website. Identifying these services was pretty easy. The more difficult part was to document all the changes for the other managers so that they could step in in an emergency, as well as to maintain a high degree of communication with all levels of staff. The changes were fairly significant, and as with most institutions, change required explanation, promotion, and ultimately user and staff support.

Easy to Maintain

Prior to my arrival, updating the information on the library's site required manually coding each line. This, as anyone working with the web in the "old days" knows, was an arduous and labor-intensive task. One of the key areas was the library's featured events, which were highlighted on the front page. This area suffered because of the effort required to keep it up-to-date.

I need to be clear that this was not due to any dereliction of duty. As in most publicly funded institutions, resources, such as personnel, can be scarce. The staff responsible for the library website also had to address user, network, interface, and system needs. Much of the day was devoted to troubleshooting, and because the library network is part of the larger city network, management came from several directions.

Because of this, projects like the website became dramatically out-of-date. Managers had to constantly monitor every page of the site and physically input data for every minor change. They had to delete events or programs that were out of date, update email addresses to reflect staff changes, and update any variation in library hours—the list could seem endless. To accurately represent all the activity in a vital library, an administrator had to dedicate immense amounts of time to removing old information and adding the new events or programs. Enabling easier maintenance was critical. This was true not only from an events point of view but also in terms of other resources, such as book and account tracking, books available, and any other information that might change regarding the facility, programs, training, etc.

The first, and most essential, element in mashing up data is to have a way to separate *content* from *container* so that information stored in one place can be automatically reflected elsewhere. This would allow an easier way to maintain the site, making manual updates unnecessary or only occasionally necessary. When I'm looking for tools, a major requirement is that they must provide a way to reuse the information I provide. Technologies such as RSS, badges, application programming interfaces (APIs), and iCal all make this possible.

Active and Vital

Creating a more accurate representation of the library was also essential. My impression on first viewing its old site was that it was static, academic, not much fun, and pretty much a dusty old library (Figure 6.1). I was amazed when I actually set foot in the facility because what I encountered was nothing like what was represented on the website.

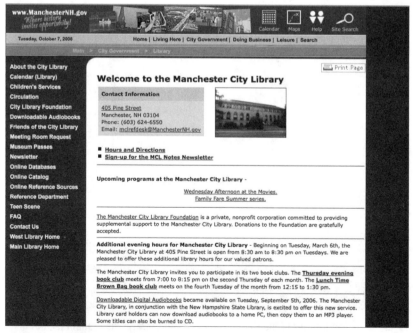

Figure 6.1   Manchester City Library website on July 15, 2007

For one, the building itself was interesting, beautiful, and dynamic. It possessed enough of an "academic" feel to convince anyone that it was indeed a library, but it also provided rich architecture, an interesting layout, and a friendly casualness that was not captured adequately on the web. From the marble edifice to the three-story-high rotunda, visitors then and now are not only embraced by the warmth of the building and its staff but also impressed by the grand nature of the entire library (Figure 6.2). Contrary to what you would have expected from its website, you truly felt you had arrived at a destination, and I wanted my new web initiatives to represent that fact.

Figure 6.2   The interior of the Carpenter Memorial Library, the main branch of the Manchester City Library (Courtesy of the Manchester City Library)

I asked myself, What accounts for the comforting welcome I felt on entering? What does the physical library have that the website doesn't, and is it possible to translate that? The answer would define my ambition to build an interactive "virtual" library that would provide all the services found in our library building, namely,

- Librarians

- Patrons

- Programs

- A collection

- Local resources

The simplest way to communicate the library and its spirit was to show it. I opened a Flickr (www.flickr.com) account in the library's name. This allowed us to share photos of the library and capture some of the warmth, diversity, culture, and social benefit, as well as give the public some insight into the lives, professional and otherwise, of the staff. A picture is worth a thousand words, and our photos show the public what is going on at the library and the many different roles the library plays as an institution and pillar of the greater community (Figure 6.3).

Figure 6.3   The library's Flickr page at www.flickr.com/photos/manchesterlibrary

In addition to being easy to use, Flickr provides a built-in option for displaying your photos on a website. I created a badge that replaced the front-page photo of the building's exterior with the latest seven photos uploaded to our Flickr account (Figure 6.4). This means that the website is automatically updated whenever any staff member uploads a new photo to Flickr, with no need for anyone to poke at the site's code to make the change. Things couldn't get much easier to maintain than that!

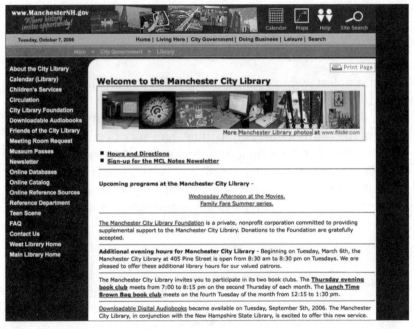

Figure 6.4   The library website featuring the new Flickr badge

Our children's department hosted a New Year's party for city children, at which they "confettied" and "noise-makered" 2008 in at the stroke of noon on January 2 (Figure 6.5). One of the photos we took at the party ended up being our first entry into the "365 Library Days" project, a collection on Flickr of libraries that all made a commitment to upload one photo for every day of the year (www.flickr.com/groups/365libs). This was partly an act of public self-discipline to help me commit to regularly adding more photos, but it also served to create the momentum for other changes to Manchester's website. Once it caught on, adding other features and benefits was easy. I knew we had started getting somewhere when I

Figure 6.5   The New Year's party marks the beginning of our 365 Library Days Project (www.flickr.com/photos/manchesterlibrary/2159938682).

entered a craft program, camera in hand, and a mother, on seeing me, asked, "Oh! What day are we on?"

Our Flickr badge served as a first step for revitalizing the main site and beginning to add features that end users would appreciate. In addition, it allowed us to track which aspects of the library generated the most interest via web traffic and actual comments from visitors.

Expose Library Resources

The second major component I added was a search box up front on the main page (Figure 6.6). This allowed users to

- Search for items in Manchester's collection, as well as those owned by other libraries in the consortium

- Determine the availability of an item in and out of the library

- View their accounts to see what materials they have out and when they are due

- Renew items the patron has not finished using

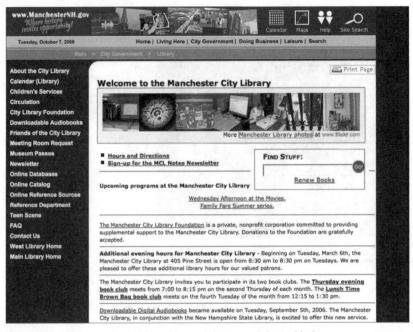

Figure 6.6 The library website with a catalog search box added

This simple function went a long way to making the main library website more dynamic and thus more productive for everyone. Previously, to search for a book, the end user had to click four times before arriving at a search page with an entirely different interface.

The same logic applied to viewing a library account. People can access their entire library account from their desktop. Except for picking up the book, everything else related to the transaction can be managed from home; users can put their names on wait lists for popular books, DVDs, or almost anything owned by any library in the consortium, and the user will be alerted when the item is in. For busy users, this makes visiting the library much easier.

Although this "access your account" feature had always been available, it was difficult to find and so under-promoted that web users were unaware of the service. Most users thought a phone call or a visit to the library was required to perform this type of library business.

The search box also serves to raise the profile of the library's resources and provide the public with an easy way to utilize the resources in person or via their home computers. Manchester is the largest public library in the state. However, looking at its old website, you would not necessarily have known it owned expensive and high-quality materials—many of which are prohibitively expensive for other public libraries to provide. As with many publicly funded institutions, Manchester's site provided the basics, but there was little reason to stay there beyond getting snippets of information about the facility. Visiting it in person offered the only option for gaining some cultural exposure.

Libraries that feature their collection, making it easy to find materials, are libraries that seem proud of the resources they provide. A proud library is the first step toward having a community that is proud of it—especially important during budget season. Highlighting the library's collection by making it accessible from the website's front page delivers the message that "this is what we are about; this is what we are proud to be able to provide to our community."

Add Opportunity for Interactivity

Even with our collections featured online, we were still missing a piece: the librarians. Previously, the library functioned as libraries have for centuries: storing books, cataloging them, serving some sort of public interest. Any patron interaction took place in person or via some other form of direct communication, such as postal mail or phone. Even once we made the collection readily available via the search box, we lacked a way to expose users to the wealth of information from other libraries and other sources around the state, region, country, and world. Basically, what you saw was what you got—and if the website did not have the information you were looking for, you were out of luck. We needed a system that engaged the viewer, allowed for automatic updates of information, and really served as a "companion" for anyone who wanted to use it.

I wanted to highlight these external resources on the website in the same way a librarian might recommend resources for a project, providing a brief orientation and perhaps a bit of comforting advice. There's no shortage of socially oriented websites that facilitate casual information exchange. While it's important to participate in as many social sites as possible, the library website should also *be* one as much as possible. Mashing up content from those sites could help me not only capture the spirit of other social sites but also represent that spirit on the library site and associate it with our institution.

A WordPress (wordpress.com) blog provided a ready solution (Figure 6.7). WordPress is quick to set up and easy to use; its built-in WYSIWYG (What You See Is What You Get) editor makes it similar to word processing applications. Those familiar with blogs expect a certain amount of casual language; posts are not necessarily press releases or "official communication." Instead, blogs are for musings; a discussion of your passion; showing your natural voice. We know that librarians don't become librarians for the money or the glamor; we do it because we love it. Here's a format for us to show our users why. If we don't love the library, we can't expect others to do so.

Figure 6.7   The library's blog (www.manchesterlibrary.org), which allows us to easily maintain the website

The blog (found on the home page, www.manchesterlibrary.org), not only allowed librarians to write in a conversational format but also made it possible for patrons to contribute (through comments) to an institution that was previously strictly for consumption. Now a conversation can take place on the website—not only between library and patron but between patrons themselves, much as they do inside library walls.

To repurpose blog content, I exploit the fact that blogs provide content in RSS. This allows me to republish blogs' content elsewhere on our website. To assist in this, I created a FeedBurner

(feedburner.google.com) account. Give FeedBurner the feed (RSS) address for your blog, and it provides a collection of information and services related to the content you produce. Among these is BuzzBoost, which "republishes your burned feed's content as go-anywhere HTML." This works much like the Flickr badge: Simply choose how you would like your blog content to appear on your website, and FeedBurner provides you with a bit of code to paste into your page. That's it. From there the website automatically updates with any new blog content.

Our front page now features a library program, a collection of resources, and an explanation of library events (last week our bottom floor was closed because of flooding, for example!). The front page updates automatically whenever a staff member writes a new blog post. For instance, with the passing of actor Paul Newman, I highlighted the events of his death as well as his life (manchester library.org/read/523). I included links to other library resources that covered this legend's career, personal life, and various charitable efforts, as well as a link to his final interview with Barbara Walters (it made me cry).

By highlighting various current events, we can also help expand public knowledge. Unfortunately, users do not always rely on the library to provide information on current events, political issues, or public debate. This new page allows us to highlight these types of issues and provide background that helps people become better informed.

The 2008 U.S. presidential race is another good example. We used the blog page to highlight developments in the race, explain the process, and otherwise inform the public about the histories of the candidates, their careers, and their positions on the issues. We have all that information at our fingertips, and the blog allows us to display it for the public in one place—serving as a starting place for the public to become better informed.

Providing library-generated and interactive content also allows patrons to communicate with staff on a more personal level. This was important because one of our mission objectives is to position the library as not just a source of information but also as a key cultural, social, and community member. Although the physical efforts of the library went a long way in this role, the virtual role of the library was reduced to merely providing information; it played no real role, nor did it provide an outlet for patrons to express views, ask questions, or interact with staff. By making its virtual presence dynamic, the library added another weapon to its arsenal, helping it promote itself as an active member of the greater community.

We can now use the blog and the website as a way to *communicate*, to relay events or programs to the public and garner feedback from patrons as to how to make the programs better, and to find out what patrons liked or did not like about a particular program. For instance, we have a page dedicated to regularly scheduled events where participants can ask questions about the event beforehand and provide feedback to us about the event after it has occurred.

This serves as an informal survey that allows us to gauge the popularity of any particular program or event. We also have easy access to reviews of the event, which allows us to capitalize on what was popular and see what needs to be modified to be more effective. We also take user suggestions about how to make events more fun, interactive, or effective.

Most of all, blog comments allow our patrons to feel like they are part of the library. This feature has increased patron participation and garnered immense goodwill. Now, when visitors want to comment on something, they do not have to track down the correct staff member and hope that their thoughts will be appreciated. All they have to do is find the topic on the site and add their input. We also allow them to provide links to other webpages if that will help them expand on the comment they are making. Because staff can comment as well, they can better explain programs or their purposes without having to reiterate their comments hundreds of times.

Integrate Content Into the Lives of Our Users

By far, however, the most dynamic modification to the Manchester City website was the new, interactive calendar. Previously, calendar entries had to be manually entered, and they stayed on the calendar until they were manually removed. The new system utilizes Google Calendar's (calendar.google.com) feature that allows calendar entries to be broadcast in RSS, iCal, and HTML.

Even more exciting is the fact that users can also *subscribe* to the iCal file from whatever calendaring program they use. This is particularly useful for our patrons who take training or use other scheduled library programs. Patrons who attend our game night or our various cultural events no longer have to check the site to see when things are planned; they can subscribe so that their PDA, online calendars, and other electronic calendar sources are updated automatically. FeedBurner also provides an email subscription service, which will send subscribers daily emails listing upcoming library events. This all happens automatically when we post a new event.

Most important, our homepage, as well as other pages that display events, is kept up to date. The RSS feature allows me to update the calendar, which then automatically synchronizes the events on the website, using FeedBurner in the same way the blog does (Figure 6.8). This means that out-of-date events are automatically removed and new or upcoming events are automatically updated. This saves time and money and helps promote the Manchester City Library as a current and vital community resource.

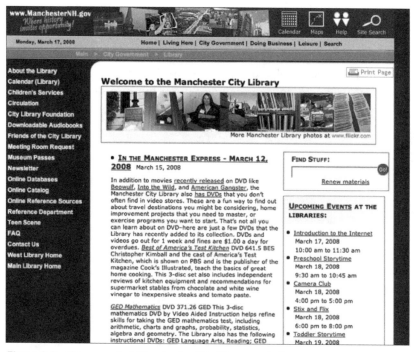

Figure 6.8   The renovated Manchester City Library website

The automatic calendar function also expanded the services and the productivity of programs the library offers. We now can offer programs, such as a lecture series, and do not have to rely on meager advertising or word of mouth to alert our constituencies. By offering more services and promoting them via the calendar, we not only expand our role in the community; we also offer residents a reliable source of information that is current.

The only investment the library had to make in achieving these first steps toward its goals for the website was in the time to plan, implement, and maintain the content; the tools we used are all available for free. These tools enabled me to create a library mashup, pulling from existing services and integrating them into a more productive website. Not only were we able to make the library more relevant; we were also able to offer several new services to the public. Our community can now take an active role in the library without having to constantly visit the website or learn how to navigate through several pages to access the information they want to see.

The Future

We're not done! I plan to continue to use tools and utilities from other sites to make our website more dynamic, informative, useful, and fun. I also plan to continue streamlining our site, with the goal of making it an indispensable part of our staff's and our patrons' lives.

CHAPTER 7

Piping Out Library Data

Nicole C. Engard
LibLime

Introducing Yahoo! Pipes

Yahoo! Pipes (pipes.yahoo.com) hit the web in early 2007. Even though it was covered by every news source I follow, I just didn't get it. Everyone said that it was a powerful mashup tool, but no matter how hard I tried, I could not find a use for it in my day-to-day work. It took an amazing article by Jody Condit Fagan in *Computers in Libraries*[1] to get me to try one last time—and I am so happy I did!

This simple little tool allows you to create mashups using a graphical interface made up of "pipes" that can flow to and from various different sources. According to Yahoo!, "Pipes is a powerful composition tool to aggregate, manipulate, and mashup content from around the web."[2] What the heck does that mean? It means that, using the Yahoo! Pipes interface, you can take data from multiple sources and mash it together to create a whole new beast. It means that, even if a site doesn't have an application programming interface (API), you may still be able to grab the site's data and create a mashup of your own.

Yahoo! Pipes provides several information gathering tools that you simply drag and drop into the editing interface to gather information in a flowchart style. There are modules that allow you to fetch, combine, filter, search, and sort information from RSS feeds, CSV (comma separated value) files, and other data formats. Yahoo! Pipes even includes some Web 2.0 sites that you can automatically mash data from and to, such as Yahoo! Local (local.yahoo.com), Google Base (www.google.com/base), and Flickr (www.flickr.com).

The purpose of this chapter is to show you how Yahoo! Pipes[3] can help you push your data out to patrons, as well as how you can bring data into your library website. I will go over some simple mashups that you can create on your own and then share some real-life examples from other libraries. By the end of this chapter, you should be comfortable enough with Yahoo! Pipes (from here on referred to just as Pipes) to try creating some simple mashups for your library website.

Merging Feeds

The most basic type of pipe is one that brings together multiple RSS feeds into one. Libraries are trying to deliver as much news as possible via RSS feeds but sometimes forget that it would make things much easier for the patrons if a library provided one feed for all news, events, and blog posts. This was an issue with LibLime (www.liblime. com). LibLime had several feeds, and I didn't want to subscribe to each individually, so I created a pipe to merge them all together in order to get all updates in one place.

The first step is to visit the Pipes page and click the Create a Pipe button. This will open up the Pipes editor. On the left-hand side, you'll find several modules for gathering and sorting information. To the right of that, you'll see the main editing area. To create pipes, you just need to drag modules from the left to the editing area on the right, and you're set to go.

For a pipe that merges multiple RSS feeds, you will need the Fetch Feed module. Drag the Fetch Feed module out from under the Sources heading and drop it in the editing area. Grab a feed address from your library site and paste it into the blank box. To add multiple boxes for multiple feeds, click the plus sign to the left of the URL (Uniform Resource Locator) heading.

Once you have all your feeds listed in the Fetch Feed box, you can drag a pipe from the dot at the bottom of the module to the dot at the top of the Pipe Output box (Figure 7.1).

You can even take your pipe one step further and sort the results by date so that the newest items float to the top (by default, the results are sorted by feed). To do this, you simply drag a Sort module out from under the Operators heading and put it in the editing area. After attaching the Sort module to the Fetch Feed module, you will be able to sort by any field found in the RSS feed; I chose to sort on the publication date (Figure 7.2). You can view the output and the source of this pipe online at pipes.yahoo.com/liblime/news. Once you publish a feed, it is publicly viewable by anyone, making it easier for your

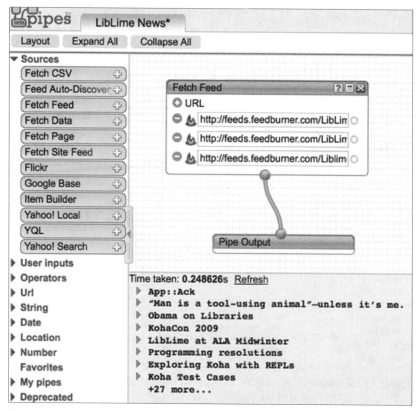

Figure 7.1   A simple pipe that merges three RSS feeds together

users to find your feeds, subscribe to them, and duplicate (clone) them for easy altering.

Finding New Books

These days, several integrated library systems (ILSs) and journal databases are offering RSS feeds for search results. Using the data pulled from these feeds, we can generate a subject-specific (or author-specific) alert for new titles added to the library catalog or database. In this example, I'm going to use RSS feeds from two library systems in Kansas, both of which are using the Koha ILS. First I'm going to run a search on the Northeast Kansas Library System (NEKLS) OPAC (Online Public Access Catalog) (nekls.kohalibrary. com) for *library science*, and then I'm going to repeat the same search on the Southeast Kansas Library System OPAC (seknfind.koha

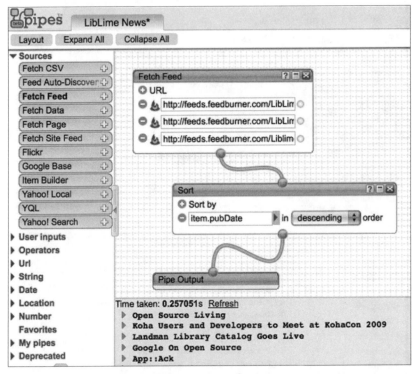

Figure 7.2 A simple pipe sorts the results from three feeds so that the most recent items appear at the top.

library.com). This is a perfect example of how someone who lives between the areas these two library systems serve can benefit from data that has been mashed together.

Using the Pipes interface, I drag the Fetch Feed box to the editing area and then add the two feeds I pulled from the two Kansas library systems (Figure 7.3).

You can preview your output by clicking on the Pipe Output box, or you can click "Run this Pipe" at the top of the screen and see what the pipe looks like when displayed on a webpage (Figure 7.4).

Once you get the hang of merging simple data sets together, you can play with some of the filters to clean up the data that is presented. Let's say you want to sort the list to show the most recently published title first and remove all duplicate titles. This can be done using two of the items found under the Operators menu, Sort and Unique (Figure 7.5).

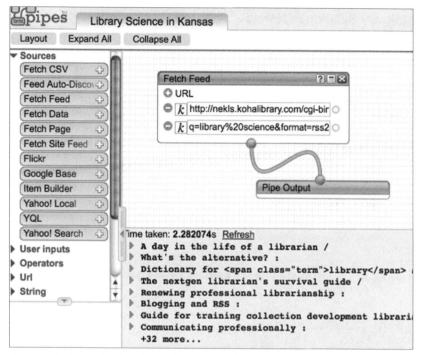

Figure 7.3 A simple pipe that pulls in two RSS feeds and merges them together

Pipes Badges

After running the pipe, you have the option of grabbing the RSS feed for the pipe, adding it to your Yahoo! or Google homepage, or remixing the data in several other ways. The easiest way to grab your pipe output and publish it on your library website is to use the badge functionality. To add a Pipes badge, you just need to copy and paste three lines of code from Pipes to where you'd like your badge to appear:

```
<script src="http://pipes.yahoo.com/js/
listbadge.js">
{ "pipe_id" : "PIPE ID HERE" }
</script>
```

Although this badge can be styled using CSS (Cascading Style Sheets), there isn't usually much need for that. This simple bit of code will print a list of the results right to your website (Figure 7.6).

Library Science in Kansas

Books on Library Science from NEKLS & SEKLS.

Pipe Web Address: http://pipes.yahoo.com/nengard/libsciks (edit)

☆ | Edit Source | Delete | Re-publish | Unpublish | Clone

Use this Pipe

📝Get as a Badge | ➕ MY YAHOO! | ➕ Google | 📶Get as RSS 📶Get as JSON More options▶

List   40 items

A day in the life of a librarian /
- 24 p. :

What's the alternative? :
- p. cm.

Dictionary for library and information science.
- 788 p.

The nextgen librarian's survival guide /
- xiv, 208 p. ;

Figure 7.4   The results of a pipe that searches for library science in two Kansas libraries

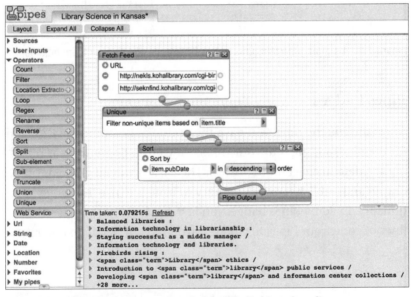

Figure 7.5   *Library science* search sorted and limited to unique items (pipes.yahoo.com/nengard/libsciks)

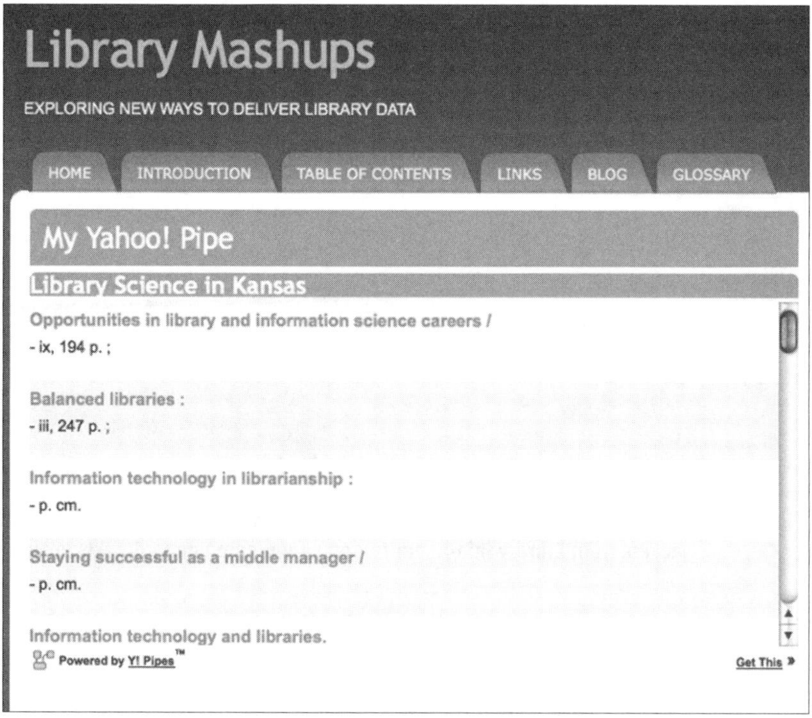

Figure 7.6 Yahoo! Pipes badge on Library Mashups website

Searchable Pipes

What if we want to give people the option of running their own search on our RSS feeds? Using the NEKLS library catalog, why don't we let people run their own search and enhance the results with book jackets? This sounds pretty complicated, but it's actually rather easy once you have played with Pipes enough. Figure 7.7 shows you how you can create a searchable pipe and bring data in from another source. You can see this pipe in action online at pipes.yahoo.com/nengard/neklscovers and clone it to alter it for a search on your own catalog.

Libraries Using Pipes

Although all my examples were created purely for this book, many libraries are using Pipes to create enhanced content for their patrons. A search of the Pipes database for *library* turns up more than 250 results, some of which are simple RSS feed mashups and

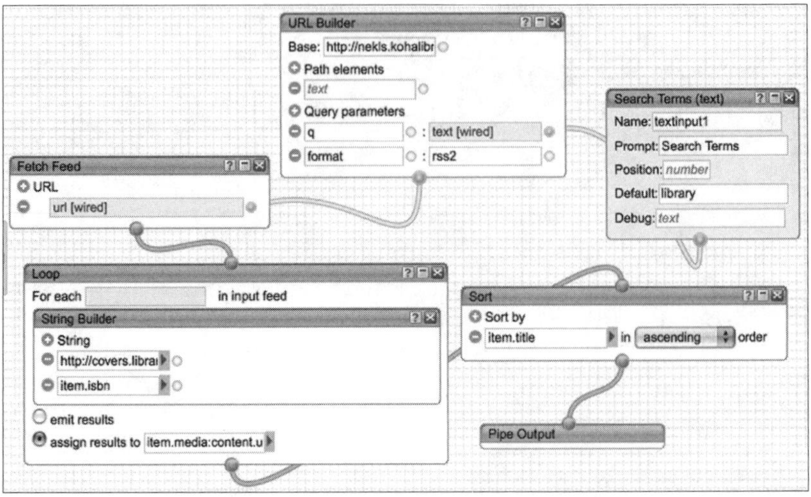

Figure 7.7   A pipe that searches a library catalog and merges the results with book jackets from LibraryThing.com (pipes.yahoo.com/nengard/neklscovers)

some of which are advanced searches on catalogs and subscription databases.

One example from the Cambridge Libraries (www.cambridge libraries.ca) maps catalog search results based on publication location by letting the patrons run a search on their catalog via the Pipes website (pipes.yahoo.com/pipes/pipe.info?_id=SrPHCrkv3BGClBN9m LokhQ). This tool can be used for research or just for fun; either way it adds value to the library's content that wasn't there before.

Another example comes from Derik Badman at Temple University in Philadelphia. Derik's mashup takes the tables of contents from numerous library literature journals and links the articles directly into Temple's subscription databases (pipes.yahoo.com/madink beard/NlG6cYgE3BG6qtZJmLokhQ). Although this tool is specific to those with a login at Temple University, it's a great example of how you can add value (like a table of contents) to an existing library service and keep it all linked together.

Last, the people at the Wakefield Library (UK) put together a pipe that pulls local news from several sources into one place for their patrons (pipes.yahoo.com/pipes/pipe.info?_id=VCj4DCfZ2xGLha UFEpPZnA). This kind of service is great for public libraries: You can grab this data, create a badge, and paste it on your library site so that community members can see the local news right on the library website without having to do the searches themselves.

Looking for more great Pipes ideas? You can search the Pipes database for the type of pipe you want, or you can check out some of the online lists of popular and useful pipes. ReadWriteWeb has one such list (www.readwriteweb.com/archives/the_ultimate_yahoo_pipes_list.php) that includes great Pipes to check out.

Conclusion

As you'll learn throughout this book, some mashups require a lot of skill and time, while others are as simple as filling in a form and copying some code. Yahoo! Pipes fits somewhere in between those two extremes—and is well worth getting the hang of. Although you may feel overwhelmed now, I promise that a little bit of playing with Yahoo! Pipes will get you hooked. Take a few minutes to recreate some of the examples I provided in this chapter, or search the Yahoo! Pipes site for pipes that might interest you and view their source for inspiration.

As in all new experiences, taking a little bit of time to get comfortable and learn the ropes will pay off in the end. Yahoo! Pipes is a great tool to get you started on the road to adding amazing mashups to your library's site.

Endnotes

1. Jody Condit Fagan, "Mashing Up Multiple Web Feeds Using Yahoo! Pipes," *Computers in Libraries* 27 (January 1, 2007): 10–17.

2. "About Pipes." Yahoo! blog.pipes.yahoo.net/about-pipes (accessed April 9, 2009).

3. You will need to sign up for a Yahoo! account before being able to create your own Pipes.

CHAPTER 8

Mashups @ Libraries Interact

Corey Wallis
Flinders University

Collaborative Mashups and Sharing Information

Libraries Interact is a cooperative blog managed by a small and committed group of librarians (and one or two others who share an interest in libraries and sharing information). The group's primary goal is to create an online space that can be used by librarians and other interested parties to share ideas and work together in exploring the ever-changing online environment. The group was formed in July 2006 and has always used online technologies such as email, instant messaging, collaborative bookmarking, and wikis to coordinate its activities. The experiences of members of the group, from across Australia, have shown that collaborative blogging can be a rewarding experience; this perspective was shown to be common among group bloggers in a 2008 survey.[1]

The group behind Libraries Interact (librariesinteract.info) includes members who work in public, academic, and special libraries; a representative from a library vendor; and an information professional. Posts to Libraries Interact are typically about broad topics or cover events such as conferences, meetings, and unconferences. Group members also have their own individual blogs, hosted on a variety of different platforms, where they post about their own areas of interest. The group works together on administering the blog, and discussions on such things as ideas for future posts and other topics are common. Members each bring their own special skills to the group, making the skill set of the group greater than the skill set of the individual members.

The members of the group are geographically diverse, and they rely on Web 2.0 and other online technologies to communicate and coordinate their activities. A lack of face-to-face communication has not had a detrimental effect on the effectiveness of the group or on how rewarding members find their participation. As one member wrote, "We can tend to be locked into our workplace's worldview, but working virtually with colleagues from different sectors and different states brings a fresh outlook on things."[2] By working together and incorporating their individual skills, the group has been able to create a series of useful mashups.

The Life Cycle of a Libraries Interact Mashup

The group's strong focus on collaboration and working together is reflected in the way it has approached the development of mashups. Each of the three mashups featured in this chapter started as an idea that was proposed to the group; the idea was then discussed, evaluated, and refined until a plan of action was determined. It is important to the group that the mashups that it develops, and continues to support, provide benefits to the community of readers that has formed around the Libraries Interact blog. Once proven on the Libraries Interact blog, the mashups are released to the wider online community in the hope that others will find them useful.

Each member of the group brings special skills to the development process. Not everyone in the group is skilled in programming or web development work. Members contribute by bringing fresh ideas, providing insights and new perspectives during testing, or simply promoting a supportive atmosphere within the group. In this way the group is able to develop mashups that would not be possible if each member was working independently. Although mashups and other aspects of online technologies and Web 2.0 can be dismissed as being only for "techies," a collaborative group approach has proven to be very effective. A mashup produced by the Libraries Interact group is truly a collaborative and collective activity.

The Libraries Interact blog is built on the WordPress blogging platform (wordpress.org). A key factor in the choice to use WordPress was that it is an open source application with a dedicated and robust community of developers. Many of the capabilities of the site rely on plug-ins and other enhancements that have been developed by the WordPress community; the primary website for locating plug-ins is the plug-in directory hosted by the WordPress team (wordpress.org/extend/plugins). At the time of this writing, the directory lists more than 3,300 plug-ins, each contributing an enhancement to the WordPress platform. As the Libraries Interact blog uses a number of plug-ins, the group has made a commitment to releasing its mashups that integrate with WordPress as open source plug-ins when possible. In this way the mashups developed by the group can provide benefits to the wider online community, in the same way that plug-ins developed by others have proved beneficial to us. To date, we have developed three mashup plug-ins:

- Blogroll to Google Custom Search Engine (CSE)

- Citation Aggregator

- Diverse Group Tag Cloud

The remainder of this chapter is dedicated to outlining how each of these mashups works and covers some of the development process that was undertaken, as a way to illustrate the cooperative and inclusive nature of the way the group approached each project.

Blogroll to Google CSE

One of the most frequently visited pages on the Libraries Interact blog is the list of Aussie Library blogs (librariesinteract.info/australian-library-blogs). This initiative meets a need perceived by the group a few months after the blog was started. At the time there was no central register of Australian library blogs. In particular, no list included both personal blogs, started by librarians as their own personal part of cyberspace, and those started by a library, typically as part of their promotional activities. The list of Australian library blogs started by the group and maintained on the Libraries Interact blog meets this need.

Initially the list was developed as a hand-edited page on the blog. Over time, however, the list grew, and its maintenance became increasingly burdensome. Each time a blog was added, the list had to be reworked, particularly as the alphabetical ordering of the list was to be maintained. Another complication was that different members added new blogs in different ways; for example, some used the appropriate HTML markup for a list, while others did not. As the list grew, the group determined that there was a great deal of information contained in the blogs on the list that would be of interest to the members of the community that was forming around the blog. Growing interest in the Libraries Interact blog can be seen in the consistent increase in the amount of traffic that the site has received over the past year. At the time of this writing, the list of Australian Library blogs accounts for more than 11 percent of the total traffic for the Libraries Interact blog, and it is the second-most-visited page, after the homepage.

It was determined that the community would gain greater benefit from the list if members could search across the content of the blogs listed on the page. To address this need, the group decided to create a Google CSE (www.google.com/coop/cse). At its core, a Google CSE is a search of the Google index that is restricted to a list of specific websites. The CSE proved popular with the Libraries Interact community, and the list of included websites continued to grow. Over time two challenges became clear:

1. Maintaining the list on the page was becoming increasingly burdensome, especially as it needed to be stored in two independent systems, the WordPress blog and the Google CSE system.

2. A way of filtering out websites that were considered abandoned would be useful. An abandoned blog may continue to contain useful information, but it also adds clutter to the list.

A new Google initiative, the ability to have a Linked CSE (www.google.com/coop/docs/cse/cref.html), presented the group with a way of solving the first challenge. A Linked CSE provides a mechanism whereby the list of websites used by the CSE can be stored outside the Google systems and hosted on a separate website. The list of websites for the CSE needed to be made available on the Libraries Interact website in a specially formatted XML (eXtensible Markup Language) file that the Google system would retrieve when needed. The possibility of using a Linked CSE provided an opportunity to resolve the problems inherent in maintaining the list—if a way could be found to automate the process.

A development plan was formed that would allow the group to automate the creation of the necessary XML file for the Linked CSE. This plan would also reduce the administrative burden of maintaining the list and provide the additional filtering functionality. We decided to construct a WordPress plug-in that was capable of

- Listing links to websites that would be categorized in primary and secondary categories

- Storing the list of links inside the WordPress system

- Integrating the Linked CSE into the blog with a minimum of effort

- Automating the update of links within the Linked CSE

The plan resulted in the development of the Blogroll to Google CSE plug-in (techxplorer.com/projects/blogroll-google-cse). The bulk of the development work would be undertaken by one group member, with other members providing support in the form of testing and giving insights into the way users of the plug-in would expect to use it.

How the Plug-In Works

Wherever possible a WordPress plug-in should use existing functionality provided by the underlying system. With this in mind, the Blogroll to Google CSE plug-in integrates with the Link Manager functionality of WordPress and uses it to mash up the data into a CSE. The Link Manager functionality of WordPress provides a mechanism whereby users can manage a list of links. These links are typically displayed in a blogroll and can be associated with one or more categories. The Link Manager provided the ideal mechanism for managing links that would be used by the plug-in. When a link is added to the system via the Link Manager, it is associated with a primary category. This category is used to identify links that are to be included in the list of links and in the CSE; an optional secondary category can also be used as a way of refining the list. In the case of Libraries Interact, the primary category is used to identify personal blogs and corporate blogs. The optional secondary category is used to differentiate those blogs that the group has determined have been abandoned from those that are still active. The process of adding a new link can be seen in Figure 8.1.

When the list of links is displayed to a visitor to the Libraries Interact blog, it is divided into separate lists, one for personal blogs and the other for corporate blogs. A user viewing the list can restrict the lists to only live blogs or only abandoned blogs or choose to see all links. The plug-in has configuration options that provide sufficient flexibility so that links can be categorized in various ways. For example, it is possible to have numerous primary categories and only two secondary categories. The names of these two secondary categories are configurable and so could be used to restrict the list of links in different ways.

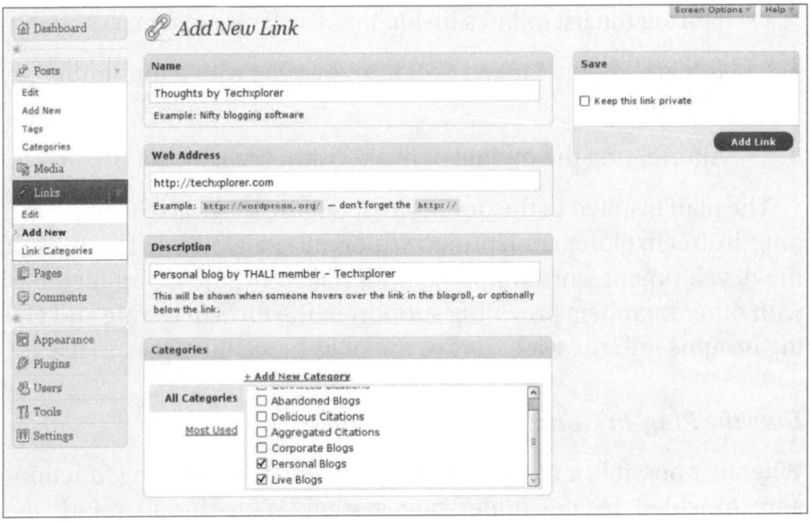

Figure 8.1 Adding a link using the WordPress Link Manager

A Google Linked CSE has a number of other options, including a description and optional keywords that can be used to further refine the way the CSE works. These options can all be set using the plug-in. In particular, the colors of the search results can be specified using a color wheel if a user of the plug-in is unfamiliar with the way colors are specified in HTML markup.

Integration with WordPress is achieved by using two shortcodes. One is used where the list of links and search box are displayed. The other is used for the page that displays the search results. Conceptually, a shortcode is similar to HTML tag and is used to integrate a plug-in with the generation of a page or post in the WordPress system. When a shortcode is encountered, the plug-in associated with that shortcode is activated, and the results of the plug-in execution will replace the shortcode in the page or post. This means that authors can create a post or page in the WordPress system as they normally would. They can include any text, images, or other media, such as an embedded YouTube (www.youtube.com) video, into the post and be confident that the shortcode will be replaced with the output of the plug-in. For example, an author could add explanatory text about why the list of links has been collected, a video about how to use the search functionality, or text explaining how readers of the blog can suggest additional links to be added to the list.

The plug-in automatically generates the XML file that specifies the websites that are to be used with the Google Linked CSE. When a search is conducted, the XML file is retrieved by the Google servers and cached for a time. This ensures that a minimum load is placed on the website hosting the file but can introduce a synchronization issue in which the list of websites cached by the Google servers becomes out-of-date. The plug-in deals with this possibility by ensuring that the Google server reloads the XML file when the CSE is used for the first time following a change to the list of links stored in the WordPress system.

The plug-in achieves the two goals that the Libraries Interact group initially set out to achieve. Maintaining the list of Australian library blogs is less administratively burdensome, and the list can be filtered using the association with the secondary categories. This plug-in has been released to the online community by means of an open source license and has been used by a number of other websites looking to achieve this type of functionality with their own blogs. The development of the plug-in is a true group collaborative effort that is now assisting others with their blogging and community development.

Citation Aggregator

The Libraries Interact group regularly shares links to resources and other interesting websites among its members. This can be done by posting these to the group's internal discussion list, adding them to the group wiki, or posting on individual group members' blogs. The most efficient way of sharing links, though, is through a social bookmarking website. These websites are designed to allow users to add bookmarks, categorize them using tags, and share the bookmarks (for instance, via RSS or by automatically posting them to a blog).

The Libraries Interact group felt these links deserved a wider audience and thought that by sharing bookmarks, the group could increase community interest in the blog. Letting others add to the list of bookmarks would also allow members of the community to contribute in a new way. This functionality is particularly useful to those who wish to contribute but are not ready to contribute regular posts. Following the discussions held by the group, a development plan for the Citation Aggregator plug-in (techxplorer.com/projects/citation-aggregator) was initiated.

We first needed to decide which of the social bookmarking websites would be used to source bookmarks. Members of the group each had their own preference for social bookmarking websites they used regularly. Following a discussion among the group, a consensus view was reached that the development of the plug-in would start by targeting the two most popular social bookmarking websites within the membership, Delicious (delicious.com) and Connotea (www.connotea.org).

The plan was to construct a WordPress plug-in capable of

- Retrieving lists of bookmarks from both services using RSS

- Storing the aggregated list of bookmarks inside the WordPress system

- Allowing filtering of the list to remove bookmarks that may not be suitable for a blog post

- Filtering out any bookmarks submitted by people who were not authorized

- Displaying a list of aggregated bookmarks in a post or page in a WordPress blog

- Being extensible enough to allow aggregating bookmarks or links from other services

Both of the chosen services allow users to tag bookmarks they add; the bookmarks associated with an individual tag are available via an RSS feed. By accessing and retrieving these feeds, the plug-in is able to achieve all of the goals the group had proposed.

How the Plug-In Works

Approximately every hour, the Citation Aggregator plug-in retrieves the RSS feed for a specific tag at the Delicious and Connotea websites. The RSS feeds produced by the Delicious and Connotea websites are complex because of the additional bibliographic and other information embedded within them. This complexity means that the Citation Aggregator plug-in must be able to work with feeds that are more complicated than those produced by a blog. To read and extract information from these complex types of RSS feeds, the Citation Aggregator plug-in uses the SimplePie (simplepie.org) PHP class. Later versions of WordPress include this class by default, but if it is not available, the Citation Aggregator plug-in will make use of a copy of the class bundled with the plug-in. The SimplePie class is able to work with RSS feeds that contain complex data structures and provides an easy way to extract data from an RSS feed.

Each bookmark in the RSS feed identifies the user that added that bookmark. To ensure that only bookmarks from trusted users are aggregated, the user identified in the RSS feed is checked against a list of known and trusted users configured in the plug-in. If the user in the RSS feed matches one of those that are trusted, the bookmark is considered for aggregation. If the user does not match, the bookmark is discarded.

Before adding the bookmark, a duplicate check is made to ensure that only unique links are stored. When a bookmark is added, the current date is also recorded. This date can be used for ordering the list of bookmarks and making it easier to select those to output in a post or page. If bookmarks are successfully aggregated, an optional email can be sent that includes details of those links that have been successfully aggregated.

A blog administrator can use a date range to specify the bookmarks that are to be included in a particular post or page. The administrator can also "suspend" a bookmark rather than delete it entirely. A suspended bookmark will not be used in a post, and this will ensure that it will not be added again the next time a check for new bookmarks is run. After an appropriate period, the blog administrator can delete any suspended bookmarks, ensuring the database does not become unnecessarily large.

To add a list of bookmarks into a post or page, a shortcode is used. The shortcode uses five attributes to build the list of bookmarks:

- Bookmark category – Used to define the category of bookmarks that should be used (a primary category is defined, as well as categories for each website from which bookmarks are sourced).

- Start date – Used to define the start of a date range to select a list of bookmarks.

- End date – Used to define the end of the date range.

- Order – Used to order the list of bookmarks, either alphabetically by title or by the date they were added to the list.

- List type – Either an ordered (numbered) list or an unordered (bulleted) list.

By using a shortcode, any additional text, images, or media can also be included in the post or page, as required. An example post created with the plug-in can be seen in Figure 8.2.

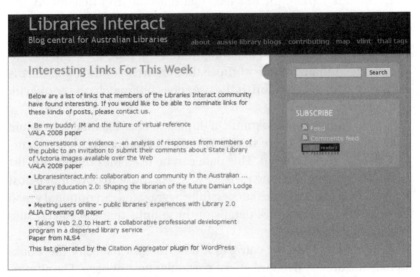

Figure 8.2 A sample list of links aggregated by the Citation Aggregator

The functionality provided by the plug-in allows the Libraries Interact group to expand the participation of the community that surrounds the Libraries Interact blog. Members of the community can be nominated as trusted users for inclusion and have their bookmarks aggregated by the plug-in into lists that can be included in posts or pages on the blog. With the functionality provided by the social bookmarking websites, the collective knowledge of the community, as represented in bookmarks, can be aggregated, mashed up, and shared with the rest of the community. Through the use of a standard data interchange format at its core, RSS, it is also possible to expand the plug-in and integrate it with other services that collect bookmarks, such as items shared via RSS aggregators such as Google Reader (www.google.com/reader). It is hoped that the plug-in will be of interest to other collaborative blogs and will prove useful in helping them build their communities as well.

Diverse Group Tag Cloud

Members of the group behind the Libraries Interact blog each have their own personal blog where they write about topics of interest to them. This often creates tension between writing for Libraries Interact and writing for an individual blog. At times, posts are made by members of the group to their own individual blog that may also be of interest to the community of readers that has formed around the Libraries Interact blog. The group identified this as a potential issue and initiated a project to develop the THALI-Tags page.

The idea for this page stemmed from a post on Dave Pattern's blog.[3] Dave had created a webpage that aggregated RSS feeds from a variety of different blogs written by librarians or focused on library-related issues. The aggregated data was used to create a tag cloud that identified the "hot topics" these bloggers were writing about. This inspired the group to use the RSS feeds from their own personal blogs and build a tag cloud that could be displayed on the Libraries Interact site.

The project proposed to the group had the goal of building a tag cloud representing posts on each member's individual blog. The tag cloud would list tags derived from the content of posts aggregated from each of these blogs. The larger the font size used to display the tag, the more times the tag was associated with posts. One initial challenge here was that group members used different platforms for their blogs. Some were self-hosted, while others used hosting providers such as Blogger (www.blogger.com). Not every blog had tags available, and those that did implemented them differently.

To solve this problem, tags would need to be derived from the content of each post. This presented an opportunity to use Yahoo! Pipes (pipes.yahoo.com), which is covered in detail in Chapter 7. The Yahoo! Pipe would analyze the content of each post and derive a few significant keywords; these keywords would be used as the basis for the tags. The initial development project produced a website separate from the Libraries Interact blog. An unfortunate side effect of being separate from the blog was an increased administrative burden on the group managing the site. This became particularly obvious when the Libraries Interact group initiated a project to change the look and feel of the blog in early 2008. With this in mind, the group initiated a project to develop their third WordPress plug-in. This plug-in would build on the existing experiences of the group and allow the generation of the tag cloud inside the WordPress system. The project resulted in the development of the Diverse Group Tag Cloud plug-in (techxplorer.com/projects/diverse-group-tag-cloud).

How the Plug-In Works

Each plug-in developed by the Libraries Interact group is designed to leverage the existing functionality provided by the WordPress platform wherever possible. Therefore, the URL (Uniform Resource Locator) for the RSS feed from each of the individual blogs is stored in the WordPress system by means of the Link Manager functionality and is associated with the same common category. (The group also had existing experience in using the Link Manager functionality for managing links as part of the Blogroll to Google CSE plug-in outlined earlier.) By using existing WordPress functionality, management of the settings for the plug-in could be simplified, as seen in Figure 8.3.

Approximately hourly, the plug-in uses a Yahoo! Pipe to derive the few most significant keywords from the content of each post in the feed. The Yahoo! Pipe takes the URL of an RSS feed as an input and

Diverse Group Tag Cloud

Email Address	Enter an email address that will receive email notifications when things do not work as expected Leave blank to disable this feature
Default Link Category	Tag Cloud ▾ Select the default category for all links aggregated by the plugin It is recommended that you create a new link category specifically for this purpose
Display Plugin Link	☐ Tick this box to display a link to the plugin project page at the end of the list of links (disabled by default)

Save Changes

Blog Name / Description	Blog Link	Blog RSS Link
Blisspix Blog of THALI member Fiona	Visit the blog	Check the RSS feed
Connecting Librarian Blog of THALI member Michelle	Visit the blog	Check the RSS feed
Innovate Blog of THALI member Peta	Visit the blog	Check the RSS feed
Librarians Matter Blog of THALI member Kathryn	Visit the blog	Check the RSS feed
Libraries Interact Our collaborative blog	Visit the blog	Check the RSS feed
snail Blog of THALI member snail	Visit the blog	Check the RSS feed
Thoughts by Techxplorer Blog of THALI member techxplorer	Visit the blog	Check the RSS feed
Blog Name / Description	Blog Link	Blog RSS Link

Figure 8.3 Configuring the Diverse Group Tag Cloud plug-in

uses the term extractor module to derive keywords. The output of the Yahoo! Pipe is an RSS feed containing the title, URL, and keywords for each post found in the input feed. The list of keywords is filtered against a list of common stop words to ensure that small, often-occurring words do not have an adverse impact on the tag cloud.

The filtered list of keywords is used to create a record for the post in a database table inside the WordPress system. Each record in the table contains a single keyword, as well as the direct URL and title for the post. Storing individual keywords makes it a simple process to derive a count of each time the keyword is associated with a post and thereby build the tag cloud. The more times a keyword appears in the table, the larger the font used to display the keyword.

As with the other plug-ins, the tag cloud is embedded in a WordPress page through the use of a shortcode. The use of a short-code allows blog administrators to put any text, images, or media that they choose around the tag cloud. When users visiting the site see the tag cloud, they can click on one of the keywords in the cloud to see a list of posts associated with that tag and then can choose which posts they want to visit. This achieves the goal of highlighting posts in the individual members' blogs.

In addition to the tag cloud, the plug-in can generate an RSS feed containing the top 10 tags. Each item in the feed is a link back to the page that displays the list of posts associated with the tag. The RSS feed is useful in making the data represented in the tag cloud available to other systems and for other uses, such as including the list of the top five keywords in the sidebar of the Libraries Interact blog or providing a mechanism for members of the community surrounding the blog to keep up-to-date with topical posts from members of the Libraries Interact group.

The tag cloud has proven useful to members of the Libraries Interact community, and it is hoped that by releasing the plug-in to the wider WordPress community, other collaborative blogs can derive similar benefits.

Final Thoughts on Mashups at Libraries Interact

The primary goal of the Libraries Interact website is to share information with the community of readers that has formed around the blog. This has been achieved by forming a collaborative, cooperative group of interested people who contribute posts to the blog.

Members of the Libraries Interact group support each other, which is shown in the way in which the development of these mashups has been undertaken. Each member of the group brings unique skills to the group, so what the group can achieve is greater than what any independent member could achieve.

As the group continues to grow and evolve, other opportunities for mashups and other activities will be discussed, evaluated, and acted on. The Libraries Interact group has shown that a bunch of interested people can get together to use Web 2.0 and other online technologies to achieve great things. One of the goals of this book is to show that mashups can be of significant use to librarians, libraries, their patrons, and the communities that form around initiatives such as blogs, wikis, and other websites. Building and developing a mashup is not as difficult as it first may seem, particularly if there is a committed and passionate group involved in the development process. The experiences of the Libraries Interact group illustrate that a group of dedicated people from diverse backgrounds and with diverse skills can successfully build mashups and use them to successfully build a community of users.

Endnotes

1. Fiona Bradley, Kathryn Greenhill, and Constance Wiebrands, "LibrariesInteract. info collaboration and community in the Australian Library blogosphere" (paper presented to the 14th biennial VALA Conference, Melbourne, February 5–7, 2008).

2. Peta Hopkins, "Libraries Interact—a personal view of practical 2.0" (paper presented to Beyond the Hype: Web 2.0 symposium, Brisbane, Australia, February 1–2, 2008).

3. Dave Pattern, "whatcha talking 'bout? Version 4!" www.daveyp.com/blog/archives/146.

Part III

Mashing Up Catalog Data

CHAPTER 9

Library Catalog Mashup: Using Blacklight to Expose Collections

Bess Sadler, Joseph Gilbert, and Matt Mitchell
University of Virginia Library

Blacklight (rubyforge.org/projects/blacklight) is an open source OPAC (Online Public Access Catalog) solution developed at the University of Virginia (UVA) Library. With this new tool, Blacklight's developers hope to solve many long-standing problems with online catalogs as well as make a strong case for the support of open source, web-services-based software development in academic environments.

Blacklight is free and provided under the Apache License, Version 2.0 (www.apache.org/licenses/LICENSE-2.0.html).

Mashups: More Than Juxtaposition

Like the music mashups that preceded them, web application mashups rely on the reuse of multiple sources of preexisting content to create something new. Although the term *mashup* suggests a loose grouping or juxtaposition of content, web application mashups instead allow for entirely new user experiences and offer a platform for the dynamic flow of information on the web. Mashups are more than a consolidation of information: They involve the use of existing tools or the creation of entirely new interfaces to explore and expose information in new ways.

This understanding of the principles of mashups is central to the structure and design philosophy of Blacklight. Blacklight combines several internal and external data resources in an innovative interface, which is in turn composed of multiple open source elements. Beyond this new approach to online catalogs, the content and interface components of Blacklight can be incorporated into other academic tools and resources, creating a vibrant flow of information that can facilitate uses beyond the capability of any individual data source or application.

Blacklight as OPAC Mashup

Online catalog systems have long been a source of frustration for librarians and patrons alike. This frustration is due in part to librarians' desire—and patrons' expectations—for their online catalog to keep pace with the rapid development seen in other web applications, in contrast to the slower progress of new library catalog features. The relatively slow development of new features for library catalogs is in part caused by most catalogs' close ties to the integrated library systems (ILSs) that run all of a library's transactions. Upgrading an ILS is a difficult and expensive process that has the potential to disrupt workflows throughout the library and is undertaken only when absolutely necessary. This is a suitable pace of change for business and workflow operations but not for front-end systems used by patrons accustomed to the pace of development of services like Netflix (www.netflix.com), Facebook (www.facebook.com), Google (www.google.com), and Flickr (www.flickr.com), each of which rolls out new features every few months.

North Carolina State University's 2005 adoption of the Endeca (www.endeca.com) platform as a front end to its OPAC was an inspiration to many, thanks to its well-designed interface and innovative decoupling of online catalog and ILS, allowing for independent growth of each piece. As groundbreaking as the Endeca system was, however, jumping from one commercial product to another was not an ideal solution for UVA. The UVA Library has a strong commitment to open source software, and the ability to shape the catalog interface, mashing up data into it and allowing for mashups elsewhere, was important to local librarians even if the term *mashup* hadn't yet entered their vocabulary.

By lucky coincidence, a project founded on open source- and mashup-friendly principles was already being developed by scholars at UVA. Collex, designed by Bethany Nowviskie for the NINES project (nines.org), offered an innovative—and just as important, open source—approach to collecting and displaying catalogs of information. Collex uses Solr and Ruby on Rails[1] to index a large number of metadata records and full-text resources from a variety of sources that can then be searched, faceted, bookmarked, tagged, and generally mashed-up in compelling ways. Collex was created especially for digital scholarship surrounding 19th-century studies but was also designed as a generalized browsing system. In 2006, developers from Collex and the UVA Library began efforts to capitalize on Collex's strengths and incorporate new types of input, specifically MARC (MAchine-Readable Cataloging) and Fedora objects (www.fedora-commons.org), in an effort to make a better library catalog.

The problem proved to be more complex than simply adapting Collex for use with different content. In fact, although it started as an effort to create a better library catalog, Blacklight is now best thought of not as a discrete piece of software but as an infrastructure project that can be used to support all kinds of applications, only one of which is an improved library catalog.

At the core of this infrastructure lies a Lucene (lucene.apache.org) search engine and Apache Solr (lucene.apache.org/solr), a web services wrapper for Lucene. Lucene has been recognized for almost a decade as a fast, scalable, general purpose, open source search engine, but before the development of Solr, it was necessary to write custom Java code to make use of Lucene. This created an insurmountably high technical barrier for many otherwise interested libraries. The development of Solr over the past several years, however, has meant that anyone who can read and write XML (eXtensible Markup Language) files can make use of Lucene by posting and retrieving XML files through HTTP. This makes Solr an ideal mashup platform because there are such a wide variety of applications and programming languages that can read and write XML. By adding as much content as possible into Solr, mashups of almost every aspect of the catalog become feasible. Once someone learns the simple Lucene query structure, he or she can then query the Solr index at will and retrieve search results in a variety of formats.

Reclaiming the Catalog

One of the greatest benefits of moving to a flexible, mashup-like method for indexing and displaying the library's catalog proved to be the ability to expose partially obscured, or even totally hidden, data to users. In traditional vendor relationships, a library that purchases an ILS often agrees to certain ways of indexing its data to make it searchable. Certain fields might be made searchable under title and others searchable under author, for example. After the vendor performs the indexing, often very little tweaking or customization occurs, and revisiting the setup is expensive and time-consuming.

In an era when free and open source software can index and search terabytes of data, this model of "search scarcity" no longer makes sense. For example, if a library is limited to a certain number of indexes—also known as *access points*—for its entire collection, those indexes are necessarily defined broadly in order to serve the greatest number of people, leading to a limited set of search possibilities, such as title, author, subject, format, and maybe half a dozen others. Similarly, if it is hard to make changes to a catalog's interface, a general interface is needed, one that can do a good enough job for most people.

With new tools such as Solr enabling the creation of flexible catalog indexes and interfaces, libraries are free to rethink assumptions about library catalog design. If designing an interface to the catalog is sufficiently easy, it becomes affordable to produce interfaces tailored to specific populations. Custom interfaces for each of UVA's branch libraries (Humanities and Social Sciences, Art and Architecture, Music, Science and Engineering) are natural places to start, but from there one could easily envision viewing library collections through lenses of arbitrary specificity, not just the pathfinders or subject guides of old, but full-featured, tailored library catalogs with tweaked relevancy ranking for searches and customized faceting to group collections into meaningful subject-specific categories. This model retains positive aspects of pathfinders, too, such as the ability to directly reference any especially exemplary items. Instead of a standard catalog of collections, a series of curated exhibits is possible. Because data indexes are no longer scarce, we can define special access points for specific needs.

Digital Library Content

In addition to remixing the content already found in the library's catalog, creating a unified search interface for all of the data in the UVA Library's collection, including items not previously searchable by the existing OPAC, became a chief goal. Of particular interest were the thousands of digital objects in UVA's institutional repository. Before Blacklight, these items were searchable only via a separate webpage. Most users either did not know about this interface or seldom thought to use it, obscuring a large portion of the library's collection from public view.

Previous attempts to highlight these hidden collections focused on the creation of MARC records for every item in the repository. This approach was quickly found to be unworkable for a variety of reasons, not the least of which was that digital objects are not books and do not share the same requirements for description and display. Attempts to express these objects with MARC vocabulary and access them with an interface designed for books proved strained and cumbersome.

The flexible design of Blacklight allows for indexing multiple types of objects from the repository with separate metadata standards. Without a rigidly defined set of access points, Blacklight has the ability to create new interface features when it is taking in new forms of content. For example, the library's digitized images are usually organized by a collection name, so when Blacklight is ingesting these images, a collection access point is created, allowing users to easily reference all of the items belonging, for example, to the Catlin Indian Paintings (Figure 9.1).

Blacklight's user interface, written in the adaptable Ruby on Rails framework, also allows for the creation of specific behaviors for specific kinds of objects. A book has a behavior profile that includes fetching its cover from a variety of book cover services, while a digitized image object instead has an action for displaying a thumbnail (Figure 9.2). In the future, embedded players for digitized audio and video files in our collection will be included, so that the user can interact with each object immediately on discovery. This arrangement allows one to imagine many future mashup opportunities, such as contextual menus for various kinds of objects allowing one to post an image to a blog, add a digitized piece of music to a personalized internet radio station, or add a video to an internet television queue for watching at home.

Digital Scholarship Content

Many of the fruits of digital scholarship at UVA are not part of our repository and too often exist in unrelated silos of content, available

Figure 9.1   Search limited to the Catlin Indian Paintings

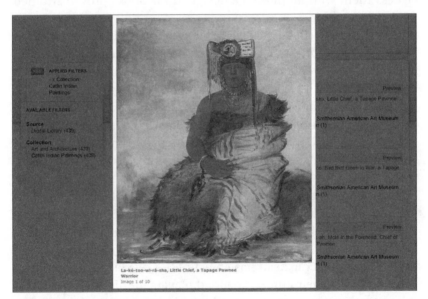

Figure 9.2   Digitized image thumbnail

only to a self-selecting few. Blacklight attempts to minimize the effort required to unify these isolated sources of information with the catalog as a whole, thus providing a more comprehensive view of all the material available at UVA, regardless of whether it has been formally collected by the library.

Ethan Gruber's work on digitizing UVA's collection of Greek and Roman coins provides a strong example of Blacklight's flexibility for ingesting content. In cooperation with the UVA Art Museum and the Classical Art and Archaeology program, Gruber created a painstakingly detailed guide to UVA's numismatic collection, along with detailed high-resolution photographs of each coin. Although the site (coins.lib.virginia.edu) is internally searchable and eventually will be findable by general internet search engines, scholars using our library catalog to find numismatics materials or to research the culture of ancient Rome would previously have been unable to discover one of our most valuable digital resources. Because the technical barriers to entry into Blacklight are so low, Gruber was able to incorporate his collection into our central catalog within a matter of hours.

To ingest items in Blacklight, a data provider needs to index objects in Solr, and—assuming these objects require unique styles or behaviors in the user interface—create ways of displaying the objects in Ruby on Rails. This means creating a Solr "add" document and a Rails "view." (You can see an example of a Solr "add" document in this XML.com article: www.xml.com/pub/a/2006/08/09/solr-indexing-xml-with-lucene-andrest.html.) POSTing this file to Solr adds the documents to Blacklight's overall index. Anyone who knows HTML should be able to write a Rails view in short order.

The coins site is based on XML-encoded EAD documents (www.loc.gov/ead). Ethan Gruber transformed those EAD documents into a Solr "add" document using XSLT (XML Stylesheet Language Transformation), then wrote two short view partials (basically HTML with a little Ruby code) in Ruby on Rails: one for the list view (Figure 9.3) and one for the item view (Figure 9.4). Here's the "show item" code: *blacklight.rubyforge.org/svn/trunk/rails/app/views/catalog/_show_partials/_lib_coins.html.erb*. Where possible, descriptors for coins were added under existing access points (notice in Figure 9.3 that *coin* has been added as a format, and The Oliver's Orchard Hoard has been added under Collection), but some numismatics-specific access points, such as *mint*, were also created, as was a numismatics-specific display behavior to take advantage of these fields (Figure 9.4).

Here, Blacklight exhibits its strength as a general browsing tool, as the numismatic collection looks nothing like a typical library catalog item. Serendipitous moments of collection discovery are possible with a system built on polymorphous content consumption and generation. Imagine glancing through the list of item types and stumbling on *coin format* as a choice. Click through, and suddenly, typical facets such as *language* and *subject* are replaced by collection-specific terms such as *dynastic period* and *deity depicted*. In a few clicks or a well-phrased search, one can go from viewing the entire library collection to focusing on only those Roman coins in the catalog that were minted during Hadrian's rule.

Figure 9.3   *Coin* has been added as a format, and The Oliver's Orchard Hoard has been added under Collection

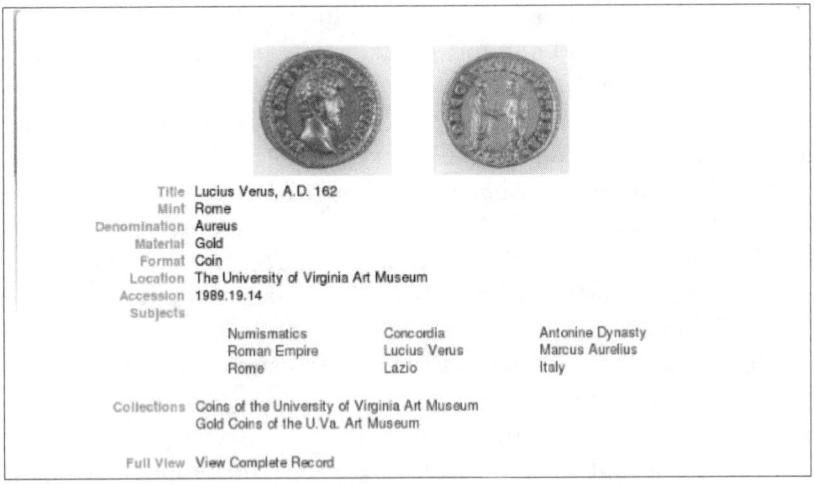

Figure 9.4   Note that *mint* has been set up as a numismatics-specific access point

Using Blacklight Services Elsewhere

Mashups in Blacklight are not just an internal process; they flow outwardly as well. In an attempt to structure our data and services in a way that makes them accessible and useful to other applications, several web services are made available. These services require almost no programming maintenance, allowing developers to focus on adding new features rather than on keeping up existing ones.

Direct Solr Service

Because Solr is one of Blacklight's core components, the catalog data is available directly as a web service. Books, movies, faculty research projects, and everything else indexed by Solr is available as a mashup source. Search results are available in a wide variety of formats, such as JSON (JavaScript Object Notation), Ruby, XML, and PHP.

Availability and Holdings Information

Like most current catalog systems, UVA has implemented a Z39.50 server that allows access to real-time status of its catalog items. Communicating directly with the Z39.50 server requires a special set of libraries for requests and knowledge of a complex query language, so direct connections are seldom used. By wrapping our internal Z39.50 server's application programming interface (API) into a web service, this complicated process is transformed into a simpler web API or querying item availability and holdings. As with Solr results, a variety of response formats is possible.

Book Cover Service

Blacklight's book cover service is able to find cover images from multiple sources, including Google Book Search (books.google.com) and Syndetics (www.syndetics.com), and can be extended to use any other compatible service. When a book cover is requested, each of the sources is queried in parallel, and the first found book cover is used.

Permanent URIs for Items and Searches

The simplest of all web services, the availability of stable and meaningful URIs (Uniform Resource Identifiers) enables anyone to reference an item or a search in his or her website, blog, class syllabus, email, or application.

User Tags

With Blacklight, users can designate any catalog item of interest with a custom tag. In the future, those tags could be made available as a web service. An external application could then query the user tag service and either mine the tags for data or generate an interesting visualization, such as a tag cloud.

RSS of Filtered Search

Blacklight's search result pages are available as standard RSS feeds. The search results change when a new item that matches your search is added to the Solr index. While useful in and of themselves, RSS feeds also allow users to take advantage of a plethora of mashup services, many of which ingest RSS. One might bring a search feed for a favorite topic into Yahoo! Pipes (pipes.yahoo.com), allowing anyone to create a cut-and-paste piece of code to include on a blog, add a feed to their personalized Yahoo! or Google pages, receive updates by email or phone, tweet[2] the feed, post the feed to Facebook, or even remix the remix!

Recently, subject librarians have begun using LibGuides (guides.lib.virginia.edu) to deliver subject-specific guides to library content online. The features made available through Blacklight's web

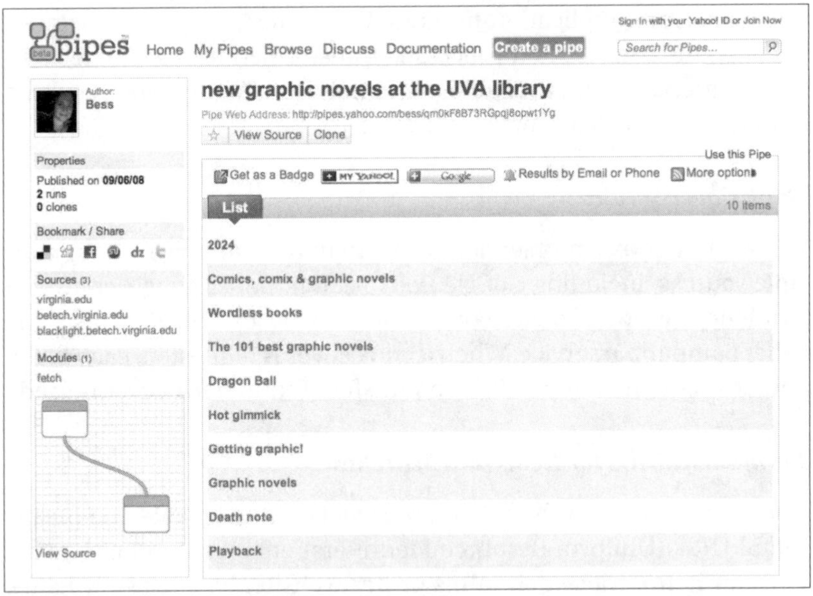

Figure 9.5   Yahoo! Pipe for new graphic novels in the UVA library

services allow these guides to deliver more robust content than was previously possible. Rather than a simple list of annotated links to the front pages of popular journal databases, librarians can provide a feed for the newest additions to relevant holdings or direct, stable links to catalog entries of popular reference works (Figure 9.5).

All of these services mean that data from our catalog can be mashed up and remixed as users see fit. As the number of easy-to-use mashup tools grows, and as users increasingly come to expect the ability to remix data, providing services such as those just mentioned will help to ensure that people continue to think of libraries as important centers for their information needs.

Leveraging the Power of Blacklight: An Example

Let's say you would like to display the book jackets for the books most recently added to Blacklight in a carousel widget. This could be achieved using nothing more than JavaScript. The first step is to build a query URL (Uniform Resource Locator), specifying JSON as the response format, and send the query to Solr. Once you receive the most recent books from Solr, each of the book covers can be collected from the book cover service. The code for the carousel widget can then ingest this JSON-formatted book cover data for display.

```
// Thanks to Doug Chestnut for this idea!
// This semi-pseudocode is using jQuery
var url = 'http://solrpowr.lib.virginia.
edu:8080/select/?';

var query = 'q=*:*&format_facet=Book&sort=
date_received_facet desc&rows=10&wt=json';

$.getJSON(url + query, function(data){
  for(i in data){
```

```
        data[i]['cover']=fetch_book_cover(data
['isbn']);
      add_item_to_carousel(data[i]);
   }
});

function fetch_book_cover(isbn){
  $.getJSON('http://blacklightdev.lib.
  virginia.edu/book covers/?isbn=' + isbn,
  function(data){
    return data['image_url'];
  });
}

function add_item_to_carousel(data){
// ...
}
```

The add_item_to_carousel function would employ the desired carousel widget. With just a small amount of code, it is possible to create a dynamic carousel without much fuss and little need to massage the data. To expand on this example a bit, let's change the query so that Solr will return the 10 books most recently acquired by the music library.

```
var
url='http://solrpowr.lib.virginia.edu:8080/
solr/select/?q=*:*&format_facet=Book&sort=
date_received_facet
desc&rows=10&wt=json&library_facet=Music';
```

The only difference here is the appended "library_facet=Music." Adding more filters to the query can focus the results further.

Adding availability and holdings information for each of the books would involve creating another function like "fetch_book_cover" but would instead query the availability service:

```
http://blacklightdev.lib.virginia.edu/virgo
/availability.json?ckey=u11111
```

The "ckey" param is the unique ID for the book. Because the returned data is formatted in JSON once again, using and manipulating these data are as simple as writing more JavaScript.

None of these services are limited to just JavaScript, of course. Most modern server-side scripting languages are capable of connecting to the internet and making requests. Although Blacklight is largely written in Ruby, other languages, such as PHP, Java, or Python, can just as easily mashup the data it provides.

Building a Web of Services

The accessibility to information provided by external web service APIs and Blacklight's flexible methods for consuming and delivering content makes providing information normally unavailable in OPACs significantly easier. One of the first attempts by Blacklight developers to leverage these methods centered on the creation of a specialized interface for the music library.

Through catalog usability testing, local music scholars expressed particular concern over the current interface, which lacked the querying functionality necessary for their research. For example, although the instruments used in a piece of music usually are cataloged and recorded in the MARC record, making these fields searchable in the online catalog has traditionally been considered too specific to include in a general search interface or to dedicate scarce resources to pursuing.

Further conversations with graduate students revealed that this was not the only issue hindering their research. The following are some requests that have since been implemented by Blacklight:

- The creation of a composition era facet. Although the composition date is recorded for all musical works, there was previously no way to quickly group, for example, everything written in the 20th century.

- The creation of a *recording OR score* facet. The commercial system currently in place can restrict results to only recordings or only scores, but not to items that are either recordings or scores.

- The ability to include metadata about a performer or work from external data sources.

In the case of this last item, finding a data source with the desired features—artist information, album art, and track listings—proved to be the first hurdle. Though sources for this kind of information are already established and growing daily, often-popular information resources make their information available only for a fee and perhaps even then only through a method unsuitable for a web services approach, such as FTP download. Although several impressive music databases exist, the Yahoo! Music API's REST-based interface, robust documentation, and rich content made it a good choice.

Much like accessing Blacklight's internal services, plucking resources from Yahoo! Music (music.yahoo.com) is as simple as constructing a URL that queries the database, finds the appropriate item in the resulting XML output, and displays it in the Blacklight record. To the end user, this content is integrated seamlessly with fields from MARC records and availability information from the ILS (Figure 9.6). Rather than tasking an army of catalogers with modifying every record with this information, we used a web services API, making it possible to add significantly more content to our music library records with just a few lines of code.

More Than Mashups: The Importance of Open, User-Driven Interfaces

Improvements to library catalog interfaces are an important step toward making the broadest amount of information available to the greatest number of people. Features such as persistent web addresses and custom feed syndication have long been lacking in commercial OPAC systems, but perhaps the most important change offered by Blacklight is the ability to modify and expand user interface functionality without impacting the underlying ILS.

At the same time, improving just one application will always have a limited effect on the general accessibility and openness of information. The principles of mashup and web-services-based design offer

Figure 9.6   Example Blacklight record

a way to look beyond the boundaries of any one application toward an overall landscape of open, user-driven web applications capable of interacting with one another and with users in innovative ways. Not only is Blacklight open source, allowing and encouraging users to download and modify the source code, but it is also open access. By consuming information from traditional and new sources and allowing others to reuse and remix this information, Blacklight fosters a flow of information that has the potential to impact users far beyond a specific library's catalog. Both open source and open data are central to the notion of software mashups, as well as strong, concrete steps toward one of librarianship's guiding principles: the freedom of information.

Endnotes

1. See www.rubyonrails.org for more details on this development framework.
2. To *tweet* is to send something via Twitter (www.twitter.com).

CHAPTER 10

Breaking Into the OPAC

Tim Spalding
LibraryThing.com

This chapter explores a number of approaches to "breaking into" a library OPAC (Online Public Access Catalog), letting you enhance your library's online catalog with useful data and powerful functionality without going to your OPAC vendor.[1]

Within a few months of founding LibraryThing (www.library thing.com), I knew that I wanted to help libraries add LibraryThing data and LibraryThing-style functionality to their catalogs. As a computer programmer with no experience in the library world, I figured this would be a simple problem to solve. Leaving aside the open systems that dominate today—Apache alone powers more than half of all websites—most enterprise closed-source systems are still designed to be extensible, with application programming interfaces (APIs) for getting data in and out and architectures that accommodate plug-ins and extensions. I figured I'd make some sort of extension that plugged into the OPAC directly, querying library data through APIs as needed.

Of course, I found out that the library world was different.[2] The code behind its systems was closed and unextensible, with virtually no APIs in or out. I found that many libraries couldn't even query their own data because it was locked up in proprietary databases. I realized library catalogs weren't like other content management systems (CMSs), databases, or web applications.

That realization started me on a process of discovery, working through the various options for "breaking into" OPACs, weighing pros and cons, and eventually developing our LibraryThing for Libraries (www.librarything.com/forlibraries) project. This chapter is the fruit of that journey.

The result is fairly light on code but heavy on the methods involved and their pros and cons. It is presumed you know HTML and something about web technologies, including concepts such as server-side versus browser-side programming. It is also assumed that you can program, or know someone who does, as you can't enhance your OPAC without some programming somewhere along the line.

Why Break Into the OPAC?

The OPAC isn't the library, but it is close. Whether from home or at the library itself, most library experiences involve using it—far more than any other finding system. Certainly patrons at most libraries check the OPAC for a book far more often than they ask a librarian.[3]

Important as they are, though, OPACs don't get the attention they deserve. Most are products of the 1990s, either essentially or literally, and they are not getting any better. Every few years, a library may upgrade its OPAC, but most upgrades are hardly deserving of the name, and almost nothing happens between upgrades. Library websites are getting better mainly because librarians understand how to use blogs and wikis. They even sign up for MySpace (www.myspace.com) and Facebook (www.facebook.com). All the while, the OPAC goes nowhere.

OPACs don't improve because libraries can't do much to them. Customization options are limited, and all but a handful[4] are essentially closed systems—shut even to professional programmers. If a library wants to start a blog or add an events section to its website, any web-savvy developer or librarian can help them. (This is surely one reason so many libraries have experimented with blogs and MySpace pages—they're easy to work with!) If a library wants to add functionality to its OPAC, though, it has to go to the OPAC vendor. If the vendor has something ready to go, it will cost you. If it doesn't, you are encouraged to wait for the next version, which will also have a cost.

Once you can "reach into" the OPAC, though, almost anything is possible. You can

1. Add alerts to the catalog so that patrons learn about upcoming events or scheduled downtimes

2. Add links to Amazon (www.amazon.com), Google Book Search (books.google.com), or Wikipedia (www.wikipedia.org)

3. Give users permanent links to catalog pages

4. Track user actions for statistical purposes

5. Add "Did you mean ... ?" spell-check functionality to search pages

6. Show a librarian-chat widget when a search turns up no results

7. Add dynamic location maps to item pages so that patrons know where on the shelf the book can be found

8. Show dynamic content on item pages, such as recommendations or links to other editions

9. Let users tag, rate, or review items in your catalog

The Problem

The task of breaking into your own OPAC can be divided into four smaller problems:

1. Changing the page – Affect some control over the OPAC.

2. Adding your own content – Put new things on the page.

3. Parsing the page – Figure out what the page is and what's on it.

4. Bringing in the catalog – Put data, functionality, or both on the page, based on information that is *not* on the page but drawn from the rest of your library's catalog.

Step 1: Change the Page

Unless your only purpose is tracking, you need some way to affect what the OPAC user sees. There are three ways to do this.

Change the Template

Most OPACs give you some sort of simple templating system, used mostly to rearrange elements on the page and to add or omit different types of bibliographic data. But a system that allows you to add a

<B> tag will, in most cases, allow an <IMAGE>, <IFRAME>, or <SCRIPT> tag as well.

"Constrained" templating is rarely a fatal problem, as any part of the page that allows HTML tags is enough. For example, a number of LibraryThing for Libraries' first customers had no access to templates for the main part of their OPAC pages and were confined to changing the "footer" alone, usually reserved for the name of the library and so forth. But once you have access to *any* page in HTML, you can insert a <SCRIPT> tag. The <SCRIPT> tags allow JavaScript to change anything on the page, from the first line to the last.

A very small number of OPACs, mostly low-end, hosted systems intended for the school market, will not allow the library to access the page templates, except to change the name of the library or add a new picture. In such cases, a "creative" developer may still find a way. Has the vendor remembered to strip <SCRIPT> tags from every textual string? Can the library change the OPAC's standard JavaScript files? Even CSS (Cascading Style Sheets) templates are not without their uses.[5]

Add a Server-Side Layer

A number of innovators, including John Blyberg and his SOPAC (www.thesocialopac.net; see Chapter 12) project and some of the work from the Dutch company AquaBrowser (www.aquabrowser.com), have solved the "change the page" problem by adding a server layer in between the OPAC and the end user. At its simplest, this approach resembles a proxy server—the user makes requests from the proxy, and the proxy requests from the target and passes the page to the user. Then, instead of echoing the page dumbly, the intermediate server can parse, change, add to, and rebuild what it receives, virtually without limits.

Powerful as it is, this approach has drawbacks. Although a server-side layer could have modest goals—adding in select enhancements and leaving the rest of the page alone—this would squander the technique's power without reducing its drawbacks. Ultimately, there is no halfway. To work correctly the new service needs to handle everything: URLs (Uniform Resource Locators) must be changed, both in HTML and JavaScript; cookies passed back and forth; and sessions maintained. Speed is a concern as every request now entails a second request and a parsing process as well. Getting in between the user and the page also introduces a new point of failure; everything will depend on keeping the intermediate servers up and running. A dedicated server is a must, with a spare too, if you can swing it.

All in all, adding a server-side layer is a good approach for anyone who wants to effect truly radical change—and has the technical and institutional support to back it up. For less grand efforts, though, it raises too many questions.

Add a Browser-Side Layer

Another less ambitious option is to enhance your OPAC with a browser-side layer. Short of writing a new browser and convincing everyone to use it, the options here are a bookmarklet or a Greasemonkey script (userscripts.org).

Bookmarklets are bookmarks (or favorites) that users add to their browsers. Unlike regular bookmarks, however, bookmarklets contain JavaScript code, not a link. When the user clicks on a bookmarklet, it executes the code against the current page and can do anything JavaScript can do—parse the page, add new elements, make additional JavaScript requests, and so forth.

The way bookmarklets are distributed limits their usefulness. A user needs to know about a bookmarklet, install it, and click it on a given page to get any value out of it. As such, bookmarklets tend to be used for highly specific, one-off tasks, such as jumping a user from an Amazon page to a local library (John Udell's "Library Lookup Project" at jonudell.net/librarylookupgenerator.html is one such effort). In theory, a library could add its bookmarklet to every public computer—for example, to show a given item's location in the building. But bookmarklets aren't widely understood and are apt to be ignored and never clicked.

Greasemonkey scripts work as bookmarklets without the clicking. Instead, JavaScript can work its magic on every page by default, without any special action on the user's part. Unfortunately, for security reasons, a Greasemonkey plug-in (addons.mozilla.org/en-US/firefox/addon/748) still needs to be installed and the script in question enabled. Worst of all, it works only on the Firefox browser! Despite these drawbacks, Greasemonkey could work within a closed environment, for example on library computers only or as a special option open to interested parties.

Perhaps its best use, however, is as a testing platform for templating changes. Greasemonkey scripts essentially pretend that a given page or set of pages has a <SCRIPT> tag on them, so it can mimic the effect of adding such a tag to a template. If you don't have a staging server, or your code isn't ready for even that yet, Greasemonkey is a powerful tool. What's good for testing can also be good for demonstrations. Before LibraryThing for Libraries had a single "reviews" customer, we were able to show people what the new enhancement would do and how it would look, just as if they had installed it in their OPAC.

Step 2: Add Your Own Content

Assuming you go with the template solution of adding HTML to the page, the next question is just what HTML you want to add. There's little point in adding static HTML as, by definition, it would be the same on every page. Instead you want an element that can change as the page changes. There are four good options, in ascending order of flexibility and ambition.

Images

The most widespread and successful library enhancements out there rely on the humble image, namely the cover services provided by Amazon and Syndetics (www.syndetics.com). These services take a standard URL structure and leave a spot for an ISBN. By filling in the ISBN, either in your templating solution or with additional JavaScript, an image is requested. A simple program on the other side—not just a server but a server running a program—sends back the appropriate book cover.[6] To get past the problem of broken images, when it doesn't have a cover, Amazon returns a 1 x 1 pixel transparent GIF—the closest thing to nothing in the world of images.

There is no reason this approach couldn't be extended to other data. Instead of sending back a cover image, the program could send back star ratings or author photos. If the URL sent call numbers instead of ISBNs, a very ambitious image program could send back a shelf-location map.

The advantage of covers is their simplicity. On the browser side, simple image requests require no scripting, and there are no cross-domain security issues, such as those that can arise with Ajax (Asynchronous JavaScript and XML), frames, and JavaScript. Covers, however, are also extremely limited; they just sit there, and they only work for a few image-based applications.[7]

It should be mentioned that images could be tortured to do more. An image request on every page can be used to track catalog usage; every URL would return a blank image, but the program that received the request would log it. (Email spammers and the CIA use this "web bug" technique.) Similarly, LibraryThing's ratings widget originally used only image requests; the image URL also saved the data to the database, returning the appropriate number of stars. On the return, images can be parsed for their height and width—cross-domain Ajax for people with very little to say.

IFRAMES

Have you ever wondered how Google puts those ads on other people's websites? The answer is the <IFRAME> tag.[8] The IFRAME, or inline frame, allows a page to set aside a part of itself—a rectangle—and load a separate page within that area. If the "parent" page and the IFRAME page have the same background color, the effect can be seamless.

IFRAMES have all the advantages and disadvantages of separate pages. On one hand, an IFRAME is free of the styles and scripts of the enclosing page—it is its own little world within the larger universe. Given the chaos and ineptitude that characterizes many OPACs' layout and stylesheets, this can be a real blessing. On the other hand, a page and its IFRAME are so separate that the page doesn't know if the IFRAME is full or not and can't give the frame more room if it needs it. As a result, IFRAMES work best when you know exactly how much content is coming back or when you have a lot of space to burn.

The separation has a security component. To prevent "foreign" IFRAMES from causing harm, IFRAMES coming from different domains are completely sandboxed, with no potential for communication from one to the other. If the IFRAME needs to know about the page it's on, it's going to need to find out through its URL query string or conceivably by parsing the referrer string. Within the same domain, however, page and IFRAME can communicate, although the JavaScript to implement this can get hairy. Finally, because IFRAMES are of a set size, they don't slow the main page down.[9]

Ajax

Ajax is probably the best-known way of dynamically adding content to webpages. Using Ajax, a web application can pull in information (XML or not) just like an IFRAME and parse and integrate it into the page itself. So many sites use it that it has become virtually synonymous with Web 2.0.

Unfortunately, Ajax has one major drawback: You can't request across domains, or even across subdomains. In the context of the

OPAC, this deficiency can be severe. Whatever server-side scripts you create have to run off the same domain and subdomain as the catalog itself. Provided you can run scripts off the OPAC's server directly, do you want to? OPACs are expensive, fiddly, and proprietary things—unless you know exactly what you're doing, it might not be a good move to test and run your enhancement applications off them.

The cross-domain problem has a number of work-arounds. There is a popular, if complex, technique that routes requests through Flash. More simply, you can set up a proxy, catch Ajax requests, and proxy them to another server and domain. (Just be very careful how you set the proxy up, or you may find the server fetching a lot more than library records.)

JavaScript

For most solutions, the answer is heavy use of cross-site JavaScript, which can fetch content like Ajax but is not subject to the same domain restrictions as Ajax is.

At its simplest, JavaScript exists as a script tag, with a URL parameterized somehow.

```
<SCRIPT TYPE="TEXT/JAVASCRIPT"
SRC="http://www.library.org/recommend.
js?isbn=0123456789"></SCRIPT>
```

At the server end, "recommend.js" wouldn't be a static JavaScript file but a file that generates valid JavaScript with the appropriate content baked in. So, for example, recommend.js with the query string "isbn=0123456789" would return data about books recommended for readers of ISBN 0123456789.

Best results are obtained when you use JavaScript and the document object model (DOM) to request more JavaScript scripts, containing added functionality or data. Although there is no "normal" way for JavaScript to ask for new scripts, a trick of sorts works on every modern browser and has become very common: Creating a new script element and inserting it into the head of the document, which, when it sees it, sends out the request.[10] A basic function looks like this:

```
function requestScript(url)
{
var script = document.createElement('script');
script.type = 'text/javascript';
```

```
script.src = url;
this.dochead.appendChild(script);
}
```

The request path of a LibraryThing tag cloud shows a typical pattern of JavaScript requests:

1. Page requests Widget.js, sending the library's ID in the query string.

2. Widget.js does nothing but establish a few helper functions, such as a script requester function, and make a new request for Connector.js.

3. Connector.js comes back with a host of functions for parsing the content of the page. These figure out what kind of page it is, what content is called for, and what ISBNs are involved. It requests a third JavaScript, Widget_Response. js, adding what it's learned, including the ISBN, to the query string.

4. Widget_Response.js comes back with the appropriate tag cloud in a JavaScript variable. Previously loaded code finds where the content needs to go and puts it there.

And that just sets up the tags. When a tag is actually clicked, more JavaScript scripts are loaded.

Here are some JavaScript tips that may prove helpful:

1. Don't get caught by caching. You can't roll out, let alone test, a complex JavaScript system like this unless you control how the scripts cache themselves. Although some caching can be useful, you never want to cache data, and it may prove best to thwart all caching, for example by adding a random item to each script's query string.

2. Wall off your code. All JavaScript plays in the same sandbox, so same-named functions and variables can wreak havoc. For example, if you make a createButton() function on WebPac Pro, you'll destroy III's function of the same name. Instead, use highly original names or stick your functions and globals under a convenience object.

3. Avoid inline scripts. Few web developers understand a basic fact about JavaScript: Because JavaScript can change

the page while it's loading, requesting and parsing JavaScript is an exclusive, synchronous action. That is, while your script loads, nothing else is loading! Unless your enhancements are more important than what comes after them, put JavaScript at the bottom of the page or attach external JavaScript to a document "onload" event so that nothing happens until the page is drawn.

4. Separate logic and content. It is tempting to make just one JavaScript request, but you can take best advantage of caching and keep your code clean by having one script for code, and have all others transmit only data, using JavaScript's handy JSON (JavaScript Object Notation) data format.

Step 3: Parse the Page

Perhaps the most painful part of enhancing your OPAC may be when you are forced to parse information from a page. OPAC HTML is notoriously slovenly and arcane, a big ball of unstructured gunk.[11]

Within that gunk lurks the information you need—the page type, or identifiers like ISBNs, LCCNs, OCLC numbers, and accession numbers, as well as item title, author, and holding status. Because LibraryThing for Libraries has a number of enhancements and allows you to control their positioning with <DIV> tags, it also parses the page for these, so it knows what content to fetch and where to put it.

There are three basic ways of parsing the page:

1. Package it up and send it to a server-side script for parsing. This is a cowardly act and will often exceed the POST limitation anyway.

2. Make a big lump of the text and probe it with regular expressions.

3. Use the DOM to find exactly the right content.

The "big lump" model works surprisingly well, particularly when searching for clearly identifiable data. You can, for example, get most of the potential ISBNs on the page in three lines of code.

```
var biglump = document.body.innerHTML;
//make the lump
```

```
var searchExpression = /[^i]([0-9]{13}
|[0-9]{10}|[0-9]{9}[x])/gi; //regular
expression to catch ISBNs

var potential_isbns = ( page.match
(searchExpression) || [] ); //find
everything that fits the regular expression
```

To really get it right, however, you may need to do more. LibraryThing spends more than 100 more lines weeding the possibles down and dealing with edge cases.

Using the DOM is conceptually the best option, but is too often thwarted by bad HTML. Retrieving a simple piece of content from the "big table in the middle" may end up involving "the second table with the 100 percent width after the cover image." If you control the page template, however, you can add as many uniquely named <DIV>s as will be helpful.

Step 4: Bringing In the Catalog

Many widgets can get away with parsing the OPAC page and drawing on outside data to add something to it. The most valuable ones, however, need to go further and draw on cataloging data from other OPAC pages entirely.

For example, it's relatively easy to parse a page for "No results found," query Google for the search string, and if Google provides a "Did you mean?" bring that suggestion into your OPAC. But who's to say the new search has any results, either? "Whoops, we don't have any books about that after all!" doesn't inspire a lot of confidence.

The problem gets worse when you are linking to items in your catalog. Everyone loves a recommended reading list, but how does the system know when the library has only 30 percent of the recommended books?

Create a Copy of Your Data

Export your MARC (MAchine-Readable Cataloging) records or just a few fields and load them into a secondary database. This is the technique used by LibraryThing for Libraries to recommend only books in your local library. This is a clean solution, but it can require considerable server resources, as well as scripts to parse the data. (Fortunately, LibraryThing has both.)

Screen-Scrape Your Own Catalog With Ajax

If you need it, same-domain Ajax screen-scraping can give you the information you need. But the process is slow and can put a lot of strain on your servers. Executing a single search to see whether there are any results might not be too bad, but if every book page sends out 10 Ajax requests for other book pages, your server might melt under the strain of a 10-fold increase in traffic.

The worst-case scenario argues strongly for using this technique only when a single answer is needed and in conjunction with database storage of the results. Unfortunately, the latter involves the potential for stale data.

Screen-Scrape Your Catalog From the Outside

If 10 simultaneous requests is a problem, you can try spacing requests out over days, weeks, or months, slowly amassing the data necessary to make a feature work.

In theory, this is a good idea. But, as with Ajax screen-scraping, stale data may still be a problem. And you have to be careful. Early on, LibraryThing screen-scraped a major Massachusetts consortium, hitting it once every 4 seconds (the industry standard is once per second) overnight. We brought the whole system down. Apparently our ISBN URL started a new session for every request, and sessions took hours to expire. The server filled up with session data and stopped responding to requests. That sort of glitch is possible only in the library world, where applications costing hundreds of thousands of dollars scale worse than a blog on a $10 per year hosting plan. But it shows what can happen.

Build Up a Second Copy Over Time

Instead of screen scraping at need, or ingesting a complete copy of the database, build up a database store slowly, by leveraging every script hit. That way, if you hit the *Da Vinci Code* today, it may show up in recommendations tomorrow, but not before.

Query an External Service

A few OPACs have APIs into one or more database features. LibraryThing is planning on releasing a JSON API to our customers' data. There is also some indication that the OCLC may be considering adding JSON APIs to its WorldCat Search API.

Conclusion

The techniques discussed in this chapter are designed to give your thinking a boost and clear the way for the real work of adding functionality to your library catalog. Although hardly "simple," enhancing your OPAC without permission is now within the reach of any competent web developer.

Ideally, however, new enhancements would be developed collaboratively, with many sharing the credit—and the bug fixing!

Endnotes

1. This chapter owes a great deal to the thought and work of other LibraryThing past and current employees, including Altay Güvenç, Casey Durfee, and Chris Holland. Whatever is good in here may well be theirs; what's bad is certainly mine.

2. The closed nature of library software is mirrored by the situation with library data. This would be remarkable enough in any industry. Within the context of libraries—the historic cornerstone of freedom of expression and free access—it is a scandal.

3. And unlike the most important library experience—using the library's holdings—the OPAC is the library's alone. If a patron reads a great new book, the author gets most of the credit, not the library the patron checked it out from. But nobody blames Steven King because his books are hard to find in an OPAC!

4. From this point forward I will restrict myself to discussing these closed systems. Open systems, like Koha and Evergreen, are still a tiny fraction of the market. Further, all of the solutions that work for closed OPACs also work for open ones.

5. With CSS alone, you're pretty much restricted to adding images. CSS2 has a Generated Content concept that allows stylesheets to change documents, not just style them. But no current version of Internet Explorer supports it.

6. It wouldn't even be entirely necessary to send the ISBN, as the image-processing program could examine the document referrer, fetch the page, and parse out the ISBN.

7. A special LibraryThing.com widget, not available to libraries, returns some of the user's book titles drawn in the image itself. We made this "graphical widget" for users to deploy on sites that forbid all other widgets, JavaScript, frames, Flash, etc. I can't imagine a library would ever go this route, cute as it is.

8. To be accurate, Google Adsense is a SCRIPT that inserts an IFRAME.

9. I have left out any discussion of other embedded solutions, including Flash, Silverlight, and Java. I don't think their discussion would add much to the capabilities of IFRAMEs with JavaScript.

10. The same technique works with CSS elements. This is how LibraryThing for Libraries allows all the elements to be stylized without changing OPAC-level templates.

11. For example, one of the major OPACs comically generates list items by making a table and filling it with lines like `<code><tr><td><li> </li></td><td>List item</td></tr></code>`.

CHAPTER 11

Mashing Up Open Data With ‡biblios.net Web Services

Joshua Ferraro
LibLime

Introduction to ‡biblios.net

In early 2009, LibLime (www.liblime.com) launched a free, browser-based cataloging service with a data store containing tens of millions of openly licensed library records (liblime.com/news-items/press-releases/announcing-biblios-net-the-worlds-largest-database-of-freely-licensed-library-records). This chapter introduces ‡biblios.net (biblios.net)—in particular, ‡biblios.net Web Services (BWS; bws.biblios.net)—and provides examples of how BWS can be used to create useful mashups of open data.

Open Data and ‡biblios.net

The philosophy behind the open data movement scarcely needs an explanation to a library audience. The mission of many libraries is to provide *open access to ideas and information*. Certainly, that same mission applies to the metadata created *by* libraries.

Open data, especially when accessible via open application programming interfaces (APIs), is essential in creating useful services, including mashups. Yet historically, there have been no openly licensed, community-maintained sources of library metadata. As a result, libraries have traditionally been restricted to providing mashups on a tiny subset of the rich semantic content available in their metadata.

So what's the tipping point for open data? There have been a number of barriers, including access to the data itself (often stuck in the silos we call Integrated Library Systems), confusion about licensing issues, and a lack of supporting technology.

Over the past few years, however, the pieces have started to fall into place; we're now seeing the beginnings of an open data movement. Let's review a few of these key developments.

Large Amounts of Public Domain Data Are Now Available

2007 saw the launch of the Open Library (openlibrary.org), with a goal of creating "One web page for every book." Libraries responded in droves to support this project, contributing more than 30 million bibliographic records in MARC (MAchine-Readable Cataloging) format. Most of the contributions were made freely available by uploading them to the Internet Archive (www.archive.org), thereby placing them forever into the public domain. Open Library itself has created a host of useful APIs for accessing these records, some of which are documented in other chapters of this book.

Around the same time that Open Library was getting started, the Library of Congress Authority File surfaced publicly in MARCXML format. Also, the Library of Congress itself opened up access to its records via an XML (eXtensible Markup Language) web service (lccn.loc.gov) using LCCN (Library of Congress Control Number) as an identifier, making it possible to access newly created and modified records more easily and programmatically.

The First Open Data License

Also in 2007, the U.K. software vendor Talis (www.talis.com) spearheaded the creation of the Open Data Commons Public Domain Dedication and License (PDDL; www.opendatacommons.org). This was a significant development because PDDL is the first license to address data, and in particular, sets of data as part of a database. As such it's suitable for licensing individual records as well as large sets of bibliographic, authority, and other library metadata.

The PDDL does for data what open source licenses such as the GNU General Public License (www.gnu.org/copyleft/gpl.html) do for software: PDDL ensures that anyone can use, modify, and distribute records, or the entire database itself.

The Web Really Took Off as an Application Environment

Momentum has been building around the web as an application environment. The days when the web consisted of a bunch of static, clunky HTML pages are long gone. Full-featured desktop-style applications like Gmail (www.gmail.com) and Google Maps (maps.google.com) surfaced, and some larger organizations and communities have seen the benefit in releasing the toolkits they used to create these applications as open source tools for all developers to use. For instance, Yahoo! released the YUI toolkit (developer.yahoo.com/yui) for building cross-browser-compatible user interface widgets, followed by other JavaScript toolkits from the open source community, such as Ext JS (extjs.com). Google released Gears (gears.google.com), a powerful tool permitting offline persistent data storage in a local MySQLite database. Cross-platform, open architecture, rich internet applications (RIAs), with functionality as smooth and usable as found in desktop applications, were becoming a reality.

RIAs were all the rave when LibLime was selected as a 2007 Google Summer of Code (code.google.com/soc) mentor. Thus was born ‡biblios, an open source, web-based metadata editor. LibLime has since released ‡biblios under the GPL (General Public License), and the software is freely available for download from the project website (biblios.org).

‡biblios is itself a mashup of several services, as we'll see later in this chapter. If you're interested in learning more about ‡biblios the editor, a great article written by one of the lead programmers in *The Code4Lib Journal*[1] gives a history and overview of ‡biblios functionality and future directions.

Putting It All Together … ‡biblios.net

‡biblios the editor provides one part of a technology framework for community-maintained data. The other part, a web-scale, network-level service where catalogers can search, create, share, and collaborate, is where ‡biblios.net comes in. This is the world's first community-maintained database of openly licensed library records. Far more than just a cataloging editor, ‡biblios.net is a comprehensive cataloging productivity suite including the following components:

- A rich cataloging editor with support for both original and copy-cataloging

- An integrated metasearch engine for finding records within the ‡biblios.net database and any other database that supports Z39.50

- A search target registry, seeded with more than 2,000 Z39.50 servers, allowing users to find, create, and share useful Z39.50 targets

- Social cataloging features like forums and built-in messaging

- Context-sensitive, field-specific help available within the editor itself

- Community-maintained, wiki-style access to the ‡biblios. net master bibliographic data store

- Future-thinking design that will easily adapt to changing metadata and search standards (e.g., RDA, linked data)

- Free access for all to ‡biblios.net as a Z39.50 target

- BWS, a set of open APIs that enable programmers to write applications to interact with the ‡biblios.net database

Perhaps best of all, not only does ‡biblios.net contain openly licensed library records, but the service itself, including the cataloging editor, is made available for use at no cost. That's right, *it's free.*

BWS

BWS is a simple set of APIs designed to allow programmers to write applications that interact with the ‡biblios.net database. Like the cataloging service, BWS is free. However, several of the services require a username and password. Programmers can sign up for a free account at biblios.net.

Services currently available via BWS include

- Searching for bibliographic and authority records via OpenSearch, SRW/U, and Z39.50

- Harvesting records and database changes via OAI-PMH

- Sending data to ‡biblios.net

A free service providing open data is ripe for mashing up into interesting combinations. Let's take a look at some examples of how BWS can be used to create mashups.

Authority Headings Auto-Completion

Other chapters in this book explore mashups using bibliographic SRU (Search and Retrieve URL) services. (SRU is an XML-focused search protocol for internet search queries.) The same techniques can, of course, be applied to the BWS bibliographic SRU search service. However, because ‡biblios.net also exposes its authority data store as an SRU target, some interesting possibilities arise for streamlining the process of cataloging authority-controlled fields.

Getting into the details of controlled vocabulary is a bit beyond the scope of this discussion, but the definition of *authority control* from Wikipedia may help out if you're unfamiliar with the concept:

> Authority control is a term used in library and information science to refer to the practice of creating and maintaining headings for bibliographic material in a catalog. Authority control fulfills two important functions. First, it enables catalogers to disambiguate items with similar or identical headings. For example, two authors who happen to have published under the same name can be distinguished from each other by adding middle initials, birth and/or death (or flourished, if these are unknown) dates, or a descriptive epithet to the heading of one (or both) authors. Second, authority control is used by catalogers to collocate materials that logically belong together, although they present themselves differently. For example, authority records are used to establish uniform titles, which can collocate all versions of a given work together even when they are issued under different titles.[2]

The traditional process for original cataloging with authority control may require catalogers to search in a remote database for authorized forms of a given author, uniform title, or subject heading, and then either copy and paste or retype that authorized form into the appropriate field of the record they are editing. Many records have three or more fields with authority control, so this can be a very time-consuming process. Some libraries opt to simply outsource authority control to third parties, which insert authorized forms into their records; those modified records must then be processed to overlay matching records in the library's catalog at a later time.

To help streamline the authority control process, the ‡biblios editor utilizes a mashup that queries the BWS authority SRU search service for a list of available authorized headings based on the field and user input (Figure 11.1). As the user types, the mashup continues to query the SRU service in the background and updates the auto-completion dropdown, displaying the most relevant headings. The cataloger can select from the list using the keyboard or mouse, and the system will fill in the authorized form based on the selection. The system will also fill in other relevant fields from the authority record, such as the dates associated with a name in the case of an author. Additionally, catalogers can roll their mouse cursor over the heading and view the entire authority record to verify that it is the correct selection (Figure 11.2).

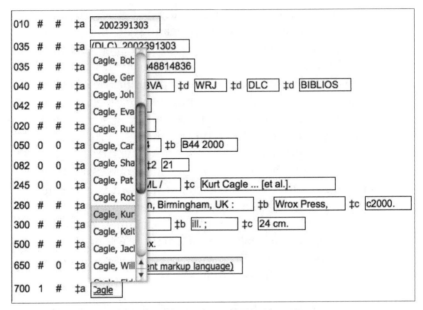

Figure 11.1 Auto-completion of authority headings in ‡biblios.net

This paradigm for authority control eliminates the need to do a separate search or to resort to copy and paste or retyping an authorized form from a separate utility or search system. A mashup like this one could be integrated into any bibliographic editor that needs to utilize a controlled vocabulary. It's an excellent example of the kind of innovation that can happen when data is both open and available via simple APIs.

Aggregating Relevant Changes With OAI-PMH, Z39.50, and RSS

One of the strengths of copy cataloging is that a single cataloger can leverage the work being done collectively by the entire community

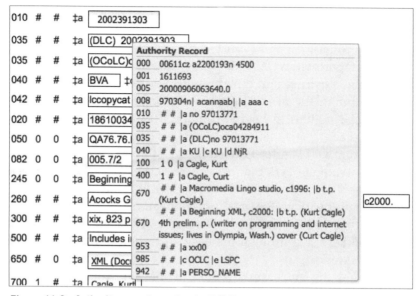

Figure 11.2   Authority record preview in ‡biblios.net

and reduce the time it takes to maintain accurate metadata for a library's collection. The traditional tools for copy cataloging are very effective in finding library records and importing them for the first time into a library's catalog, but they leave much to be desired when it comes to ongoing maintenance of that metadata.

For instance, suppose you participate in a shared cataloging environment with thousands of other catalogers. You regularly download and import records created by others, but minor typos may go unnoticed and make their way into your catalog. Some time later, perhaps someone will submit a change to the original record in the shared cataloging environment, fixing a typo. How do you know that change has been made, and how can you harvest that record and update your catalog?

If your shared cataloging environment supports an OAI-PMH (Open Archives Initiative Protocol for Metadata Harvesting) service, it can be used to harvest changes to that database. Developed by the Open Archives Initiative (OAI; www.openarchives.org), OAI-PMH defines a set of services that let you query a database with parameters, such as a date range, and receive back a list of all the records that have been added, modified, or deleted in that database during that period. Couple this service with a way to reference which of the changed items exist in your collection and you'd be well on your way to easily identifying and harvesting useful upstream changes to metadata you use.

BWS supports all six OAI-PMH verbs against the ‡biblios.net shared cataloging environment (bws.biblios.net/doku.php/harvesting_with_oai-pmh). It's an ideal platform for experimenting with OAI-PMH-based utilities to help streamline a local catalog's metadata maintenance.

For example, Figure 11.3 shows a simple proof-of-concept mashup, written in Perl, that reads BWS's OAI-PMH feed, initiates a Z39.50 search to the specified catalog, identifies matches, and provides the user with an RSS feed containing a filtered list of changed records that could potentially affect the user's catalog. That's a mouthful! Let's step through the basic operation of this mashup to see how it works.

To review the inner workings of this mashup, you can obtain a copy of the code by downloading it from kados.org/stuff/aggregate_biblios.net_changes.pl and opening it in your favorite editor.

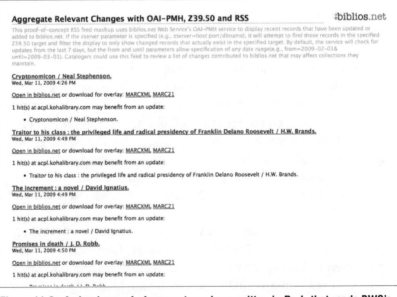

Figure 11.3   A simple proof-of-concept mashup, written in Perl, that reads BWS's OAI-PMH feed, initiates a Z39.50 search to the specified catalog, identifies matches, and provides the user with an RSS feed containing a filtered list of changed records that could potentially affect the user's catalog

By default, this script will simply convert the OAI-PMH feed from ‡biblios.net for the past 7 days into an RSS feed, suitable for reading in any RSS reader. However, the script also takes three optional parameters:

- *zserver* – The host, port, and database name to use to connect to the user's Z39.50 target (e.g., host:port/dbname); this server will be used to filter out any records that have been updated on ‡biblios.net that don't exist in your catalog)

- *from* – The starting date to retrieve changes from, in ISO format (e.g., 2009–02–01)

- *until* – The ending date to retrieve changes until, also in ISO format

For example, if you wanted to retrieve a list of all of the records that have changed in ‡biblios.net between February 1, 2009, and March 1, 2009, and cross-reference the fictional Example Library Catalog (z3950.example.com:210/bibliographic) to see if any of its records might need updating, the parameters would be

```
aggregate_biblios.net_changes.pl?zserver=
z3950.example.com:210/bibliographic&from=
2009-02-01&until=2009-03-01
```

The RSS feed helpfully provides links to download the record from ‡biblios.net (via another web service) in MARCXML and MARC21 in case you want to overlay those records into your catalog. It also offers a link to open the record directly in the ‡biblios.net record editor.

This example script is a good proof of concept mashup, but there are lots of areas for improvement. For instance, it relies on a fast Z39.50 connection, and your browser or RSS client will likely time out waiting for the feed if your Z39.50 connection is slow. One solution would be to run this as a batch job and generate the RSS feed daily. Also, the Z39.50 search function currently relies on ISBN matching, which is less than ideal because libraries catalog ISBNs differently. Also, it won't page through more than the default number of records retrieved via an OAI-PMH request, which means you can query only 50 records at a time. It could easily be enhanced to pay attention to all changes between a given date range rather than just the first page presented by the OAI-PMH request; such a request would, of course, take more time to process.

Conclusion

As outlined here, BWS offers a simple set of push/pull APIs that can be used to build interesting and useful mashups of rich library metadata. The mashup examples in this chapter show how some of the available services can be combined to enhance workflow and streamline maintenance of a library's collection. These examples just scratch the surface of possible uses for BWS. Because access to BWS is free, and the data is provided under an open license, anyone can create new mashups that utilize these resources. If you create a mashup you would like to share, or if you would like some help with an idea you have, you can sign up and submit a post to the ‡biblios.net Forums (biblios.net/forum).

Endnotes

1. Chris Catalfo, "‡biblios: An Open Source Cataloging Editor," *The Code4Lib Journal* (2008), journal.code4lib.org/articles/657.
2. Wikipedia, s.v. "Authority control," en.wikipedia.org/wiki/Authority_control (accessed March 12, 2009).

CHAPTER 12

SOPAC 2.0: The Thrashable, Mashable Catalog

John Blyberg
Darien Library

A Brief History of SOPAC

When life hands you lemons, grow grapes: That's the impetus behind the Social Online Public Access Catalog (SOPAC). In 2005, I had the privilege of helping to create the Ann Arbor (MI) District Library (AADL) website (www.aadl.org). My primary focus and responsibility was the way in which users would interact with the online catalog. Having been seriously underwhelmed by library catalogs for a very long time, I decided that success would depend on meeting one key requirement: The catalog and all its associated patron transactions needed to be seamlessly incorporated into the site. In other (and more geeky) words, the catalog and website had to be served by the same parent process. I was able to achieve this, but there were caveats.

The parent process, of course, was Apache, through which PHP and the content management system (CMS) Drupal (www.drupal. org) were instantiated. The reason this was a primary requirement is that if all catalog activity could be channeled through an open development stream (such as a PHP script), then pieces of it could be "hijacked" and modified by injecting content. This made it possible for us to provide our users with a single web address where we could not only take advantage of all the benefits of a CMS but where we could also embed a traditional catalog and account information. This bit of critical functionality would become the basis for future work on SOPAC and was nicknamed "the wrapper." The wrapper was a highly customized Drupal module that utilized the cURL (Client URL

Library; us3.php.net/curl) to do session-based screen scraping on the III Millennium catalog.

The wrapper afforded us a great deal of flexibility with the catalog, giving me the opportunity to do a fair amount of experimentation. Harnessing the power of social software within the context of a library catalog seemed like a logical trajectory for the web project. In January 2007, AADL went live with SOPAC. It gave users the ability to tag, rate, and comment on bibliographic records (www.aadl.org/catalog). There were some drawbacks to the software as it was written, however.

Despite the wrapper, the ability to customize the catalog was fairly limited. To introduce a foreign interface element, a series of very specific regular expression matches needed to be written for the desired injection point. This, in itself, is a cumbersome way to customize an interface, but we had an added frustration in that whenever we upgraded our integrated library system (ILS), we ran the risk of breaking critical functionality.

Even though the source code for SOPAC was released concurrently with its launch, I stated at the time that it would "definitely not work out-of-the-box" (www.blyberg.net/2007/01/21/aadlorg-goes-social). Because of its highly customized code, the source was released primarily as an example of how something similar could be done elsewhere. Its functionality also depended on III's Millennium OPAC and XML (eXtensible Markup Language) server product—the latter of which was later removed from the market. I began to field questions from many interested librarians who wanted to know how they could implement SOPAC and whether it would work with their ILSs. Sadly, I had to say that SOPAC would not work for them, although I dearly wanted to say, "yes, you can run SOPAC too!"

Additionally, I was frustrated by the fact that the content we were starting to get from the community was not in any way useful in the discovery process. In other words, when a user added a tag, it could not be used to later search for the tagged item. In the initial SOPAC model (now referred to as SOPAC1), user-contributed metadata was completely divorced from the record it was describing.

Last, SOPAC1 illustrated that, individually, libraries cannot reach a level of critical mass with respect to bibliographic social data. They just don't have a large enough user base to get an equalized data set that accurately reflects the sensibilities of the community a library represents. Like any social software, the success of SOPAC depends strongly on the strength of its associated network effect. The more participation a site enjoys, the more data it has to incentivize new users. It's a chicken-or-the-egg conundrum—if you don't have the data, how do you get the users? If you don't have the users, how do you get the data?

The Social Catalog Application Suite

The first version of SOPAC was clearly not a product that could be packaged and distributed for use by other libraries. Additionally, the project was shelved after I moved to Darien Library in May 2007. It remained inactive for about a year until we made the decision at Darien to go ahead with SOPAC2 in early spring 2008. While brainstorming, we recognized the importance of creating a project that could benefit not only Darien Library but others as well. Having already gone through the development process once before, I knew that if we were to create a "product," SOPAC would need to have a well-defined architecture that was self-contained and extensible. Whereas the focus for SOPAC1 was on creating a unified, Drupal-based portal, SOPAC2's main development parameters centered on its identity as an open source project for the wider library community. To that end, it was decided that SOPAC2 would satisfy the following requirements:

- Its code base would have no customizations.
- All interface elements would be 100 percent "templatable."
- It could be installed by the average IT staffer.
- It could be used on top of any ILS.
- The social data would be part of a shared repository.
- Its core functionality could be made available to any other application.

I approached these requirements by breaking up and categorizing the major functional components of SOPAC and handling them as their own distinct elements. The result was that all of the non-interface functionality was delegated to two independent software libraries. The first, Locum, handles all of the ILS abstraction and transactional pieces, and the second, Insurge, provides all of the social repository functionality. SOPAC itself is now simply an application that uses Locum and Insurge.

Locum

Over the past several years, a new third-party OPAC market has emerged that has seen a number of front-end pieces developed that will work with a number of different ILSs. So the idea of an ILS-agnostic catalog is not new. If SOPAC was to be successful as a community-driven open source project, it needed to have the potential for use across multiple systems.

Locum's job is to do just that. Locum is a software library—a collection of PHP classes that interact with the ILS. It is a stand-alone abstraction layer that functionally separates any application that is built on top of it from the business logic of whatever underlying system is in place.

Two characteristics of Locum make it very useful to developers. First, Locum is designed to have a secondary abstraction piece—an ILS connector that can be literally dropped into place to make Locum work with another system. Second, all of the methodology is standardized so that a developer can simply instantiate the desired Locum class and begin developing a third-party catalog application. Locum was designed this way as an acknowledgment that its functionality would prove very useful, not only in SOPAC, but in other applications as well. This makes Locum a development toolkit and frees it from simply being a collection of code that is dedicated to supporting the SOPAC application.

Insurge

Where Locum handles all the ILS business logic, Insurge (a loose adaptation of the abbreviation of "Independent Social Repository") provides functionality for the storage and manipulation of bibliographic social data. Following in the Locum model, Insurge is an independent software library with its own self-contained methodology. At its most basic level, Insurge pairs social data with bibliographic numbers, allowing developers to add, remove, and modify the database.

Eventually, Insurge's server code will allow libraries to create repositories of social data that can be shared between institutions in a way that will help bolster their own community-added tags, ratings, and reviews. This is an effort to try to mitigate some of the issues surrounding the lack of seed data in our systems now.

Bringing It Together

It's true that both Locum and Insurge exist as separate software libraries, but they are also designed in such a way that they can work together. As I mentioned, one of the major limitations of SOPAC1 was the inability to use contributed data for discovery. Locum addresses this because it is "Insurge-aware." It shares a database with Insurge and is pre-configured to associate social data with its corresponding bibliographic record during the indexing process. This essentially means that when Locum does a keyword search, contributed tag and review data will be used in the discovery and weighting of the result. Locum also allows developers to implement searches by tag or review content. The social data makes for some interesting sorting options as well, such as the ability to sort by the highest-rated items first.

Because Locum takes advantage of the Sphinx full-text index engine (www.sphinxsearch.com), there is a great deal of flexibility in how records are indexed. Each index is populated via a unique and customizable SQL (Structured Query Language) query that brings together the elements that you want to highlight. The result is that developers have full control over the behavior of their discovery systems, from the way the index performs all the way through the interface itself.

Let's take a look at a few examples of how Locum and Insurge might be used in a website or application. These examples assume that you have PHP installed and that you are working within a PHP file on your website. If you are not familiar with PHP or how to get it to work with Apache, a good place to start learning about these topics is www.php.net. These examples also assume that you have successfully installed Locum and Insurge. See www.thesocialopac.net for detailed instructions on how to do that.

As with any standard PHP5 class, you can bring in Locum and Insurge functionality anywhere in your existing code. So in your PHP file, you will want to start by including the client libraries for Locum and Insurge:

```
require_once('/path/to/locum-client.php');
require_once('/path/to/insurge-client.
php');
```

Then instantiate them:

```
$locum = new locum_client;
$insurge = new insurge_client;
```

You now have all the functionality of both software libraries at your disposal. So let's look at an example of how you might embed a list of your library's 50 newest books in your website. We start by grabbing a Locum search result:

```
$locum_search = $locum->search('keyword,'
'*,' 50, 0, array(1));
```

This operation will populate $locum_search with an array of the 50 newest books in the collection, sorted by cataloged date. It is doing a keyword match on "*" (anything), limiting to 50 and starting at result 0 (remember that programmers start counting at 0 instead of 1), in item type 1, which happens to be the material code for books at the Darien Library. For the purposes of what we want to do, we are primarily interested in the *results* element in the returned array that contains the actual bibliographic items:

```
[results] => Array
  (
    [0] => Array
      (
        [bnum] => 1282718
        [author] => Roberts, Nora
        [addl_author] =>
        [title] => Tribute
        [title_medium] =>
        [edition] =>
        [series] =>
        [callnum] => Fic ROBERTS
        [pub_info] => New York : G.P.
        Putnam's Sons, c2008
        [pub_year] => 2008
        [stdnum] => 9780399154911
        [lccn] => 2008000860
        [descr] => 451 p. ; 23 cm
        [notes] => a:1:{i:0;s:550:"Cilla, a
        former child star who has found
        more satisfying work as a restorer
```

of old houses, has come to her
grandmother's Shenandoah Valley
farmhouse, tools at her side, to
rescue it from ruin. In the attic,
she finds a cache of unsigned
letters suggesting that her
grandmother was pregnant when she
died and that the father was a
local married man. When Cilla
becomes the target of a series of
intimidating acts and a
frightening, violent assault, her
neighbor, graphic novelist Ford
Sawyer, steps in to help her sort
out who is targeting her and why";}
[subjects] => a:6:{i:0;s:23:"Child
actors--
Fiction";i:1;s:25:"Granddaughters--
Fiction";i:2;s:46:"Motion picture
actors and actresses--
Fiction";i:3;s:23:"Grandmothers--
Fiction";i:4;s:29:"City and town
life--Fiction";i:5;s:13:"Love
stories.";}
[lang] => eng
[loc_code] => a
[mat_code] => 1
[cover_img] =>
http://syndetics.com/hw7.pl?isbn=97
80399154911/SC.GIF&client=yourid
[modified] => 2008-08-07 19:17:57
[bib_created] => 2008-07-23
[bib_lastupdate] => 2008-08-06
[bib_prevupdate] => 2008-08-05
[bib_revs] => 23
[active] => 1

As you can see, this result set is simply an array of numbered results in a presorted order. Presenting your 50 newest books is now simply a matter of looping through the array and building your list:

```
foreach ($locum_search[results] as
$search_item) {
// Do your HTML output here
}
```

You'll notice that with a very small amount of code, you can incorporate some very useful functionality in your site. The power of the Locum and Insurge model is that it gives web developers a great deal of flexibility over how and where their own library's data is used.

The SOPAC module itself tried to follow in the same vein by allowing flexibility and customizability wherever possible. It does this by taking advantage of Drupal's extensive application programming interface (API) and hooks architecture. There are two parts to SOPAC's "mashability": first, the internal Drupal elements, such as the SOPAC configuration panel and block placement, and second, the external elements, such as the extensive availability of interface templates and the ability to create sub-modules under SOPAC.

Think of SOPAC as a module that "makes available" to Drupal all the pieces that comprise a social catalog—the search form, the side blocks, the hit list, the faceted search browser, and the item record screen. These separate pieces can then be assembled in myriad different configurations to fit the needs and sensibilities of your institution. For example, if you wanted to embed a simple search form into a blog post, you could simply enable the ability to embed PHP in your Drupal posts and include the following where you want the form to show up:

```
<?php
print sopac_search_form('basic');
?>
```

If you wanted to include the Ajax-enabled advanced search form:

```
<?php
print sopac_search_form('both');
?>
```

SOPAC then takes care of any form submittal from that point on and will send the user to the hit list of results, which presents another opportunity for mashup and customization. There are three PHP templates associated with the hit list:

- *sopac-results.tpl.php* – Frames the entire hit list page

- *sopac-results-hitlist.tpl.php* – Governs how each individual "hit" displays

- *sopac-results-nohits.php* – Used when a search yields no results

The SOPAC template system allows you to be as specific as you want to be about the layout and design of your site. You can make every bit of the SOPAC interface look and feel exactly the way you want it to, without any limitation. Furthermore, because they are standard PHP templates, developers have at their disposal all the data they need to make intelligent modifications. If you are interested in customizing the SOPAC interface via the template system, simply copy all the .tpl.php files into your theme directory and make your modifications to those copies.

If you wanted to include a bit of code that would let users preview results in Google Book Search (books.google.com), you could simply add the following in *sopac-results-hitlist.tpl.php* wherever you wanted the button to appear:

```
<script type="text/javascript"
src="http://books.google.com/books/
previewlib.js"></script>

<script type="text/javascript">
GBS_insertPreviewButtonPopup('ISBN:<?php
print $locum_result[stdnum]; ?>');
</script>
```

The result is a button that, when clicked on, will pop up a preview of that particular book, if the record exists in Google Book Search. These types of very simple, drop-in enhancements can also be carried over to the record display as well as several of the sidebar blocks that SOPAC makes available.

Blocks, as they are known to Drupal, are an important navigational element within SOPAC. They are sometimes called sidebars in other

CMSs. Drupal blocks can actually be configured to appear on the left or right side of the page, or at the top or the bottom. They can also be "weighted" so that an admin or webmaster can have a finer degree of control over where they appear. Additionally, Drupal allows administrators to associate custom PHP code to an individual block. This code can help determine where the block appears or whether it even displays at all. The benefit of the Drupal block system is that blocks can be displayed based on *context*. For instance, if a user was reading a blog post about community involvement, a small custom SOPAC sub-module could instantly formulate and display a block that suggests several bibliographic items in the catalog based on the node taxonomy or keywords in the post. This would be a great way to merge library-generated content and physical collections.

The most important thing to remember about the Social Catalog Application Suite (SOPAC plus its two supporting libraries, Locum and Insurge) is that SOPAC and its supporting libraries are designed modularly. Each bit of discrete functionality is self-contained and presents its own programming interface so that it can be reused in myriad different PHP applications. Within SOPAC itself, the various elements can be individually configured or modified without touching any of the core functionality. This makes this model a very flexible and powerful set of tools for webmasters and ILS administrators alike who want to step beyond the bounds of the traditional OPAC. Even if you are not interested in the "social" component of the Social OPAC, there are still a number of compelling reasons these tools might be useful to you.

The long-term vision and hope for the Social Catalog Application Suite is that a community of open source developers will help improve the existing code and offer their expertise to write interesting new sub-modules. The project is still young, but it will be exciting to see the user base and the limitless number of ideas that have been coming in take shape. We'll look for you at thesocialopac.net!

CHAPTER 13

Mashups With the WorldCat Affiliate Services

Karen A. Coombs
University of Houston Libraries

What Are the WorldCat Affiliate Services?

Over the past year, OCLC has been making a series of web services available to its member libraries for accessing bibliographic data. Many of the tools and services were originally piloted by OCLC Research Works (www.oclc.org/research/researchworks). Currently the production web services that OCLC offers as part of WorldCat Affiliate Services include WorldCat Registry Search, WorldCat Registry Detail, xISBN, xISSN, and OpenURL Gateway. In addition, OCLC conducted a beta test of a new service over the summer of 2008 and made it available in August of the same year: the WorldCat Search application programming interface (API). While all of these web services provide valuable data to libraries, some are more valuable in creating mashups than others.

The WorldCat Registry Search and WorldCat Registry Detail services are similar in that both provide information about institutions or consortia in the WorldCat Registry based on their organization's profile. Where they differ is that the WorldCat Registry Search retrieves basic information about multiple WorldCat institutions and consortia, while the WorldCat Registry Detail retrieves detailed information about a single institution or consortium. These services could be of use to libraries interested in creating mashups that combine map data from a search (such as on Google Maps; maps.google.com) and data about libraries.

The xISBN and xISSN services are also similar in nature. Their basic purpose is to help libraries collocate related standard numbers, either for books (xISBN) or serials (xISSN). The xISBN service allows libraries to submit an ISBN to the service and receive a list of related ISBNs and selected metadata. This data could be used by libraries to show patrons and librarians a given book's other editions and formats (such as an ebook or audiobook). Mashing this data up with information from the library catalog could potentially create a user-friendly browsing experience, similar to Amazon (www.amazon.com). The xISSN service works in a similar fashion by allowing libraries to submit an ISSN to the service and retrieving a list of related ISSNs and other selected metadata. This information helps libraries relate different editions of the same serial (such as print and online editions) and to show historical relationships (ISSN changes that result from title changes, mergers, splits, etc.). Although data from the xISSN service can be mashed up with catalog data to enhance user interfaces, the most likely mashup using this data would be invisible to users. Libraries could use the xISSN service to enhance their OpenURL resolver to guarantee more consistent matching and linking to full text.

The OpenURL Gateway service is different from many of the other services in that it doesn't provide data directly back to the library. Instead, its purpose is to direct web users to full-text and other online resources at an appropriate library based on the user's IP (Internet Protocol) address. This service is useful for libraries that want to provide local users with links to their local resources.

Introduction to the WorldCat Search API

Probably the service that holds the most promise for libraries creating mashups, though, is the WorldCat Search API. The basic concept of the WorldCat Search API is to allow a search to be submitted to the WorldCat database and results to be retrieved in a machine-readable format. The beta version of the WorldCat Search API can return search results in four machine-readable formats: MARCXML, Dublin Core, Atom, and RSS. Libraries submitting queries to the services can specify which format they want their results returned in. The WorldCat Search API makes available many of the same search indexes as the standard WorldCat (www.worldcat.org) interface; however, the indexes available depend on the service level being used. The default service level allows libraries to search by keyword, title, author, ISBN, ISSN, and OCLC number and return a limited set of bibliographic data. The full service level allows libraries to search by all of the indexes available in WorldCat and returns more complete bibliographic data. For libraries that include all their holdings in OCLC but don't have an API for their catalog, this functionality is a huge advantage because it gives them programmatic access to bibliographic data.

Currently the WorldCat Search API is available only to OCLC member libraries that maintain a cataloging subscription, and in Europe to libraries cataloging in the Dutch GGC and the CBS systems. This is something I hope changes as WorldCat.org would benefit greatly from individual bloggers' and website maintainers' linking back to it. The easiest way to facilitate this linking is by providing the right tool.

Before we get started, the WorldCat Search API has some important terms and conditions worth summarizing:

- Bibliographic records and holdings information are to be used only for discovery purposes.

- The WorldCat Search API cannot be used to enhance any commercial service.

- Discovery cannot be used as part of the cataloging process.

- Institutions are responsible for maintaining the appropriate level of service requirements. The service level determines which indexes may be searched and whether a link to holding libraries and their OPACs (Online Public Access Catalogs) must be present within the application created.

- Any website using the WorldCat Search API agrees to display the "This site uses WorldCat" badge graphic on the website and provide it as clickable access to WorldCat.org.

To use the service, libraries are required to get an API key and sign the terms of service (TOS) agreement. Qualifying institutions can sign up at www.worldcat.org/affiliate/tools?atype=wcapi.

Searching WorldCat

In addition to its basic functionality, the WorldCat Search API lets you limit searches to a particular location based on ZIP code, IP address, or the xxx index (the OCLC symbol for the library). Using the library holdings index, libraries can limit their search results to a specific library based on OCLC symbol, ZIP code, or IP address. Search results can then be sorted based on relevancy, author, title, date, and number of libraries with holdings. Additionally, you can retrieve a library catalog URL (Uniform Resource Locator) for a specific library and record from the service.

The service also allows you to reformat records retrieved into standard citation formats, including American Psychological Association (APA), Chicago, Harvard, Modern Language Association (MLA), and Turabian.

Let's look at how a search API request is constructed. WorldCat Search API requests can be sent in one of two ways: by OpenSearch or by Search and Retrieve URL (SRU) service and CQL (Contextual Query Language). I will demonstrate how to submit searches to the WorldCat Search API using both these methods.

OpenSearch

OpenSearch (www.opensearch.org) requests allow only for keyword searching. This makes it the simpler of the two methods for searching the WorldCat Search API. The simplest form of an OpenSearch request is made up of three parts: the base URL, the query, and the API key.

```
http://www.worldcat.org/webservices/
catalog/search/opensearch?q=[search terms]
&wskey=[your key]
```

So if you wanted to search for the keyword "Ambient Findability," then the query would be q=Ambient%20Findability.

Results returned via OpenSearch can be formatted using the Atom or RSS specification. By default, results to search requests sent via OpenSearch are returned in Atom (Figure 13.1).

To specify a format for results, you need to add the "format" parameter to your request. So for a search for "Ambient Findability" that returns the results in RSS, the request would be as follows:

```
http://www.worldcat.org/webservices/
catalog/search/opensearch?q=ambient%20
findability&wskey=[your key]&format=rss
```

Figure 13.1   Example of Atom returned from OpenSearch

OpenSearch results formatted in Atom and RSS are extremely easy to read and use. However, the bibliographic information in them is not as robust as the information contained in results formatted using Dublin Core or MARCXML. Subject information in particular is missing from the Atom and RSS versions. Still, submitting queries via OpenSearch has the advantage that results can include citations in one of the predominant citation formats (APA, Chicago, Harvard, MLA, and Turabian) simply by addition of the "cformat" parameter. So if I wanted to do a search for "Ambient Findability" and return the results in RSS format with APA citation information, the request would be as follows:

```
http://www.worldcat.org/webservices/
catalog/search/opensearch?q=ambient%20
findability&wskey=[your key]&format=
rss&cformat=apa
```

This would return the results seen in Figure 13.2.

You can see that the WorldCat Search API is extremely powerful. However, using it requires some familiarity with the methods for submitting searches and the formats in which data is returned. If you are just getting started, the OpenSearch method of submitting searches and its corresponding result formats have the lowest learning curve.

Figure 13.2   Example of RSS returned from OpenSearch

SRU

In contrast, the SRU method for submitting allows you to return a fuller set of bibliographic data by providing access to more search indexes.

The simplest form of an SRU request is made up of three parts: the base URL, the query, and the API key:

```
http://www.worldcat.org/webservices/
catalog/search/sru?query=[search terms]
&wskey=[key]
```

However, unlike in OpenSearch requests, the search portion of the request can contain CQL. Using CQL, you can specify a particular field to search. So if you want to send a search for the title Ambient Findability, then the search portion would be

```
query=srw.ti%3D%22ambient%20findability%22
```

Results to search requests sent via SRU can be returned in MARCXML or Dublin Core. By default, results to search requests sent via SRU are returned in MARCXML (Figure 13.3).

To specify a format for results, you need to add the recordSchema parameter to your request. So for a search for the title Ambient Findability that returns the results in Dublin Core, the request would be as follows:

Figure 13.3 MARCXML returned from SRU request

```
http://www.worldcat.org/webservices/
catalog/search/sru?query=srw.ti%3D%22
ambient%20findability%22&wskey=[key]&record
Schema=info%3Asrw%2Fschema%2F1%2Fdc
```

This would return the results seen in Figure 13.4.

For those who want to go beyond OpenSearch to use SRU but are having difficulties building search requests, check out the Explain page for the API (worldcat.org/webservices/catalog/search/sru? wskey=[your key]). This page consists of a form that you can fill out and have your search request created for you. I have often used this feature to make sure my requests were properly created and to build code to parse search results in a particular format.

WorldCat Search API Examples in Action

The OCLC Developers' Network website (worldcat.org/devnet/index .php/SearchAPIDemos) includes several examples of how the WorldCat Search API can be used to create a mashup. One example mashup listed there is the WorldCat Facebook Application. The WorldCat Facebook Application allows users to search WorldCat and retrieve results from within Facebook (www.facebook.com) (Figure

```
Source of: http://www.worldcat.org/webservices/catalog/search/sru?query=srw.kw%3D%22ambient%20findability%22&wskey=obmCLoEUxfTLlAfCh7LoUWNnaMCTvS0RzAXKEO0IYB8plT9dY...

<?xml version="1.0" encoding="UTF-8" standalone="no"?>
<?xml-stylesheet type="text/xsl" href="/webservices/catalog/xsl/searchRetrieveResponse.xsl"?>
<searchRetrieveResponse xmlns="http://www.loc.gov/zing/srw/" xmlns:xsi="http://www.w3.org/2001/XMLSchema-instance" xmlns:oclcterms="http://purl.org/oclc/terms/"
xmlns:dc="http://purl.org/dc/elements/1.1/">
<version>1.1</version>
<numberOfRecords>1</numberOfRecords>
<records>
<record>
<recordSchema>info:srw/schema/1/dc-v1.1</recordSchema>
<recordPacking>xml</recordPacking>
<recordData>
<oclcdcs>
<oclcterms:recordIdentifier>61260129</oclcterms:recordIdentifier>
<dc:title>Ambient findability</dc:title>
<dc:creator>Morville, Peter.</dc:creator>
<dc:type>text</dc:type>
<dc:publisher>O'Reilly</dc:publisher>
<dc:date>2005.</dc:date>
<dc:format>xiv, 188 : ill. (some col.) ; 23 cm.</dc:format>
<dc:language xsi:type="http://purl.org/dc/terms/ISO639-2">eng</dc:language>
<dc:description>How do you find your way in an age of information overload? How can you filter streams of complex information to pull out only what you want? Why
does it matter how information is structured when Google seems to magically bring up the right answer to your questions? What does it mean to be "findable" in this
day and age? This eye-opening new book examines the convergence of information and connectivity. Written by Peter Morville, author of the groundbreaking Information
Architecture for the World Wide Web, the book defines our current age as a state of unlimited findability. In other words, anyone can find anything at any time.
Complete navigability. Morville discusses the Internet, GIS, and other network technologies that are coming together to make unlimited findability possible. He
explores how the melding of these innovations impacts society, since Web access is now a standard requirement for successful people and businesses. But before he
does that, Morville looks back at the history of wayfinding and human evolution, suggesting that our fear of being lost has driven us to create maps, charts, and
now, the mobile Internet. The book's central thesis is that information literacy, information architecture, and usability are all critical components of this new
world order. Hand in hand with that is the contention that only by planning and designing the best possible software, devices, and Internet, will we be able to
maintain this connectivity in the future. Morville's book is highlighted with full color illustrations and rich examples that bring his prose to life. Ambient
Findability doesn't preach or pretend to know all the answers. Instead, it presents research, stories, and examples in support of its novel ideas. Are we truly at a
critical point in our evolution where the quality of our digital networks will dictate how we behave as a species? Is findability indeed the primary key to a
successful global marketplace in the 21st century and beyond. Peter Morville takes you on a thought-provoking tour of these memes and more -- ideas that will not
only fascinate but will stir your creativity in practical ways that you can apply to your work immediately.</dc:description>
<dc:description>Lost and found. Definition -- Information literacy -- Business value -- Paradise lost -- A brief history of wayfinding. All creatures great and small
-- Human wayfinding in natural habitats -- Maps and charts -- The built environment -- Wayfinding in the noosphere -- The web -- The Baldwin effect -- Information
interaction. Defining information -- Information retrieval -- Language and representation -- The people problem -- Information interaction -- Intertwingled.
Everyware -- Wayfinding 2.0 -- Findable objects -- Imports -- Exports -- Convergence -- Asylum -- Push and pull. Marketing -- Design -- Findability hacks --
Personalization -- Ebb and flow -- The sociosemantic web. Us and them -- The social life of metadata -- Documents -- A walk in the park -- Inspired decisions.
Bounded irrationality -- Informed decisions -- Network culture -- The body politic -- Information overload -- Graffiti theory -- Sources of inspiration -- Ambient
findability.</dc:description>
<dc:subject xsi:type="http://purl.org/dc/terms/LCSH">Database design.</dc:subject>
<dc:subject xsi:type="http://purl.org/dc/terms/LCSH">Database searching.</dc:subject>
<dc:subject xsi:type="http://purl.org/dc/terms/LCSH">Information and retrieval systems -- Design.</dc:subject>
<dc:identifier>0596007655 (pbk.)</dc:identifier>
<dc:identifier>9780596007652 (pbk.)</dc:identifier>
</oclcdcs>
</recordData>
</record>
</records>
<nextRecordPosition/>
<resultSetIdleTime/>
<echoedSearchRetrieveRequest xmlns:srw="http://www.loc.gov/zing/srw/">
<version>1.1</version>
<query>srw.kw%3D%22ambient+findability%22</query>
<maximumRecords>10</maximumRecords>
<recordPacking>xml</recordPacking>
<startRecord>1</startRecord>
```

Figure 13.4 **Dublin Core returned from SRU request**

13.5). It also provides a way for users to see the proper citation format for items retrieved.

This mashup of Facebook and WorldCat would not be possible without the WorldCat Search API.

Additionally, David Walker at California State University is piloting several services using the WorldCat Search API. He is building a next-generation catalog interface that incorporates book jackets from Amazon and allows users to view search results from their local library, their consortia, or libraries worldwide, within a single interface. Walker is also using the WorldCat Search API in conjunction with other APIs to build a single seamless search interface that matches his library's website. With these tools, Walker is able to mash up the library website with search interfaces, two tools that have traditionally been separate and distinct. At the University of Houston Libraries, my department has prototyped two applications: plug-ins for WYSIWYG (What You See Is What You Get) editors FCKeditor and TinyMCE and a WordPress WorldCat Search Widget.

WorldCat Plug-In for FCKEditor and TinyMCE

FCKeditor (www.fckeditor.net) and TinyMCE (tinymce.moxiecode. com) are open source WYSIWYG editors that can be included in web

Figure 13.5 WorldCat Facebook Application

applications to allow users to easily format text and other elements of a web page. WordPress (wordpress.org), the most popular open source blogging software, uses a version of TinyMCE to allow bloggers to format their posts. At the University of Houston, we use WordPress for our libraries' blogs, and our content management system (CMS) uses FCKeditor to format page content. Often, our librarians want to include links to books, media, or other items from our catalog in their course- or subject-related pages. This process is somewhat tedious because they have to locate the item in the library's catalog, copy the relevant bibliographic information into the page they are working on, and then copy the persistent link to the item in our catalog. If they want to include any other relevant information, such as a book jacket or links to reviews, they have to find the items and add them by hand. This is time-consuming, to say the least.

We thought a better approach would be to allow the librarians to search for the item they wanted to add and select the additional information to include from within the blogging or CMS interface itself. However, with no API to access the data in our catalog, this was nearly impossible—until, of course, the WorldCat Search API came along. We began by examining the ways in which we wanted to allow our librarians to search for materials in WorldCat and add them to the posts and pages. It seemed pretty clear that searches by keyword, title, and author were necessary. Next, we examined what bibliographic data we wanted to retrieve from WorldCat and display on the page. Title and author seemed like the most important. However, as we went forward, we realized that we had an opportunity to enhance our interface tremendously if we also included COinS (Context Objects in Spans) for each of the items retrieved from WorldCat and embedded in the page.

The purpose of COinS is to allow bibliographic information to be embedded into a webpage in a machine-readable format. The advantage of COinS is that they make this information available for other applications, such as Zotero. Zotero (www.zotero.org) is a Firefox add-on that allows users to store and manipulate citation information. Because Zotero can recognize and read COinS, users can take COinS-embedded bibliographic information and add it to their Zotero personal data store automatically.

Bibliographic data retrieved from WorldCat was just one piece of information we wanted to use. Other information, such as book jackets, reviews, ratings, links to other editions, and full-text, could also be used to enhance our links. Ultimately we decided to keep this particular display simple and incorporate only book jackets. Currently book jackets are available via a variety of free sources, including Amazon, LibraryThing (www.librarything.com), and Open Library (openlibrary.org), as well as via subscription services such as Syndetics (www.syndetics.com). Because of the limitations placed on jackets retrieved from Amazon and LibraryThing, we decided to retrieve our jackets from Syndetics.

The plug-in allows our librarians developing a webpage to decide to embed a link to a book without having to leave the CMS. They click on the WorldCat link in the toolbar and are able to input a search (Figure 13.6).

When search results are retrieved, they can choose a result to add to the webpage they are working on (Figure 13.7).

The plug-in adds a book jacket, embeds citation information using COinS, and creates a link back to WorldCat containing the title and author information (Figure 13.8).

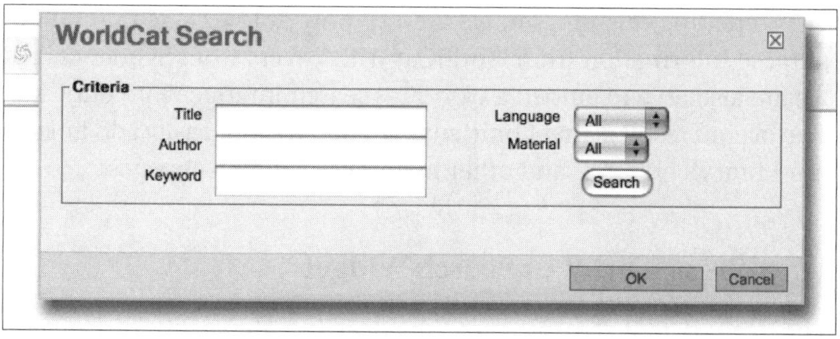

Figure 13.6   WorldCat search pop-up

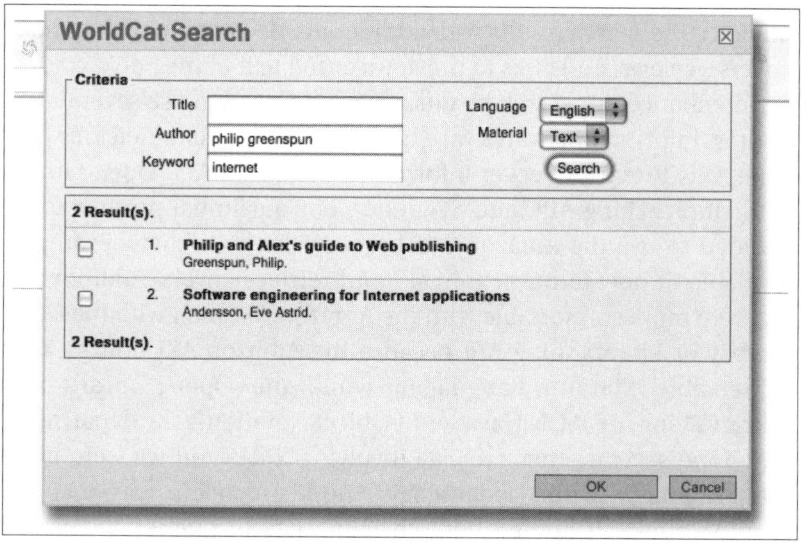

Figure 13.7   WorldCat search results pop-up

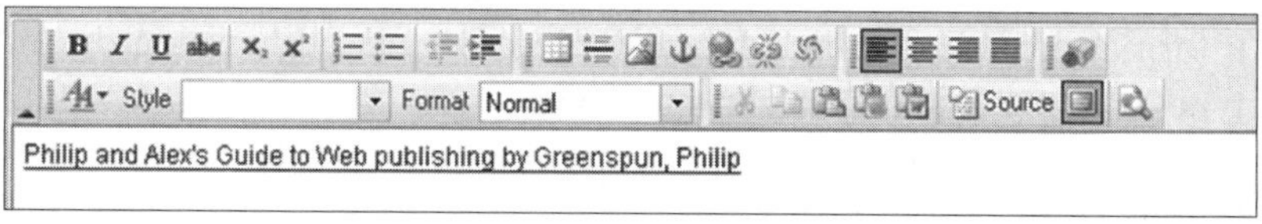

Figure 13.8   Link created by the plug-in

By creating this plug-in, we are not only able to mash up bibliographic information from WorldCat with covers from Syndetics, but we are also able to embed a WorldCat search interface into our CMS. The overall result is that librarians are able to more easily add links to our library's holdings and other materials to their webpages.

WordPress WorldCat Search Widget

The second tool that we prototyped at the University of Houston Libraries was a WorldCat Search Sidebar Widget. We decided to build this widget because we saw a need for librarians to display search results from WorldCat as part of their blog sidebar. However, in addition to the bibliographic information in WorldCat, we wanted to enhance the search results with additional information, such as book covers, reviews, and links to previews or full text of the book.

To enhance our search results, we would need to use several APIs to draw information from a variety of sources. We examined four possible APIs to retrieve cover information: Amazon API, Open Library API, LibraryThing API, and Syndetics. For our initial prototype, we decided to use the Amazon API because there are many examples available of how to query this API and retrieve covers. Additionally, we were more comfortable with the Amazon API than with the Open Library or LibraryThing API because the Amazon API utilizes XML (eXtensible Markup Language), while the Open Library and LibraryThing use JSON (JavaScript Object Notation). The department had done several other projects involving XML, and we were more comfortable with this technology. Another concern was that the LibraryThing API limited both the numbers of queries a day and access to client-side scripting (JavaScript). Using client-side scripting would create potential accessibility issues that would have to be worked around.

In terms of reviews and ratings, there were two possible sources of information: Amazon and LibraryThing. Because this was a prototype and we wanted experience working with a variety of data sources and API formats, we chose to use rating information from LibraryThing for our prototype.

For links to previews, full text, or both, there were two possible sources: the Google Book Viewability API and the Open Library API. At the time of the initial pilot, the Open Library API was less than a month old. Very few examples of its use existed. In contrast, the

Google Book Viewability API had been around for 4 to 5 months, and Google had posted several examples of its use on the API website. For these reasons we decided to only incorporate data from the Google Book Viewability API into our prototype.

Having decided on the information we wanted to include and what the sources for that data would be, our next step was to design the interface, which the librarians would use to create their WorldCat Search sidebar (Figure 13.9).

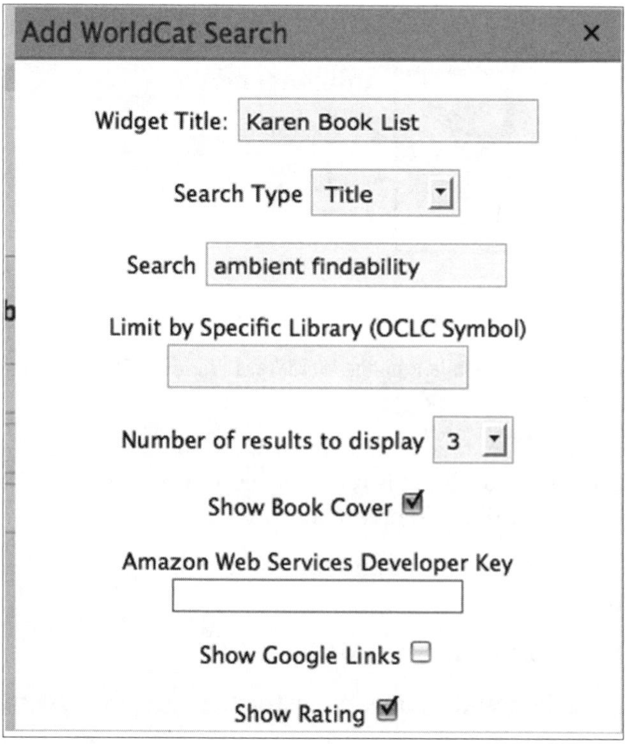

Figure 13.9   WordPress WorldCat Search Widget backend

The interface for the widget is fairly simple. Librarians are asked to input a search by keyword, title, or author. They can limit it to a particular library based on OCLC symbol. Additionally, they can choose whether to display book covers, ratings, or links to preview or full text. The initial prototype also provides them a required field for an Amazon API key and a WorldCat Search API key. However, we hope to move this to the WordPress settings area in a future version of the widget.

Once a librarian has configured the widget and saved the settings, a listing of the results retrieved will appear in the blog sidebar. You can see that the widget displays a book jacket, title, and author of the book and a star rating from LibraryThing (Figure 13.10).

Figure 13.10 Display results from the WordPress WorldCat Search Widget

The code for this widget is relatively complex because of the number of sources for data. To create the sidebar

- The search must first be submitted to the WorldCat Search API.

- Results are returned in MARCXML.

- From the results, ISBNs are extracted. (This step is crucial because ISBNs are necessary to retrieve the covers, ratings, and previews.)

- After this the results are processed to retrieve the title and author to display.

- Covers are then retrieved from Amazon.

- Then we check Google Book Search (books.google.com) for a preview and retrieve the URL if a preview is available.

- Finally we get the rating from LibraryThing.

The final result is a sidebar that includes a book cover, title and author information, rating from LibraryThing, and a link to a preview or full text if available. By mashing up data from these different sources, we are able to create a more dynamic and robust interface for our library users.

While building our prototype, we encountered several problems. The first was how to retrieve data from Amazon, LibraryThing, and Google Book Search. Many of these APIs allow you to retrieve information based on both OCLC number and ISBN. Because there is only one OCLC number in a bibliographic record, we felt it would be easier to retrieve data using this number rather than ISBN, multiples of which can be in a record. Although this logic should have been sound, our development and testing illustrated that we could not get consistent results from the APIs if we used the OCLC number. The Google Book Availability API was particularly troubling. The OCLC number from a particular record would not retrieve a preview, but the ISBN from the same record would retrieve one. This was extremely frustrating and led us to switch to using ISBN to retrieve covers, ratings, and reviews.

Additionally, we realized that several enhancements would be desirable in the next version of the widget. First, we realized that by adding the xISBN service, we would be able to more thoroughly check for covers, ratings, and previews or full text. Second, we would like to incorporate links to any possible preview or full text available. This means checking both Open Library and our own ebook holdings. Third, with the release of the WorldCat Identities service (orlabs.oclc.org/identities), we would like to consider incorporating links from authors to their WorldCat Identities page. Last, we need to rewrite our code to retrieve covers from Syndetics instead of Amazon. All of these are relatively minor changes, and we hope to complete them early in fall 2009 so that we can make the widget available to our librarians as soon as possible.

Conclusion

As you can see from the description of the services and the examples provided, WorldCat Affiliate Services provide a wealth of data that can be used to build mashups and enhance library interfaces. These services are interoperable both with each other and with other APIs. This makes them very useful for incorporating library data into different systems, mashing up bibliographic data with information from other APIs, enhancing existing services, and building new tools and services for library users. Conversations on the WorldCat Developer's list, as well as the current sample applications, demonstrate the diversity of ways in which these services can be used. Only time will tell what new tools people will build and how libraries will use this data to create mashups.

Additional Resources

Amazon Web Services Discussion Forums, developer.amazonwebservices.com/connect/index.jspa

Google Book Search APIs, code.google.com/apis/books

LibraryThing APIs, librarything.com/wiki/index.php/LibraryThing_APIs

Open Library API, openlibrary.org/dev/docs/api

Part IV

Maps, Pictures, and Video … Oh My!

CHAPTER 14

Flickr and Digital Image Collections

Mark Dahl and Jeremy McWilliams
Watzek Library, Lewis & Clark College

Introduction

Many academic libraries and cultural institutions build online image collections. One popular approach involves scanning analog slides and photos and then cataloging them with the use of digital collections software designed for this task. This approach mirrors a traditional library or archival workflow in which a significant body of work is processed, organized, and made available to the public by the staff of a particular organization. When a collection is made available on the web by means of library-managed software such as CONTENTdm (www.contentdm.com), search engine indexing can make the images accessible to a worldwide audience, thus extending the benefits of the collection well beyond the organization doing the digitizing.

This method allows a library with an interest in a particular collection of resources to care for it and curate it, while also sharing the work with the world. It has worked well for a decade or so, but in today's Web 2.0 world, it is beginning to show its limitations:

- The images and metadata reside in a data silo that does not easily allow the data to be intermixed with other images and metadata in mashup-type fashion.

- The software systems used to mount these types of collections tend to be relatively outdated, installed and upgraded on year-long upgrade cycles. They don't offer the end-user features that web-scale applications do.

- The images and metadata are created and improved in a one-way fashion by the staff of the library or archives administering the collection.

Some significant developments in the digital delivery of cultural collections have begun to address these limitations. ARTstor (www.artstor.org) is an example of a web-scale collection of images and metadata whose software is a single instance maintained centrally on the network. ARTstor's aggregated nature allows it to easily and quickly offer improvements to its users. It recently added a feature that clusters multiple images of the same work of art together in search results, something that would be much harder to do if it were not a single, unified database. The ARTstor collection is built in a mostly one-way fashion, though it is beginning to allow libraries to create their own subcollections.

Omeka (www.omeka.org), an open source digital collections management system offered by the Center for History and New Media at George Mason University, breaks the one-way model of digital collection building to which libraries and academic institutions have become accustomed. Effectively, Omeka allows an organization to "crowdsource" a collection of digital artifacts. The software powers a project called the Hurricane Digital Memory Bank, in which survivors of Hurricane Katrina can upload images, videos, and personal accounts of their experience with Katrina. Omeka allows an institution to create a hybrid digital collection that encompasses both centrally managed and community contributed content.

Since 2004, the social photo sharing website Flickr (www.flickr.com) has offered consumers a web application for managing images online. It's known particularly for its Web 2.0 features such as community tagging and a flexible application programming interface (API), which allows Flickr content to be repurposed in multiple contexts. Flickr's design centers around individual image collections connected to a Yahoo! account; it isn't really geared toward organization-level collections. A recent exception, however, is the Flickr Commons project (www.flickr.com/commons). Launched in January 2008, The Commons on Flickr project invites cultural heritage institutions to mount their digital image collections on Flickr. Putting their digital collections on the Flickr platform makes them more findable because it places these images in the Flickr pool. It also allows the public to add their own tags and comments to the images, thus enriching the metadata for each image. Furthermore, the Flickr platform's API (www.flickr.com/services/api) tools are available for mashing up these images.

In 2008, Watzek Library and the Department of Art at Lewis & Clark College implemented Flickr as the digital collections software for accessCeramics (accessceramics.org), an online collection of contemporary ceramics images. Our use of Flickr for this project was not motivated by a desire to launch a cutting edge model of digital collection development or to go Web 2.0 for the sake of doing so. Rather we were looking for a low-cost, lightweight software system that would help solve our collection building challenge. Unlike some digital collections projects, we did not have a central pool of images and metadata to mount online. We needed to ask artists dispersed throughout the U.S. and beyond to contribute images and metadata of their work to the collection. We knew that asking them to email files of images and spreadsheets with metadata would be an overly complex option for them and us.

Our familiarity with Flickr through organizing our own photo collections and as a demo application for mashups got us thinking about the possibilities. Though not designed for organizational use, Flickr did have some pretty compelling features that we figured might help solve our problem:

- Individual accounts that our contributors could use to privately control their own images

- Excellent software for uploading and managing sets of images online

- A system for bringing images together from individual collections into selective groups (Flickr Groups)

In this chapter, we will discuss how Flickr can be used as a digital image collection platform. First, we will investigate the Flickr API, tags, and machine tags. We will then outline the accessCeramics model and future possibilities for an "academic Flickr."

The Flickr API

Flickr is a developer's dream, primarily due to its extensive API. The API lets programmers communicate with Flickr using a REST-style format—a query is sent to Flickr in the form of a URL (Uniform Resource Locator), and Flickr responds with XML (eXtensible Markup Language). It includes more than 100 methods, each of which performs a certain function. A full list is available at www.flickr.com/services/api and includes extensive documentation and test areas for each method. Flickr also has an API discussion group focused on developer support, which includes more than 6,000 Flickr users (www.flickr.com/groups/api). At the Flickr Code blog (code.flickr.com), Flickr's developers announce news related to the API, code samples, and other ideas on developing applications to work with Flickr.

Although Flickr users have created a number of language-specific kits to make using the API simpler (also available at flickr.com/ services/api), it's worth showing the basic format of a REST (REpresentational State Transfer) request. The following example shows a query of the images tagged with "stella" (Jeremy's dog) and "beach" in Jeremy's Flickr account, using the flickr.photos.search API method:

```
http://api.flickr.com/services/rest/?method
=flickr.photos.search&api_key=7ad1d7c3a5f1b
239574437d87409f604&user_id=64194819@N00&
tags=stella,+beach&tag_mode=all
```

Analyzing this URL, you can see the following parameters and values that comprise the query:

```
api_key=7ad1d7c3a5f1b239574437d87409f604
```

Users of the Flickr API must obtain an API key, available at flickr.com/services/api/keys.

This is my Flickr user ID, which is included in order to limit the query to the images on my Flickr account:

```
user_id=64194819@N00
```

This limits the search to images with the tags "stella" or "beach:"

```
tags=stella,+beach
```

Setting the tag_mode to all changes the Boolean logic so images must have the tags "stella" AND "beach:"

```
tag_mode=all
```

The default value is "any," which equates to the Boolean OR. This yields the XML response (Figure 14.1).

```
- <rsp stat="ok">
  - <photos page="1" pages="1" perpage="100" total="6">
      <photo id="2762148880" owner="64194819@N00" secret="5b508517ba" server="3277" farm="4" title="resting" ispublic="1" isfriend="0" isfamily="0"/>
      <photo id="2761287319" owner="64194819@N00" secret="1f94c88f6a" server="3227" farm="4" title="stella on sand dune" ispublic="1" isfriend="0" isfamily="0"/>
      <photo id="439834825" owner="64194819@N00" secret="5b2229ed76" server="161" farm="1" title="Stella on beach" ispublic="1" isfriend="0" isfamily="0"/>
      <photo id="315726420" owner="64194819@N00" secret="8f0ec364e" server="107" farm="1" title="Stella investigating" ispublic="1" isfriend="0" isfamily="0"/>
      <photo id="315726415" owner="64194819@N00" secret="3012e2b8e2" server="115" farm="1" title="Stella as a puppy" ispublic="1" isfriend="0" isfamily="0"/>
      <photo id="315726412" owner="64194819@N00" secret="92de8b6f1c" server="119" farm="1" title="Stella's first beach run" ispublic="1" isfriend="0" isfamily="0"/>
  </photos>
</rsp>
```

Figure 14.1   XML response from Flickr API query

You can now use the language of your choice to parse this XML response and create an HTML output. Figure 14.2 shows a PHP code sample that makes the request, and creates a simple HTML table of images.

Figure 14.3 shows the output.

```php
<?php
    $url="http://api.flickr.com/services/rest/?method=flickr.photos.search"
    "&api_key7ad1d7c3a5f1b239574437d87409f604&user_id=64194819@N00&tags=stella,+beach&tag
    _mode=all";
    $xml=simplexml_load_file($url);     //Gets the xml response from the url query.
                                         //For production, you may want to use a PHP Curl function instead.

    $total = $xml->photos->attributes()->total;     //Gets the 'total' attribute in the 'photos' element.

    if ($total>0){
        $table="<table>";
        $cpr=3; //table cells per row
        $c=0;   //counter for the table rows
        foreach ($xml->photos->photo as $photo){   //cycles through each 'photo' element
            if ($c==0 or (is_int($c/$cpr))){$table.="<tr>";}     //adds a table row

            //these lines get the various attribute values for a 'photo' element
            $id=$photo->attributes()->id;
            $secret=$photo->attributes()->secret;
            $server=$photo->attributes()->server;
            $farm=$photo->attributes()->farm;
            $title=$photo->attributes()->title;

            //formats the attributes into a URL for a Flickr 'small' image
            $img="http://farm".$farm.".static.flickr.com/".$server."/".$id."_".$secret."_m.jpg";
            $table.="<td><img src='$img'><br>$title</td>";     //adds the table cell

            if (is_int(($c+1)/$cpr) or ($c==$total-1)){$table.="<tr>\n";}     //ends table row when appropriate

            unset($id, $secret, $server, $farm, $title);     //empties variables
            $c++;     //adds one to counter
        }
        $table.="</table>\n";
        echo $table;
    }
    else{echo "Query did not return any results.";}
?>
```

Figure 14.2   PHP code to convert API XML response into an HTML table of images

Tags and Machine Tags

The ability to tag images with descriptive keywords is arguably the bread and butter of Flickr and other Web 2.0 applications. Tagging provides the backbone for the development of folksonomies and plays a significant role in the social aspects that make sites like Flickr

accounts, upload images, and contribute images to a Flickr Group. We just had to create a website to facilitate the process, set up our Flickr Group, and convince ceramic artists to contribute images.

Much of the early site development consisted of testing various methods of the Flickr API. This included functions such as authentication, uploading images, assigning tags, adding images to groups, and searching. Once we felt comfortable with these tasks, we began creating the site using PHP and the jQuery JavaScript library (jquery.com). Rather than creating a database layer, we hoped such data storage needs could be met entirely by Flickr (Figure 14.5).

After a few months of development and testing, we were ready to start building the collection. The group's ceramic artist, Ted Vogel, invited a handful of his colleagues to get Flickr accounts and join our Flickr Group. Once artists joined the group, they were asked to visit accessCeramics.org. On the site, artists would log in with their Flickr username and password and would then either upload a new image to the account or select an existing Flickr image. The artist would then catalog the image, using a standard form (Figure 14.6). When the form was submitted, PHP code would convert the entered form values into a REST URL and generate machine tags in Flickr via the flickr.photos.addTags method. The form also includes options for assigning a Creative Commons License (using flickr.com/services/api/flickr.photos.licenses.setLicense.html) and a safety level (using flickr.com/services/api/flickr.photos.setSafetyLevel.html).

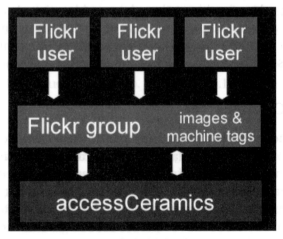

Figure 14.5 Initial model of accessCeramics

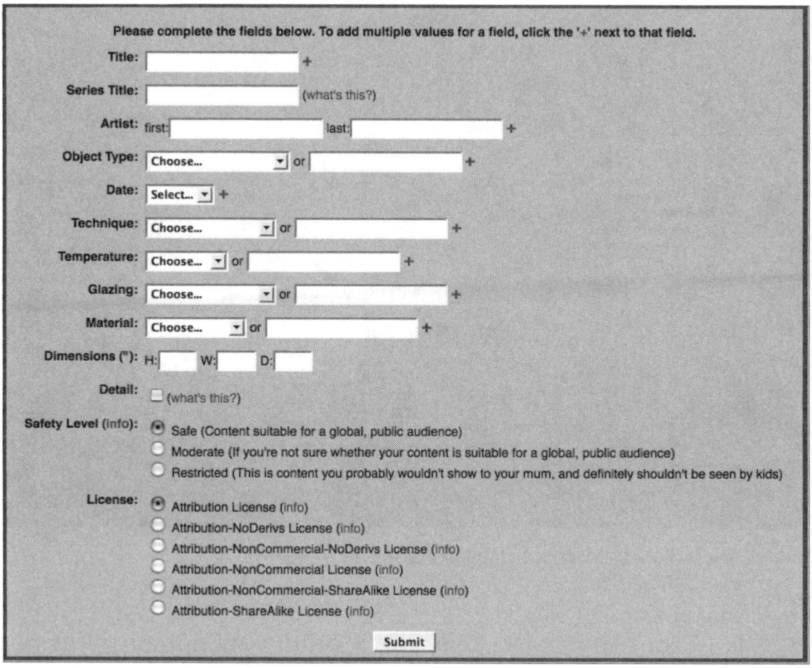

Figure 14.6   Web form, which transforms submitted values into Flickr
machine tags

In addition to the submission portion, we developed the general interface for browsing the images by field. And in an attempt to take advantage of the high-quality images, we made accessCeramics Cooliris compatible (see www.cooliris.com for details). This enabled full-screen viewing of each image and a virtual wall of images for each result set (Figure 14.7). In the near future, we plan to add more features to facilitate educational use of the images.

As the collection slowly grew, we came to a crossroads regarding metadata storage and bibliographic control. If a contributing artist wanted to make a correction on a given piece of metadata, we had to work with that artist to remove the incorrect machine tag on Flickr and add a new one with the exact syntax. Because the original generated machine tag was "owned" by that artist, we had no authority to edit it directly using a different Flickr account. It immediately became apparent that this approach was not practical. We needed a solution in which all metadata could be edited centrally so as not to bother our generous artists with annoying details.

To gain some control, we shifted our model to include a MySQL database. At the point of cataloging, we rerouted metadata from

Figure 14.7   accessCeramics images viewed with Cooliris

Flickr to our database. We then built functionality for an accessCeramics administrator to gather the metadata for each newly submitted image and add machine tags to the images in Flickr via the API. This gave "ownership" of the tags to the administrative account, allowing us to remove any erroneous tags without involving the artists. Granted, the artists themselves, as owners of the images on Flickr, could still remove the tags, so our control gains were still somewhat limited.

With the MySQL database in place, we then began to investigate how this might affect the functionality of the site. One obvious area was the ability to browse by field. When we relied solely on Flickr machine tags, creating the ability to browse by field was somewhat impractical; it required an API query for every image in the collection, followed by code to parse each XML and organize all possible field values into arrays and then generate the browse menu. This approach might work for a collection of 10 or fewer images but would be unbearably slow for a larger collection. Conversely, one simple SQL (Structured Query Language) query to our MySQL database accomplished the task almost instantaneously. Thus we began reworking our model to incorporate the MySQL database for metadata storage and site functionality, though we still added machine tags using our administrative account for experimental purposes (Figure 14.8).

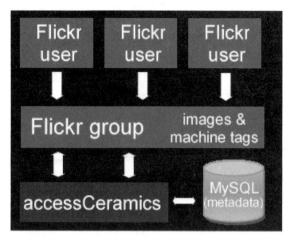

Figure 14.8 Revised accessCeramics model

Mashable Collections for Research and Teaching

Although the accessCeramics submission system and public website are themselves mashups, the accessCeramics metadata and images can also be thought of as fodder for other third-party mashups and Web 2.0 applications. We hope to encourage educational technologists, librarians, arts instructors, students of the arts and art history, and humanities scholars to do creative things with accessCeramics that we never imagined. Flickr's extensible platform provides many of the prerequisites for reference and reuse of content in other contexts, including Creative Commons copyright licensing, ready-made code for embedding images in other websites, and community tagging and commenting. The ability to view accessCeramics images in Flickr and on accessceramics.org using the Cooliris (previously known as PicLens) browser extension for Firefox (addons.mozilla.org/en-US/firefox/addon/5579) serves as a good example of Flickr's extensibility.

College educators are becoming increasingly interested in the concept of new media literacy. The idea is that a liberal education in the early 21st century should prepare students to make an argument or tell a story using the current communication media of the networked digital environment: blogs, wikis, podcasts, mashups. We can imagine ways in which the rich metadata and flexible platform of accessCeramics could facilitate critical projects that enhanced this type of literacy among students. For example:

- Students composing an essay about works in the collection in an online format such as a blog could use tags to reference aspects of the collection, such as all works created by a certain artist, made from a certain material, etc.

- To demonstrate how a certain artistic approach to ceramic artwork is distributed geographically, a scholar could tag and geocode works in accessCeramics on Flickr and then display them in a web mapping application.

- As an assignment, a college instructor might ask students to create a virtual exhibition of works in accessCeramics, a task that could be facilitated by Flickr's tools for embedding images or slideshows based on a certain tag.

- As a collaborative assignment, an undergraduate course could tag images in the collection based on any number of perspectives—the influences apparent in a work of art, the emotions evoked, or a political statement. Although these tags could be useful in the short term as an educational exercise, they could also enrich the metadata describing the collection overall.

Bringing third parties into the process of metadata enrichment is a somewhat unfamiliar notion to librarians and arts professionals. For them, the intellectual description of a work is an area customarily controlled by professionals. The idea that anyone can come in and tag a work seems a bit dangerous. Indeed, for the initial metadata in accessCeramics, we have eschewed open tagging and instead collect high-quality, controlled metadata in a distributed fashion. Nevertheless, projects like Flickr Commons have demonstrated the value of nonprofessional metadata contribution, or "crowd-sourcing." In fact, the Powerhouse Museum in Australia is re-ingesting metadata contributed by Flickr users to their Flickr Commons images into its native digital asset management system (www.powerhouse museum.com/dmsblog/index.php/2008/07/25/re-ingesting-flickr-tags-from-the-commons-back-into-our-collection-opac). The messy process of developing folksonomies truly enriches a digital collection and provides opportunities for educational exercises. Although our focus on building accessCeramics has been on controlled metadata, we hope that others will add uncontrolled tags to accessCeramics and enrich the collection.

Thinking Big: An "Academic Flickr"

In an April 2008 blog post, executive director of the Digital Library Federation Peter Brantley argued for the creation of an "Academic Flickr" (blogs.lib.berkeley.edu/shimenawa.php/2008/04/17/ah_screw_the_interface). He envisions an online application with the rich user experience of Flickr that would allow academics to contribute content to a digital repository without the involvement of a library or other intermediaries. One of the most important aspects of such a digital content repository would be the ability to disintermediate the content from the application through APIs, one of Flickr's strongest suits.

Our experience attempting to adapt Flickr as it currently stands for an organizationally sponsored digital collection of cultural objects has led us to do some thinking about what an ideal digital asset management system for such digital collections would look like. We believe that it would look much as Flickr does now and would possess some of the same characteristics, including

- An aggregate collection to which every digital asset belongs by default. The capability would exist to make a collection private or restricted, but the default would be to be part of a large public collection that could be parsed, searched, commented on, and remixed as a whole.

- A cloud computing model for the application, in which all software would be run centrally at web scale. Any improvements or upgrades to software would occur without needed interventions by users or local systems administrators.

- A robust API like Flickr's that permits reading and writing to the collection in the widest possible number of ways.

- Excellent browser-based end user tools for loading and manipulating digital objects and their metadata, tools that would work well for building crowd-sourced, centrally curated, and hybrid collections.

- Social web features such as tagging, commenting, and sharing.

- The ability to bring objects together selectively in groups.

- Easy ways to add Creative Commons licensing.

The academic Flickr would take things a step further from where Flickr is right now, allowing a mixture of individual collections and more formally managed organizational collections. Characteristics of the academic Flickr would include

- Support for multiple object types including documents, images, and video.

- Organizational collections of objects that could be managed by multiple users. Currently, Flickr is not set up so that several users can collaborate on the same collection of images: One can ultimately control what is in one's own account. By contrast, our model would allow an object to be moved from an individual account to an organizationally managed collection, assuring that the longevity of that object would not depend on an individual's account.

- Support for controlling metadata at the organizational level using a more robust form of machine tag. Organizational collections could implement a formal metadata schema and update metadata centrally. This metadata could coexist along with less formal folksonomic metadata.

- Facilities for migrating and updating data in subcollections that require a different type of database structure than the default. In other words, make it easy to create a secondary website driven by data from a subcollection within the academic Flickr.

It may seem somewhat strange that a consumer web application like Flickr should serve as a model for a "serious" application designed for the needs of academia. This, however, is a manifestation of a broader trend. Jon Stokes calls this phenomenon "IT Consumerization," in which the best new hardware technology and web applications make their way into the hands of consumers before making it to enterprise applications (arstechnica.com/news.ars/post/20080706-analysis-it-consumerization-and-the-future-of-work.html). We hope that projects like ours will help bring Flickr's mashable qualities into the more "serious" organizational digital collections applications of libraries and other cultural heritage institutions.

blip.tv and Digital Video Collections in the Library

Jason A. Clark
Montana State University Libraries

Ever since I watched *Saturday Night Live*'s digital short "Lazy Sunday" (en.wikipedia.org/wiki/Lazy_Sunday) on YouTube (www.youtube. com), I recognized the fun potential of this online video phenomenon. In time, YouTube and related sites like blip.tv would deliver other priceless moments—try a Google search for "boom goes the dynamite" or "chocolate rain" to see what I'm talking about. (I say "priceless" with tongue firmly planted in cheek!) YouTube moments are usually best viewed as satire, in the spirit of lampooning the "everyone is a star" meme that this great internet enables.

What I didn't recognize at the time was the importance of two things these newer online video sites provided: a digital video infrastructure and the ability to remix content. In opening up video uploading to anyone with a webcam, online video sites were giving people a voice—but, more important, they were aggregating content. Many enterprising developers, recognizing the potential for mashups, looked to build real-world, practical applications using these sites' application programming interfaces (APIs) to remix the data stored in sites like YouTube and blip.tv. As I watched this happen, I began to take another look at these sites, which were essentially providing video distribution platforms. This was no longer just about passively consuming videos; there were other opportunities here to actively create resources. As Montana State University (MSU) Libraries moved toward providing digital videos for our patrons, I made the decision to experiment and build a data storage application as well as a search and retrieval interface in a mashup through the open web API of blip.tv. I chose blip.tv for a number of reasons:

- It scaled with our developer group of one and kept the need for extra staff to a minimum.

- It used a standard XML (eXtensible Markup Language) feed format (RSS) in responding to requests for information from the API service, making parsing and displaying of information extremely easy.

- It allowed us to "route around" the limitations of our limited bandwidth by using the blip.tv network to distribute our files.

- It allowed us to outsource the digital video conversion process as this process was part of the blip.tv upload function.

- It gave us access to group participation in metadata, tagging, and commenting.

- It created opportunities for different distribution formats (RSS) of our "signal" (project data) into many web channels—iTunes (www.apple.com/itunes), Google Reader (google.com/reader), Yahoo! homepage (www.yahoo.com).

TERRApod (www.terrapodcast.com) was the digital library project that resulted from this experiment. TERRApod is a working digital video library utilizing the blip.tv infrastructure to host and distribute content. The TERRApod site features a robust XML metadata architecture that enables podcasting and syndication of content. It also features social networking functionality, with ratings and comments for each video (Figure 15.1).

In this chapter, I will discuss how TERRApod uses blip.tv as a digital video collection platform. First, I will give a quick background about the TERRApod group and project. Then, I will investigate and explain the blip.tv API, as well as the important role that blip.tv metadata and the automated file conversion processes play in creating the TERRApod mashup. Next, I will outline the ingest and display model for TERRApod and walk through some of the methods that make the mashup possible. Finally, I'll talk a bit about some of the lessons learned and look closely at future possibilities for digital library collections working together with digital video sites like YouTube and blip.tv.

Figure 15.1   Individual film view of TERRApod

Project and Group Details

The TERRApod group is a pilot project from MSU and Montana 4H. It involves graduate students from the Media and Theatre Arts department traveling to remote areas of Montana and running workshops on filmmaking for middle school and high school students. At the end of a workshop, participants are divided into working groups, video recording equipment is provided, and an assignment is given to each working group to create a film on a given subject. Given a focus on improving science curricula, TERRApod films are typically video shorts centered on themes of science and natural history. Recently taught modules include biodiversity, road ecology, and water quality. Over the course of filming, students are able to chat with workshop leaders about the filmmaking process or related questions through the TERRApod forums available on the TERRApod site. Once completed, the assigned films are uploaded to blip.tv, and the data is pulled into the TERRApod site via the blip.tv API. The initial TERRApod site was created in January 2007, and MSU Libraries was brought in to build, program, and code the site and to create a content management, metadata, and data preservation system.

The blip.tv Infrastructure and API

With a lean team of one primary web developer, I quickly looked toward leveraging the data infrastructures already in place on popular video websites. blip.tv was an easy choice because it allowed for a mashup with minimal branding, had a well-documented API, and provided a large-scale storage option for the videos TERRApod produced. Leveraging the blip.tv infrastructure also allowed us to work around local bandwidth limitations and take advantage of the digital video conversions and thumbnail and graphic creation processes that were part of uploading files to blip.tv servers. This provided us with the means to outsource some costly and time-consuming processes; without these shortcuts, the project would have been tough to get started. One of the real advantages of Web 2.0 and cloud computing is exactly this ability to leverage the web and its many data sources and services to create a "mashed up" application.

The blip.tv API allows for multiple REST (REpresentational State Transfer) methods centered on the main functions available in the native interface for the site—searching, getting metadata about videos, uploading videos, managing accounts, etc.[1] The blip.tv API, like many popular API implementations, employs an intuitive REST style format that is similar to the URL (Uniform Resource Locator) protocol that we use daily. Essentially, a query is sent to the blip.tv API in the form of a URL, and blip.tv sends back XML (or some other structured data format) that provides the raw material for a mashup. To see how this works, try to access the URL www.blip.tv/posts/?user=terrapoduser&pagelen=20&file_type=flv&skin=rss in your favorite web browser. This REST method returns a list of the most recently uploaded videos on the blip.tv instance of TERRApod. The raw XML response to this method (which you can view in the source code of the resulting page) contains detailed information on these videos, and might look something like the XML in the image shown in Figure 15.2.

The blip.tv API responds to a REST request with a richly populated XML feed that contains the requested data. It is precisely this extensive information base that makes the blip.tv API so compelling to work with as it allows developers the freedom to come up with creative new applications. Here are some relevant highlights from the blip.tv XML feed for the TERRApod mashup:

- The outermost <channel> element encloses one or more <item> elements, each representing a video matching the query. Each <item> contains further information on the video it represents.

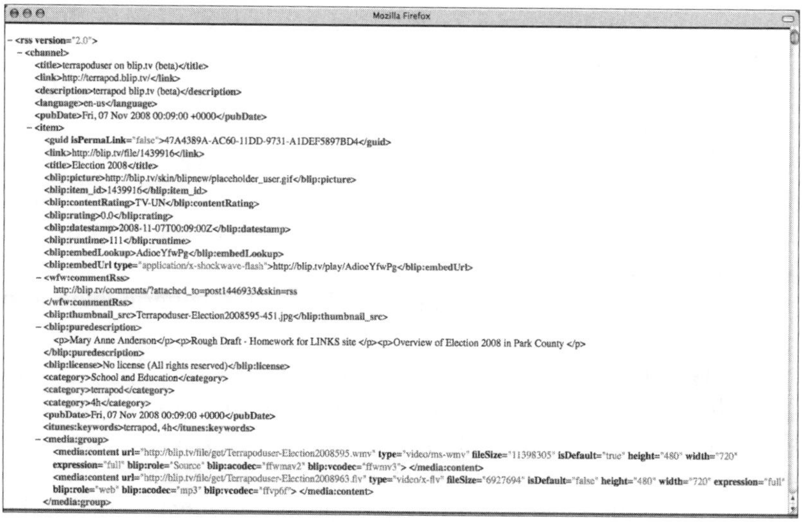

Figure 15.2   Example XML response from the blip.tv API

- The <blip:embedLookup> element provides a unique identifier for each file and will later be used to make the blip.tv player work within TERRApod.

- The <blip:puredescription> element supplies the author value as well as an explanation of what the film is about.

- The <blip:picture> and <blip:thumbnail_src> elements give us our graphic elements and video thumbnails.

- A selection of metadata elements, <category> and <itunes:keyword>, provide subject terms and tags for TERRApod.

- Additional date and duration elements, <pubDate>, <blip:datestamp, and <blip:runtime>, provide date and playing time values for our TERRApod video display.

- A <media:group> element within each <item> contains detailed information on the video file: the file size, file type, and video player links.

Making the TERRApod Mashup

With XML from the blip.tv API providing the raw material, it was a relatively easy next step to integrate this data into a new TERRApod application. The principles behind the mashup are pretty simple: Write application level code to send REST requests, parse and decode the responses, and last, integrate the resulting data into the website interface and display.

The TERRApod group decided to use the native blip.tv upload form and then harvest the metadata and digital video objects that resulted. This decision shortened development times and ensured that filmmakers and students would have a simple interface for uploading files and entering data. To this end, a generic login and password were distributed to all TERRApod participants, and all participants were directed to the TERRApod instance on blip.tv at terra pod.blip.tv. Given the emphasis on harvesting metadata after files had been uploaded, it should come as no surprise that I primarily utilized the retrieving metadata functions of the blip.tv API.

One of the first actions of the mashup was to create an editorial queue of the uploaded files. The TERRApod editors wanted a chance to review the content before elevating it into our publicly viewable database.[2] TERRApod editors see a screen that lists the most recently uploaded videos to the TERRApod blip.tv instance (Figure 15.3).

From the administration queue, editors are able to view the videos and judge the quality. In addition, the editors can check for data entry errors and contact the student filmmakers with tips or suggested revisions for their films.

Figure 15.3 Administration video queue on TERRApod

Figure 15.4   blip.tv video player on TERRApod

Our second mashup action was to push the metadata that our TERRApod participants created during the upload process into our local database. If the video appears ready for the public side of TERRApod, editors are able to click on a button that adds the video and its associated metadata to the local TERRApod database. The process is seamless, and most important, it streamlines the onerous data entry that a traditional web form requires. If you'll recall, our XML feed file returned a rich set of values from the blip.tv API, including source files, tags, durations, file formats, titles, and descriptions. Each of these values is collected in a series of variables and then submitted to a web form, which interacts with the local database.[3]

Our third mashup action was to create a display and video player for the videos by means of the blip.tv unique id and the blip.tv Flash player (Figure 15.4).

Here again we relied on collecting the metadata from each blip.tv video to enable the mashup. The important piece of data in this case was the XML element <blip:embedLookup>, which holds a unique value that can be passed to the blip.tv Flash video player (an example is in bold below). The TERRApod player code is just simple HTML:

```
<p><strong>The Green Alien</strong></p>
<object type="application/x-shockwave-
flash"
```

```
classid="clsid:D27CDB6E-AE6D-11cf-
96B8-444553540000" height="390"
width="640">
<param name="movie"
value="http://blip.tv/play/AdXyQ4fwPg">
<param name="allowScriptAccess"
value="always">
<param name="allowFullScreen" value="true">
<embed type="application/x-shockwave-flash"
src="http://blip.tv/play/AdXyQ4fwPg"
allowscriptaccess="always"
allowfullscreen="true" height="390"
width="640">
</object>
<p>01:52 (mins) | Produced by: Thomson,
Ethan and Fry, Bryn Fry, and Barre, Manon
| <a class="download"
href="http://blip.tv/file/get/Terrapoduser-
TheGreenAlien232.mov" title="Download: The
Green Alien">Download</a></p>
```

The HTML just includes some paragraph (<p>) tags, a few <object> tags, and the <embed> tag. I needed some markup to place title, duration, and creator metadata. However, the most important piece was finding a method to bring the blip.tv Flash player (along with its full screen capabilities and sharing options) into the TERRApod site. Being able to use these built-in functions and getting the unique media id (<blip:embedLookup> passed in dynamically with PHP) from the TERRApod local database to make the player run a specific video saved a tremendous amount of time as I didn't have to create a Flash video player from scratch. Again, I was able to have a robust interface in a short amount of development time by borrowing "expertise" from the markup code and scripts of blip.tv.

Future Possibilities for TERRApod and Lessons Learned

As far as what's next for TERRApod, we are just getting started. Due to its pilot project status, the TERRApod group has focused more on internal services. As we come off pilot status, I will press for us to look at the many other ways to distribute our content. The blip.tv admin interface provides many different types of XML feeds, and we have an opportunity to syndicate the TERRApod videos as podcasts and place them within iTunes. I'm also thinking about the ways that the API could enable a widget or TERRApod mobile application. A TERRApod mobile application based on the RSS feed of the blip.tv TERRApod show page would be a great source for such a project (Figure 15.5).

Figure 15.5 A possible view of TERRApod mobile

There has also been talk within the TERRApod group of the need for a "rough cuts" screening room where workshop participants and students can post their works in progress. I can imagine using the administration queue code as a foundation for this new effort.

If I had to pick a core lesson learned during the process of building the TERRApod mashup, I would point to how creating a mashup or using a web service is just a series of simple actions: Make a request, get a response in some form of structured data, and then parse and display that data in HTML. If you are willing to study the API documentation and work through a little trial and error, you can do this. I'd also point to the fact that the move to mashup can give you access to content or data stores you could not otherwise provide and enhance your site with a service that is not feasible for you to provide. TERRApod is proof that mashups can work in the library setting. In a lot of ways, the reliance on external resources and the willingness to use tools created by others is very much in line with how libraries work.

Endnotes

1. Full documentation is available at blip.tv/about/api.
2. TERRApod uses a local MySQL database to store video metadata and source files. The video metadata is used to display information about video files and allow for searching and browsing of videos. The video source files are archived for data preservation purposes but not served in the public TERRApod application. The live TERRApod application uses the networked blip.tv video files as the primary files for the TERRApod video player.
3. For those who are interested, the complete request, parse, and display code for the blip.tv API call is available on my site as a PHP file at www.lib.montana. edu/~jason/files.php.

CHAPTER 16

"Where's the Nearest Computer Lab?": Mapping Up Campus

Derik A. Badman
Temple University

"Where Is the Registrar?"

"Hi. How can I help you?"

"I need to go see the registrar, but I'm not sure where the office is."

"Okay, let's see if we can find it. We'll take a look in the phone directory ... hmm ... No entry for registrar. I think they go by a different official name. Let's try a quick search on the university website for registrar ... Ah, okay, here we go, Office of Academic Records is the name, luckily 'registrar' is in their URL ... Okay, it's in 200 Conwell Hall."

"Where's that?"

"You go out the door, turn left, follow it two blocks, then make another left, but don't cross the street, stay on this side. Then you walk two more blocks and it's on your left at the corner. It's a big, tall, thin building with steps going up to red doors, right next to Carnell Hall."

"Umm. Where?"

"Hold on, I'll find a map ... Let's see ... 'Maps and Directions' .. 'Campus Maps.' We've gotta download the PDF. Here we go. Let's see, Conwell is number 7 on the key ... and ... There's number 7. See?"

"Ah. Okay. That's right next to where I get lunch sometimes. Thanks! While you've got the map up, can you show me where the office for the economics department is?"

"Well, this map only shows building names. Let's go back to the directory."

University campuses can be complicated places. Offices, departments, computer labs, and all other sorts of places are scattered across many buildings and blocks. Finding where certain places are is often a matter of "just knowing" from previous experience. Print directories (when they are still printed) are quickly outdated, replaced by websites. Location information on websites—a mix of building names, room numbers, and street addresses (which are often not clearly marked on buildings)—often lacks consistency and clarity. Maps are found in outdated, static forms. Visitors and new students in particular will be set adrift in such conditions. At my university, no central repository of location data was available to assist in wayfinding, and the only map available was a downloadable PDF file. To find a building on the map, you had to look up the building in an alphabetical listing to get the key number, for which you then had to search on the map itself. This process was neither efficient nor data rich.

Visualization of data has become ever more prominent through the increasing use of web technologies. A number of universities have taken to creating interactive campus maps on their websites, but these maps are often homegrown systems requiring programming time and skill that is not yet ubiquitous, even in academia. I decided to find a way to map the campus that didn't require extensive programming knowledge. I knew it would involve not only some web programming skills, but also a great deal of aggregation and creation of data. Aggregating data is a traditional mission of libraries, and I see the creation of data in this case as a form of gathering data and making it discoverable. Isn't that, in the end, what libraries do? Not only can such a project be a useful service for the community, it can also be an aid in answering questions at the reference desk, as well as a good on-campus public relations opportunity for the library.

Mapping Campus

Choosing a Cartographer

My first step in this project was choosing the appropriate tools. In some sense, the first tool spurred the idea for the project itself. The Google Maps application programming interface (API) (code.google. com/apis/maps) is a tool for creating customized maps, with many well-known examples. Yelp (www.yelp.com), for instance, uses Google Maps to map reviewed locations, while HousingMaps (www.housingmaps.com) uses Google Maps to map housing ads from craigslist (www.craigslist.org). The API puts the power of Google Maps into the hands of users with a bit of programming skill, allowing for the creation of customized points, pop-up information about those points, polygons, controls, and numerous other features, all drawing on Google's reliable back end.

Although the Google Maps API does not require extensive programming knowledge to plot locations on maps and add information about those locations, I wanted to have a search and browse function on my campus map. While I was looking for an easy-to-use search interface, a fortuitous blog posting led me to MIT's SIMILE (Semantic Interoperability of Metadata and Information in unLike Environments) project (simile.mit.edu). One of SIMILE's tools is called Exhibit (simile.mit.edu/exhibit), a web framework for visualizing data. Exhibit provides an easy way to take a data file and create rich interfaces in a simple HTML page. Programmers with only basic HTML/CSS (Cascading Style Sheets) knowledge and a willingness to read the documentation (simile.mit.edu/wiki/exhibit) can quickly create timelines, tables, and maps. To generate those maps, the framework makes use of the Google Maps API.

Formatting the Key

After the framework for my map was selected, I needed to have data to map. Exhibit uses a form of JSON (JavaScript Object Notation) as the primary source of data. SIMILE's Babel project (simile.mit.edu/babel) can convert data into the proper JSON format from a number of other formats (such as tab-separated values, Excel spreadsheets, or the BibTex citation format). In my case, and I suspect in many others', the data was scattered across many locations. It was up to me to gather and format the data on my own.

Conveniently, Exhibit's JSON format is rather simple. JSON is a human-readable format for structuring data. That is, both computers and humans can "read" the data without too much trouble. Let's take a look at part of my data file:

```
{
    items: [
      { label: "Paley Library,"
        type: "Building,"
        latlng: "39.981012,-75.154571,"
        address: "1210 W Berks St,"
        contents: ["Library," "Computer Lab
        (General)"],
        classcode: "PL"
      },
    ]
}
```

This is the data for one building. It should be easy to read and identify the properties and values of those properties for, in this case, the main library on campus. The data files for Exhibit are made up of "items," anything that you want to have data for. In the preceding example, items: text tells both the program and us that what is contained in the brackets that follow are items. Each item is enclosed by braces and separated from the next item by a comma. Within the braces each item has properties (as few or as many as necessary) and values for those properties. In this case, the item has six properties that will be used in the map. Each property is named, and the value is placed after a colon. Note that the "contents" property has multiple values enclosed in brackets and separated by commas (just as the items are gathered). This group of multiple values is called an *array*. Any of the other values could also be arrays, using the same notation.[1]

The only required properties for each item in the general JSON format are "label" and "ID." The "label" is simply the way the item is referred to in the webpage. The "ID" is a unique identifier for each item. You'll note that there is no "ID" property in my example. This is because Exhibit will automatically assign the value of the "label" property to the "ID" property if no "ID" is explicitly given. In my case, each location I will be mapping has a unique name (no two buildings have the same name), so I have left out the "ID" property to simplify the data file.

The properties for each item can be anything, and items don't have to all contain all of the same properties. Because of this, the data is highly customizable and expandable, allowing a user to start with a small amount of data and slowly expand as necessary.

Data Gathering

I started my data file with two primary properties: "label" and "latlng." That is, the name of the location and its geographical coordinates (latitude and longitude). This barest of data would start off my map by replicating the data found on the old PDF campus map that was the current standard. These two properties are also the minimum data needed for Exhibit and Google Maps to create a map. Once this data was entered, I planned to continue adding properties, including street addresses, locations of academic departments and administrative offices, class codes used in the registration system, and other useful data (such as computer lab and library locations).

Data collation was the most time-consuming part of creating the map. Because none of the information could be found in any standardized format, I had to gather it all and put it into a standard format (the Exhibit JSON format). At some point, someone has to standardize data, and by taking the map one or two properties at a time, I felt the process was manageable. Also, once this data is standardized in one form, Exhibit offers exporting of data into a few alternate formats, such as XML (eXtensible Markup Language) or tab separated values. I was comforted by the knowledge that my work could be reused at a later time with more ease.

Building and Geolocating

Starting with that old PDF map, I created a data file that listed all the buildings on campus by name and looked something like this (except with many more buildings):

```
{
  items: [
    { label: "Paley Library" },
    { label: "Tuttleman Learning Center" },
    { label: "TECH Center" }
  ]
}
```

Make sure to edit your file in a text editor (not Word) and save it with the .json extension. Once I had a list of all the buildings, I needed to locate them on the map and retrieve their latitude and longitude. This process, called *geolocating,* can be done automatically at sites such as geocoder.us by using the street address, but I discovered that the street addresses of the campus buildings did not retrieve accurate enough placement on the map. An alternate way to retrieve coordinates for a location involves using Google Maps (maps.google.com) directly. First, you must navigate to the area on a regular Google map. Then, double click on the point where you want the plotted map point to appear in order to re-center the map on that location. I would click on the area near the building's main entrance. At this point you use the "link to this site" link at the upper right corner of the map to retrieve a long URL (Uniform Resource Locator), for instance:

```
http://maps.google.com/maps?f=q&hl=en&geo
code=&q=1210+W+Berks+St,+Philadelphia,+PA+1
9122&sll=40.212441,-75.273342&sspn=
0.010651,0.020192&ie=UTF8&ll=39.981134,-
75.154558&spn=0.001336,0.002524&t=h&z=19
```

The value found after "ll" ("39.981134,-75.154558" in this URL) is the center point of the map (where you clicked), written in the form of "latitude,longitude." I used this method to geolocate each of the buildings and then added that data to my file, which looked like this:

```
{
  items: [
    { label: "Paley Library",
      latlng: "39.981012,-75.154571" },
    { label: "Tuttleman Learning Center",
      latlng: "39.980565,-75.154933" },
    { label: "TECH Center",
      latlng: "39.980359,-75.153415" }
  ]
}
```

This is enough data to map all the buildings, but with such sparse information, it's not much better than a paper map.

Value Added Data

The real use of the map would lie in adding data about what the buildings house. This sort of data is dispersed across the university's websites, which brought about one of the original impetuses for the project. As a starting set of this data, I decided to collect the locations of schools, departments, administrative offices, libraries, and computer labs. Even to longtime employees, some of these places are unknown, and by centralizing a site for search and browse, all sorts of users can become more familiar with the university landscape.

I started by entering all these bits of data into a single property called *contents*, but I quickly realized that, while this was an easier way to collect the data, it was less efficient when the data was put to use. The Exhibit framework allows for the easy creation of browsable menus based on properties, and by dividing up the contents into groups, I could enable users to browse by different types of contents. I started with the *department* property, in which I entered the location of all the schools and departments in the university. I kept the contents property for libraries, computer labs, and administrative offices. I ended up with items that looked like this:

```
{ label: "Paley Library,"
  type: "Building,"
  latlng: "39.981012,-75.154571,"
  contents: ["Library," "Computer Lab
  (General)"]
},
{ label: "Ritter Annex,"
  type: "Building,"
  latlng: "39.978867,-75.156396,"
  department: ["School of Social
  Administration (SSA)," "Risk, Insurance
  and Healthcare Management," "Economics"],
  contents: ["ROTC," "Kiva Auditorium,"
  "Disability Resources and Services,"
  "Online Learning," "Summer Programs"]
},
```

You'll note that the "department" property is absent from the first item. Properties without any values can be completely left out of the data, and it is better to leave them out, as empty properties will still appear in any browse list (see following). Also take note that where a property has multiple values (as in the contents property for both items), the values are comma separated, quoted, and contained within brackets. Do not leave a comma after the last part of any list (i.e., you would not, in the example above, put a comma at the end of the line: contents: ["Library," "Computer Lab (General)"]). Doing so would cause your data file not to validate and would cause problems in Internet Explorer (though not in Firefox).

As my data collection continued, I added an "address" property for the street address of buildings (also not to be easily found in any one place) and a "dining" property for restaurants, cafes, and cafeterias. A common question at the beginning of any semester concerns the location codes used on class schedules, so I also added the "class-code" property. A sample item looked like this:

```
{ label: "Ritter Annex,"
  type: "Building,"
  latlng: "39.978867,-75.156396,"
  address: "1301 Cecil B Moore Ave,"
  department: ["School of Social
  Administration (SSA)," "Risk,
  Insurance and Healthcare Management,"
  "Economics"],
  contents: ["ROTC," "Kiva Auditorium,"
  "Disability Resources and
  Services," "Online Learning," "Summer
  Programs"],
  dining: "Lucky Cup Cafe,"
  classcode: "RA"
},
```

A plethora of other properties could be tracked. Some, such as wireless locations, could be appended as new properties for the building items. Others might require that they be separate items with their own coordinates, such as emergency phones, parking lots, and accessible entrances. All could be added to the data file as items of different types.

Plotting the Map

With some amount of data in hand, ready to be mapped, the next step is making the map and the interface to the map. This involves a few steps, which start with getting a Google Maps API key. To make use of the Google Maps API, a unique key is required. The key is a long series of letters, numbers, and symbols (mine is more than 80 characters long) used to uniquely identify your use of the API. Sign up for a free Google Maps API key at the main API site (code.google.com/apis/maps).

Starting Off

For the purposes of this project, only two files will be needed: the data file created earlier and a single HTML file to display the map. The HTML starts as a basic framework:[2]

```
<html>
<head>
<title>My Campus Map</title>
</head>
<body>

</body>
</html>
```

The first things we need to add are lines to call the JavaScripts for the Exhibit framework and its Google Map component. These JavaScripts will allow us to use special code that would normally not be understood in an HTML file. This special code is specific to Exhibit and will always begin with the prefix "ex:" as we will see in the following section. To call the JavaScripts, we add the following two lines after the <title> tags (or anywhere between the <head> and </head> tags) in our file:

```
<script src="http://static.simile.mit.edu/
exhibit/api-2.0/exhibit-api.js" type="text/
javascript"></script>
<script src="http://static.simile.mit.edu/
exhibit/extensions-2.0/map/map-extension.
js?gmapkey=XXX"></script>
```

Make sure to copy your Google Maps API key into the location where I put three X's. We also need to enter a line that will connect our HTML page to the JSON file of data:

```
<link href="buildings.json" type="
application/json" rel="exhibit/data" />
```

This line can be put after the <script> tags in the HTML file. I call my data file "buildings." Change your code so it matches the name of your file and that file's location. The file is now ready to display data.

Adding the Display

The first thing we want to add is the map itself. With a few lines of code, a map will be displayed that shows markers for all the items in our data file that contain longitude and latitude coordinates (the "latlng" property). The code for my map, using the Exhibit mapping code,[3] is

```
<div ex:role="exhibit-view"
ex:viewClass="Map"
ex:center="39.981612, -75.153571"
ex:zoom="16"
ex:size="small"
ex:latlng=".latlng"
ex:marker=".label">
</div>
```

This looks like a <div> tag that has no content in it. (Normally you would have text or images inside between the <div> and </div> tags.) Exhibit creates the content dynamically based on the properties in the tag. Each property provides a different setting for the map. The "ex:role" property tells us what the purpose of this "div" is. The "exhibit-view" value means this is a container for creating some kind of data visualization. The "ex:viewClass" tells us what kind of visualization it will be, in this case "Map" (Exhibit has a number of other options).

The next five properties are used as parameters for the map itself. "Ex:center" tells the map where it should be centered. This is important because otherwise the map will be centered above the center of the U.S., which is probably not where the markers will be. In this case, the center of the map is set to the same coordinates as the library, which is almost at the center of my campus. The "ex:zoom" property sets the level of zoom on the map. You can experiment with this number to get the right level for your map. "Ex:size" sets the size of the maps controls (small or large). "Ex:latlng" is used to tell the map what property it should read from your data file as the latitude and longitude of the items (in this case, "latlng"). When referring to a property from the data file, a period precedes the property name (e.g., ".latlng," ".label"). The "ex:marker" tells what data property should be used for the label on the map markers.

Save the HTML file (as "sometitle.html") and open it in your web browser. You should now see a map with markers for all the items that

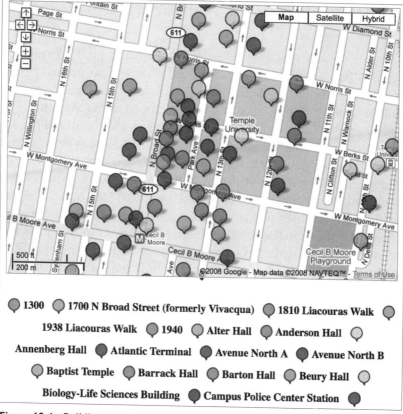

Figure 16.1 Buildings plotted onto the map

included "latlng" values in the data file (Figure 16.1). The map should be interactive: You can zoom in and out, move around, and click on markers. It is even resizable by dragging at the bottom border. You will also note that every mapped item has been listed below the map. This is all done automatically by the Exhibit code. Not bad for a few lines of code.

Browsing and Searching

Now this is a nice interactive map. But users still need to click around to find any information other than the building name. Thanks to Exhibit, we can easily add browsable lists of data to aid in discovery. These are called *facets*, and they are created with one line of code:

```
<div ex:role="facet" ex:expression=
".contents"
```

```
ex:facetLabel="What's in the building?"
ex:showMissing="false"></div>
```

Again we see the "ex:role" property, and this time the value is "facet." The "ex:expression" is used to indicate what property from the data file should be displayed. In this case, the "contents" property will be used to display a list of all the mapped items' contents. The "ex:facetLabel" sets a value for the heading at the top of the browsable list. Finally, the "ex:showMissing" property decides whether you see listings for items that have no value for the current facet (e.g., "false" means they are not shown in the browsable list, which I recommend). When this code is inserted into the HTML page (after the map code), the user will be able to browse a list of every value for "contents" found in the data file. Clicking on any of those values will cause only items with that contents value to show on the map (e.g., clicking on "Computer Labs" will cause only buildings that contain computer labs to show on the map; Figure 16.2).

Similar facets might be made for the properties "department," "label," or "classcode." This enables users to find locations without already knowing where a building is on the map. Another valuable tool for users is the ability to search. Exhibit also provides a quick way to add a search box:

```
<div ex:role="facet" ex:facetClass=
"TextSearch"
ex:queryParamName="srch"></div>
```

This is a special type of facet, so it uses the "ex:facetClass" to define its function as "TextSearch." Insert this line above the previous facet code, and the map will include a search box above the browsing options. You can limit which properties are searched by adding another element to that <div> tag:

```
<div ex:role="facet" ex:facetClass=
"TextSearch" ex:queryParamName="srch"
ex:expressions=".label, .contents,
.department"></div>
```

The ex:expressions attribute takes a comma-separated list of properties from your data file (again, don't forget that period in front of the name) to limit which fields are searched. In my case I noticed that an

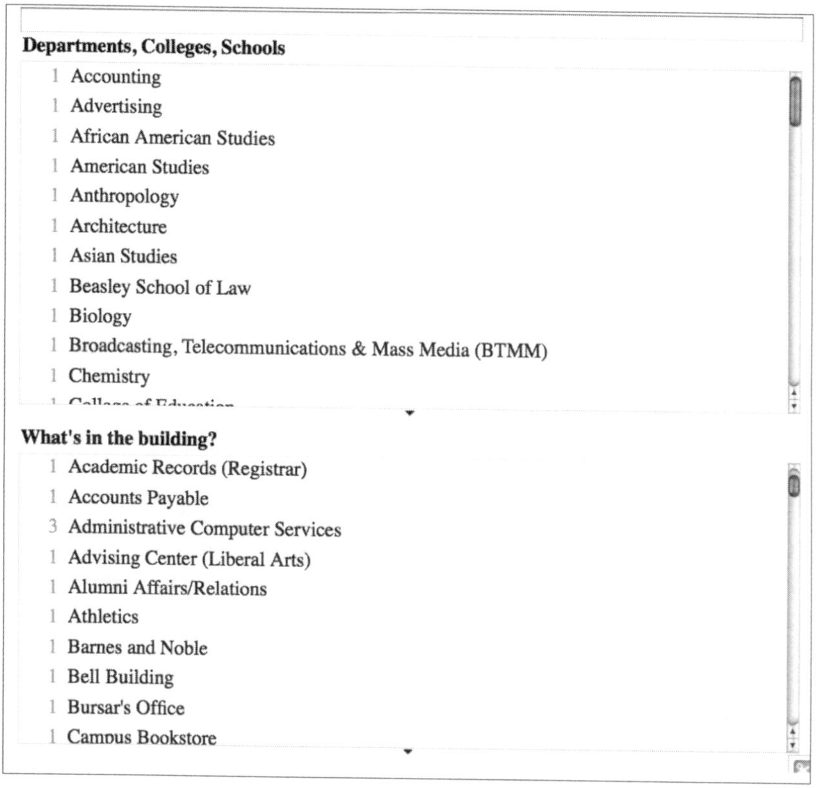

Departments, Colleges, Schools
    1 Accounting
    1 Advertising
    1 African American Studies
    1 American Studies
    1 Anthropology
    1 Architecture
    1 Asian Studies
    1 Beasley School of Law
    1 Biology
    1 Broadcasting, Telecommunications & Mass Media (BTMM)
    1 Chemistry
    1 College of Education

What's in the building?
    1 Academic Records (Registrar)
    1 Accounts Payable
    3 Administrative Computer Services
    1 Advising Center (Liberal Arts)
    1 Alumni Affairs/Relations
    1 Athletics
    1 Barnes and Noble
    1 Bell Building
    1 Bursar's Office
    1 Campus Bookstore

Figure 16.2   Search and browse facets

Exhibit created property for "URL" was causing too many search results on the search "library" because the word "library" was in the URL of my map. By setting specific properties to be searched, I avoided this problem.

Interface Design

We now have a campus map with both searching and browsing options that will allow greater and easier access to information than a static PDF map. What's left to do? While the map will work as is, some time should be spent on the visual design and page layout.

If you click on one of the map markers, a word balloon pops up showing you all the properties and values for the selected item. The design itself is unattractive, and properties such as "latlng," which users do not need to see, are displayed. Exhibit offers us the concept of a "lens" to design the display of the data for an individual item.

A basic lens is created like this:

```
<div ex:role="lens" class="lens"
style="display: none;">
<p ex:content=".label" class="name"></p>
<p ex:if-
exists=".department"><strong>Departments:</
strong> <span ex:content=".department"
class="department"></span></p>
</div>
```

The "ex:role" property specifies that the div will serve as the "lens." In all cases the "class" property is solely there for CSS styling purposes and serves no specific Exhibit function. The styling (style="display :none;") in the first "div" is important to hide the lens until an action is taken, such as clicking on a map marker. The content of the lens "div" is similar in structure to the previous examples. The "ex:content" property specifies which property from the data file is displayed (always remember to put a period before it). The "ex:if-exists" allows for an empty property (e.g., a building with no departments in it) not to be displayed so that the lens does not get jumbled up with empty properties. Continuing to add properties in this way allows you to customize which data gets displayed in the pop-up. Using CSS, you can then style it to look the way you like (Figure 16.3).

A few other simple design matters can be dealt with using CSS. You may note at this point that a list of every marker with its label appears beneath the map. I found this element unnecessary, and it was taking up too much space, so I decided to remove it. Using the Firefox plug-in Firebug (getfirebug.com), I discovered that the whole list was enclosed in a "div" tag entitled "exhibit-legendWidget." Adding a simple line to my stylesheet

```
.exhibit-legendWidget { display:none; }
```

prevented the list from appearing on the page. Other elements of the map can be altered in this way. You can find a number of settings that can be used to alter the map listed on the Exhibit documentation (simile.mit.edu/wiki/exhibit/2.0/Map_View). These settings can be put into the "exhibit-view" <div> as shown previously.

The layout of the map, as well as the search and browse panels, can be organized by using normal HTML and CSS. For public use, you will

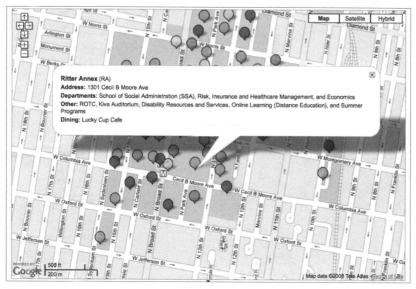

Figure 16.3 The lens shown when a marker is clicked on

probably also want to add any standard headers, footers, and navigation to the page so it will match the website it will be found on. Some value would also be found in exploring the possibilities for a mobile style sheet to optimize the display for those who might look at the map while out and about on campus.

Mapping Forward

A map at this stage should be ready for users (Figure 16.4). How you go about getting those users will depend greatly on your institution. Comments, questions, and suggestions naturally come with users. In the future, I'd like to add features for commenting or editability (wiki style) of the data. If someone knows of an office that is missing from the map, a direct user edit would be much more efficient than other methods but would involve an altered technological solution that I have not solved. In the meantime, a prominent Suggestions link on the map should help with filling in missing details. And, because a university is an ever-changing place, the map's administrator must make sure to keep up with any changes that need to be made to the data file itself.

Figure 16.4 The final map minus headers and footers

This project provided an excellent opportunity to do what librarians should do best: organize information and make it presentable and accessible for their community. All it took was some free web services, a little code, some HTML/CSS knowledge, and the time and effort to collate all my data. The end result is a useful tool for the community that shows off another function of the library.

Endnotes

1. For more on the Exhibit JSON format see
   simile.mit.edu/wiki/Exhibit/Creating%2C_Importing%2C_and_Managing_Data.
2. I use a very basic format here that is not recommended for general use. Refer to another book or website for information on properly formatting valid webpages.
3. For the Exhibit map documentation, see simile.mit.edu/wiki/Exhibit/2.0/Map_View.

CHAPTER 17

The Repository Mashup Map

Stuart Lewis
University of Auckland Library

Mashups can be created for many different reasons, but the most common purpose for creating a mashup, rather than using another form of data presentation, is to add value to the data by combining several sources in order to present new relationships between them. I created the Repository Mashup Map (maps.repository66.org) to do just this—combine data about repositories from different data providers and mash it up with Google Maps (maps.google.com) to visually display information about the repositories. In this chapter we'll examine the mashup to see why and how it was created and look at the data sources it uses in order to consider issues and considerations that affect us when mashing-up data feeds.

Background

Many universities around the world have repositories or are in the process of setting them up. Often these are called institutional repositories, open access repositories, or digital repositories. They are most commonly administered by university libraries undertaking their roles as curator of, and provider of access to, university information resources. There are many reasons that a university would want or need a repository; these include

- A need to collect, archive, and manage the research outputs of an institution

- The desire to make publicly available the results and outputs of research

- A need to comply with mandates issued by funding bodies such as the National Institutes of Health, the Wellcome Trust, or the European Research Council, which mandate the depositing of publicly funded research results in open access repositories allowing free access to the materials (see www.sherpa.ac.uk/juliet for an up-to-date list of mandates)

- A desire to create an online showcase of the research outputs of a repository

- The creation of a long-term preservation archive for digital materials such as journal articles, data sets, photographs, digitized materials, or administrative documents

Since the start of the millennium, there has been a lot of effort spent on the development of repository software to facilitate the easy creation of repositories. The repository landscape now includes a wealth of software platforms, including open source, commercial, and hosted options, and the number of items held within these repositories figures into many millions.

Table 17.1 shows some examples of the diverse range of repositories across the world and some examples of their content.

Reasons for Creating the Repository Mashup Map

Because repositories are a relatively new area for libraries, tracking their growth in size and number is interesting. Two registries of open access repositories have been created to facilitate this type of tracking:

- Registry of Open Access Repositories (ROAR; roar.eprints. org) – ROAR is run at the University of Southampton, U.K. It works by automatically collecting and analyzing the content of repositories by harvesting their contents using the Open Archives Initiative Protocol for Metadata Harvesting (OAI-PMH). Once a new repository has been added and briefly checked by an administrator, the statistics collection process is fully automatic.

- Directory of Open Access Repositories (OpenDOAR; www.opendoar.org) – OpenDOAR is run by the SHERPA (www.sherpa.ac.uk) team at Nottingham University, U.K. OpenDOAR is a human-edited registry of repositories including hand-written descriptions of each repository. The SHERPA staff members update individual repository statistics occasionally.

Both these registries present their data in a tabular form. Although this is a suitable format for examining the data record by record, it does not lend itself to providing an overall picture of repository development across the world. Being able to visualize data in an easy format can help researchers see new information that is hidden when displayed solely in a textual format. Because repositories are located at particular places, this makes an ideal key on which to display the data: on a map.

Table 17.1 Examples of the diverse range of repositories across the world

Repository	URL	Description and Examples
MIT OpenCourseware	ocw.mit.edu	An open access repository of course materials from Massachusetts Institute of Technology
MSF Field Research	msf.openrepository.com	The repository of field research undertaken by Médecins Sans Frontières
E-LIS	eprints.rclis.org	A subject-based repository for articles about library and information studies
BEACON eSpace	trs-new.jpl. nasa.gov/dspace	NASA's Jet Propulsion Laboratory published research repository
CADAIR	cadair.aber.ac.uk	A typical university institutional repository in the U.K.
ResearchSpace@ Auckland	researchspace.auckland. ac.nz	A typical university institutional repository in New Zealand

Universities and research institutions are competitive bodies. They have to compete against each other for research funding, prestige, and rankings. One side effect of this competition is that they often look sideways at what other institutions are doing in order to keep up with any developments that others are making and that they feel they need to copy. Again, a map is an ideal visualization tool as you can see what is happening at institutions near you, in your country, your continent, and across the whole world.

Repository managers also like to judge their progress in populating their repository against other repositories. They see it as a matter of professional pride to have a higher number of archived items in their repository than other repositories in similar institutions have. The vendors of repository software and services like to compare themselves to each other to see who has more installed instances of their software in comparison to others, allowing them to make claims such as "the most widely installed open source repository solution." This is a powerful marketing tool because we all feel safe following the leader—no one was ever sacked for buying IBM!

Plotting the Repository Mashup Map

So there was the statistical data available about repositories and a need for a visual representation allowing easy comparisons to be made, but there was one key bit of data missing—the geographic location of each repository in a form that could be plotted on a map.

OpenDOAR held the name and address of the institution that owned each repository, but this information cannot be directly used. A map does not know where your house is unless you code the location in a format that can be used with a map. To plot data on a map, you require a set of coordinates.

I had three options available to gather this data:

1. Locate each repository by hand.

   - Description: With a tool such as Google Maps, the locations of the institutions could be found.

   - Efficiency: Low. This is a time-consuming process as it requires human input to actually locate the repositories and to copy the data into the mashup database.

   - Accuracy: High. The accuracy should be high as each location is checked by hand.

- Issues: This option does not scale well and requires human input before a repository can appear on the map.

2. Look up the location of each repository by its IP (Internet Protocol) address.

   - Description: Every computer on the internet has a unique address, known as its IP address. This address is used to ensure network traffic is sent to the correct machine. Both open and commercial databases hold the geographic locations of IP addresses.

   - Efficiency: High. The process of finding the IP address of a computer from its URL (Uniform Resource Locator) and then using a web service to find its location can be scripted. This requires no human input.

   - Accuracy: Medium. While the coverage of the free geolocation databases is fair, and the commercial databases good, not every IP address is located accurately, and some are located only to the nearest city or region.

   - Issues: One particular issue is that repositories hosted by a commercial company are often located at the company, not the institution. Sometimes the company is in a different country from the institution, and if the hosting company has a lot of customers, you could find a cluster of repositories incorrectly located at the site of the server.

3. Use a geocoding service.

   - Description: Geocoding services take an address (typically a street address, city name, or ZIP code or postcode) and convert it to a map coordinate. This happens whenever you use an online map service to look up an address.

   - Efficiency: High. Addresses and ZIP codes or postcodes are held for each repository-owning institution in OpenDOAR and can be used to automatically look up the location by means of a geocoding service.

- Accuracy: High. Addresses are unique, and ZIP codes or postcodes refer only to a small geographic area.

- Issues: Geocoding services are either very expensive or offer partial coverage across the world. For example, Google introduced a geocoding service for U.K. locations only in July 2007.

At first the intention of the project was to make a map of U.K. repositories. Because this was a reasonably limited set of repositories (less than 100 in early 2007), I located each repository by hand. Coming from the U.K., I had a good idea about where each institution was in the country and how to locate it accurately on a map, so the job was not too difficult. However, it soon became apparent that a repository map of the whole world would be more useful, which meant that placing each repository by hand, especially in countries where I had no knowledge of the geography, was an unrealistic task.

The initial solution was to use the free IP-address-to-geographic-coordinates service "hostip" (www.hostip.info). At the same time, ROAR started using this service to collect the locations of each repository, meaning that the mashup could delegate this task to ROAR and just use that information along with the rest of the information it harvested. However, as time went on and more repositories were added, gaps in the free information started to appear. So in mid-2007, I converted the code to use a commercial web service to locate the repositories from their IP address. The accuracy was better, although not perfect.

In true Web 2.0 fashion, the repository mashup map also allows users to locate repositories on the map or to update existing repository locations. The mashup achieves this by listing repositories without locations and with locations and allowing users to place repositories on a map, recording the location in the database.

As of mid-2008, a mixture of techniques was in use to locate the repositories on the map:

- A commercial geolocation database web service

- Locations held by ROAR and OpenDOAR

- Entries entered or updated by users

- Hand location of repositories

Creating the Repository Mashup Map

This next section details how I built the repository mashup map (Figure 17.1), including the decisions I had to make and the potential benefits and trade-offs I had to consider. There are often several ways to achieve a task (e.g., aggregating a set of RSS feeds), and choosing the best solution is not always easy.

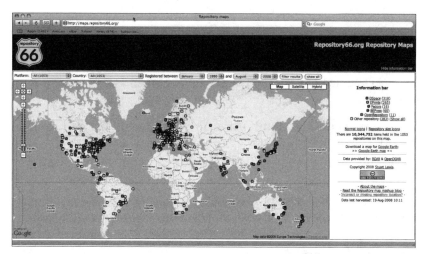

Figure 17.1   Repository Mashup Map (maps.repository66.org)

To be able to mash up data from external sources such as ROAR and OpenDOAR, you will need to find a way to grab the data. Sometimes this can be done by screen-scraping HTML, or, if you are lucky, the data providers you use will provide you with an application programming interface (API). An API is a way of easily interacting with a web service. Using an API will typically allow you to harvest the data in a formatted fashion, often with a search facility.

Harvesting Data From ROAR

ROAR offers two data-harvesting interfaces:

- An OAI-PMH interface (roar.eprints.org/oai.php?verb= ListRecords&metadataPrefix=oai_dc)

- A complete download of all repository records (roar.eprints.org/index.php?action=rawlist)

The choice of which to use was easy. Rather than making successive web requests, which are required by OAI-PMH, it was easier to download all the data in one go and parse it into individual records myself.

Harvesting Data From OpenDOAR

OpenDOAR provides a useful API (www.opendoar.org/tools/api. html). There are two ways of using it:

1. Perform a search, for example all repositories in New Zealand (www.opendoar.org/api.php?co=nz).

2. Download all the data at once (www.opendoar.org/api. php?all=y).

As with ROAR, I found it easier to download all the data at once and then process it myself.

As previously mentioned, the Repository Mashup Map is created by mashing up the data held in ROAR and OpenDOAR and combining it with geographic location coordinates supplied by various means. To mash up the data, several design decisions needed to be made.

The Common Identifier

To mash up data, you often need a common identifier that can be used to match items in each of the data sources that you are using. Often these common identifiers are unique to a given object, allowing very fine-grained matching of objects in different systems. For example, in the case of a book mashup that pulls information from different sources, you could choose the ISBN, as it will uniquely identify the same item in each system. In the case of repositories, the unique key used by both ROAR and OpenDOAR is the OAI-PMH location (a URL) of each repository. The OAI-PMH location is the web address that can be used by software to harvest metadata from a repository in order to reuse the metadata or to collate statistics.

You can see examples OAI-PMH responses by trying these URLs:

- cadair.aber.ac.uk/dspace-oai/request?verb=Identify

- cadair.aber.ac.uk/dspace-oai/request?verb=ListSets

- cadair.aber.ac.uk/dspace-oai/request?verb=ListMeta dataFormats

- cadair.aber.ac.uk/dspace-oai/request?verb=ListRecords& metadataPrefix=oai_dc

Data Source Authority

When combining two data sets that provide different types of data about a group of similar objects, you have to decide whether to use all the data provided by both systems or to consider one data source as authoritative and the other as secondary. This can be explained most easily through a traditional Venn diagram (Figure 17.2).

- Use all the data – Use data from both systems, A and B. Where they cross over at X, you have richer data; where they differ, you have less data, but at least you have the object.

- Use one authoritative system – When one system is considered authoritative, you lose any data that is stored only in the other system. In the diagram, this means you would lose data from section B.

The decision will depend on your mashup. If you are creating a mashup of products sold by an online store with reviews about those items from a product review site, there is no point in showing reviews for products that you cannot buy. Therefore, it is best to consider the store's product list as the authoritative data source. If on the other hand your mashup is to compare prices of products in different online stores, then you want to show every product, even if it is only for sale in one store.

To avoid potential duplication of data in the Repository Mashup Map, I decided to make one source the authoritative source. If all sources were used (A + X + B), then duplicates could (and do!) arise where a common identifier in A and B refers to the same object but the objects are subtly different. As of August 2008, the Repository Mashup Map used ROAR as its authoritative source because the collection policy of OpenDOAR is stricter than that of ROAR. However, I continue to monitor the situation to provide the best aggregated resource to users of the maps.

Live or Offline Processing

Mashing up data requires processing power. It takes effort to combine data sources, and this can either take place "live," as the user

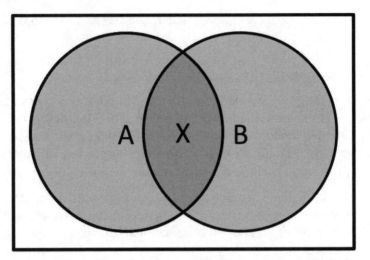

Figure 17.2 Traditional Venn diagram (en.wikipedia.org/wiki/Venn_diagram)

requires it, or "offline," in advance of the user's requiring it. Performing the processing offline is advantageous as the mashup user does not have to wait while the data is compiled. When data from different sources is being mashed up, the latency of different data sources could mean a slow and unsatisfactory mashup experience for the user. However, if the data is time critical and constantly changing (e.g., a mashup of items for sale on eBay and their geographic locations), then offline processing may not be an option as the user requires up-to-date information. One solution offering the advantages of both options is to cache a copy of data for a time (perhaps an hour) and then to refresh the data once it has expired. This means the data is reasonably up-to-date but is not being refreshed slowly for each user.

Offline processing will not be an option if the whole of a data set is not available or if you do not have the processing power or storage space to deal with it. If you were mashing up data from a large online store such as Amazon (www.amazon.com), you can only query it rather than download it all. (Even if you could download it all, the average mashup maker does not have the resources to process it.)

The Repository Mashup Map uses data sources that are manageable (in the order of thousands rather than tens of thousands) and that are not updated very often (OpenDOAR rarely, ROAR daily). Therefore, it made sense to compile the mashup data offline every day or two rather than mash up the data for each user. An additional benefit of processing the data offline is that it is less prone to errors. If one of the data sources is temporarily not working, then the site will continue to provide a full service rather then being degraded during the service outage.

Client or Server Filtering

Very often with a mashup, the user is interested in only a portion of the complete data set. When viewing a mashup of crime statistics and houses for sale, the user will most likely be interested only in certain house types in a few areas (e.g., large family homes in the suburbs). This filtering of the complete data set can take place either on the server proving the data or in the browser (client) viewing the data.

Some mashups, such as a mashup of products and reviews, require the user to enter a query before any data is shown. Only when users request reviews for a particular product or product type will they see any mashed up data. In this case, because the data set is likely to be large, it is probably most efficient to let the web server perform the work and then send the resulting smaller data set to the client.

However, if the mashup is restricted to a smaller and more specialized data set in which the user by default will see all the mashed up data (e.g., a map of zoos and wildlife parks in a country), then it would probably be most sensible for filtering to take place on the client's machine. Because the client machine already has all the data, it would be silly and slow for the mashup to request just a subset of the data to be re-sent (just zoos and wildlife parks with monkeys) when the filtering can be performed locally.

The Repository Mashup Map uses the second of these options. The entire data set of repositories and their locations is downloaded at once. If the user wishes to filter on one aspect, such as software type or date of creation, then this filtering is performed on the browser end.

Send Enough or All of the Data

When one is creating a mashup and deciding when and what data to send to a client, an additional decision that needs to be made relates to when to send the data. On first loading, mashups often just initially show a low level of detail (product names, price, and star rating) but then display a higher level of detail (product reviews and photos) once the user has selected them. There are three options of deciding what data to send to the client at which point:

1. Send all the data at once.

   - Advantages: Once the mashup has loaded, the client has all the data the client requires, so the client will experience a responsive mashup that provides additional detail quickly.

   - Disadvantages: The mashup will be slower to load as all the data needs to be transmitted at once.

2. Send the low-level detail first, and then the high-level detail once the user requires it.

   - Advantages: The mashup loads quicker as it is not loading the entire data set.

   - Disadvantages: Users may not perceive the mashup as responsive because it will take a short amount of time for the higher detail level to be fetched from the server.

3. Send the low-level detail first, and send the high-level detail in the background.

   - Advantages: The mashup loads quickly, and then in the background, while the user is interacting with it, the high level data is downloaded, meaning that the mashup will appear responsive when the user requests the high level of detail of an item whose data has been downloaded in the background.

   - Disadvantages: It is technically difficult to do this and beyond the scope of an amateur mashup creator.

Initially I decided to make the Repository Mashup Map send all the data at once. However, as the data contained in ROAR and OpenDOAR grew, the data file that was downloaded became half a megabyte in size. For users with a slow internet connection, the downloading of the file was prohibitively long. Therefore, in mid-2008 I switched to the second option and only downloaded the simple statistics of each repository. Full details, such as the repository description, were loaded only when a user requested to see it. Because each user of the mashup will probably look only at the descriptions of a few repositories, this small trade-off of loading time versus a slightly less responsive mashup made sense.

Data Source Licensing

Data sources often come with licenses describing what you are allowed to do with the data, what you are not allowed to do with the data, and whether there are any attributions to the data owners that must be shown. The data from ROAR and OpenDOAR are both shared under a Creative Commons (www.creativecommons.org) license ("by attribution" and "by attribution, noncommercial, sharealike," respectively).

It is a good idea to license your own data in order to protect your own rights. If the data you are using requires it, you may be required to pass on a similar set of rights (a share-alike license).

The Repository Mashup Map licenses its data with a Creative Commons "by attribution, noncommercial, sharealike" license.

The Mashup Website

This chapter has so far concentrated on why the mashup was created and how the data was collated. This section describes how the mashup website is constructed and what technologies power it.

The Mapping

The mapping element naturally takes up the largest area of the mashup webpage and is powered by the Google Maps API (code.google.com/apis/maps). The API allows a map to be added to any webpage with very few lines of code. Interactive features can easily be included on the maps, such as a zoom bar, mouse event handling for panning around the map, and buttons to switch between a traditional map view and a satellite view. The initial view of the map can be controlled by code and is set by default to show the whole world.

I could have used an alternative mapping API such as Yahoo! Maps Web Services (developer.yahoo.com/maps) or Bing Maps (www.microsoft.com/maps). However, for purely pragmatic reasons, I chose to use Google Maps. (Sometimes decisions I make are just based on "what I know" rather than anything more scientific!)

The Dots

The markers are placed on the map via JavaScript. The XML (eXtensible Markup Language) file containing the repository data is downloaded using JavaScript that then processes the data and places the markers. The markers are either displayed in variable sizes

(Figure 17.3) or all the same sizes (Figure 17.4), depending on the number of items in each repository. The markers are sized according to a logarithmic scale (en.wikipedia.org/wiki/Logarithmic_scale) to ensure that small repository markers are not too small and large repository markers are not too big.

The Data

To display the data held about each repository, a window appears when a user clicks on a repository marker on the map. The window that pops up uses tabs to make the best use of the space. The initial tab shows basic data about the repository: its name, date of creation, number of items it holds, and content types it holds.

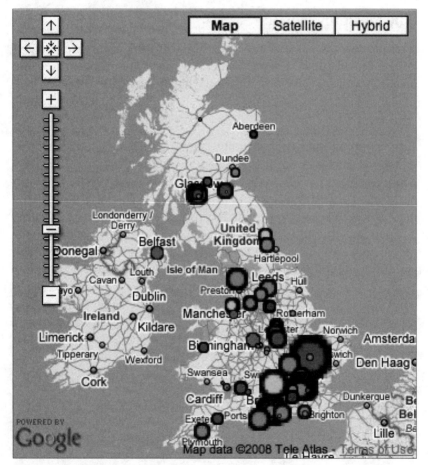

Figure 17.3 Markers are displayed in varied sizes.

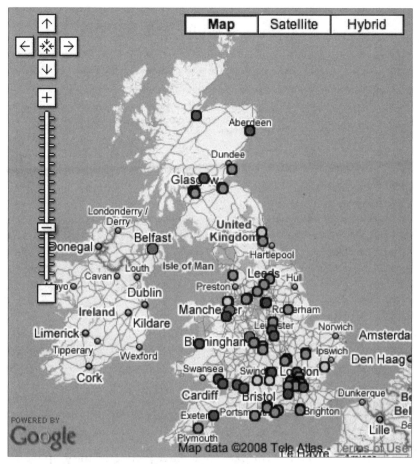

Figure 17.4 Markers are displayed all the same size.

Additional tabs show the description of the repository from OpenDOAR, a growth graph showing how the number of items in the repository has grown over time, and a search tab. The search tab allows the user to search the contents of the repository using Google, Google Scholar (scholar.google.com), or Bing (www.bing.com) (Figure 17.5).

The Growth Graphs

Growth graphs showing how the numbers of items in each repository have changed over time are generated for the site (Figure 17.6). There were several possible solutions for generating the graphs:

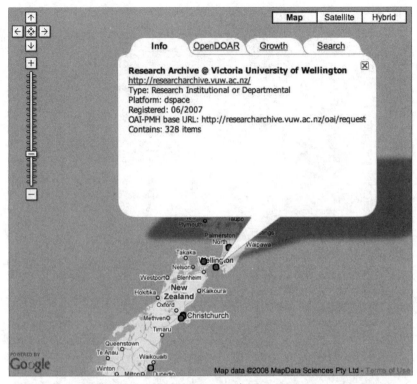

Figure 17.5   The pop-up window tabs make the best use of the space to display the data held about each repository.

- Generate graphs when the data is collated – The software written to collect the data could have generated the graphs via a software library designed to generate graphs.

- Generate graphs on the client via JavaScript – The data could be sent in its raw form to the web browser that can make use of a JavaScript charting library. Potential downsides of this option are an extended initial loading time as the charting library is also downloaded and an increased chance that the site will be incompatible with some browsers.

- Use an online charting service – Google provides an online charting library (code.google.com/apis/chart) that generates charts on the fly for inclusion in webpages. The URL of the image has to be specially constructed to contain all the chart data and metadata (type, colors, scales, etc.).

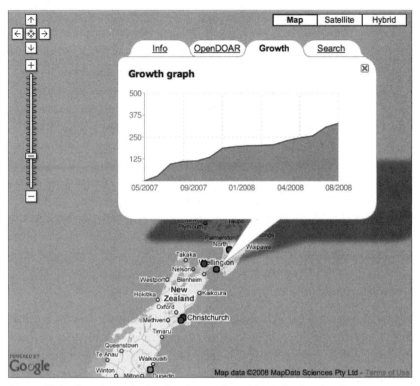

Figure 17.6 Growth graph showing the number of items in the repository

The Google charts option was chosen as it seemed most flexible. It also reduced the amount of bandwidth used by the mashup web server as Google servers would serve the images. From a lazy programmer's perspective (there is nothing wrong with being lazy—I'm just making my job easier and quicker!), this was the quickest option to develop.

The Filters

Several filtering options are available when one is selecting which repositories to display. The first filter added was for the different software platforms that are used by each repository. This showed interesting patterns of use throughout the world. Some countries have a complete mix of platforms whereas others showed more prominent usage patterns.

The second filter added shows the state of repository population at any time in the past. The user can select a month and year and see which repositories existed at that time. This allows a user to see how and where repositories developed over time (adoption trends).

A third filter was added during the editing of this book chapter (a good mashup keeps adding new features!). It allows the user to filter on repositories in one country only.

Also added during the final editing of this chapter was the automatic zoom function. Imagine using the filters to select "All repositories in the United Kingdom"; it is pretty predictable where the results will be. Therefore the mashup makes use of the Google Maps API functions that allow you to center the maps and to zoom so that the map markers are shown at an appropriate level. In this case it zooms in automatically to show the U.K.

User Contribution

Users can update the position of a current repository marker if it has been incorrectly placed or can be placed more accurately, or they can add the location of a repository that has not yet been placed on the map. A smaller Google Map is shown to the user, who can move around it and zoom in or out to find the correct location. Users can then submit the new location, which is emailed to the author as a suggestion to update the location database. I try to thank all contributors with a short personal email just so they know their contribution has been accepted and considered worthwhile and to say "Thank You!"

The Blog

The site uses a blog powered by WordPress (wordpress.org) to provide a mechanism to update users on developments and to allow users to comment on the mashup. Once again, resource issues made the choice easy. WordPress uses technologies available from my web host (PHP and MySQL) and was quick to set up and configure.

Future Developments

There are several possible areas of future developments of the Repository Mashup Map, and they include

- A timeline animation – Automate the date filter so that a Play button can be pressed to automatically view the change in the repository landscape over time, with new repository markers appearing and growing.

- Extra filters – New filters such as repository content type could be added.

- Extra search options – Extra search targets can be added for each repository (perhaps repository-specific search services such as OAIster [www.oaister.org] or Intute Repository Search [www.intute.ac.uk/irs]). Another search option might be to search groups of repositories, such as all repositories of a given type.

- Dynamic filter selection boxes – When you select a filter (e.g., "All DSpace repositories"), the other filter selections (e.g., countries) should get rewritten so that instead of showing how many repositories there are in each country, they show how many DSpace repositories there are in each country.

I would be pleased to hear of any other suggestions! Please either email me or leave a comment on the blog.

Part V

Adding Value to Your Services

CHAPTER 18

The LibraryThing API and Libraries

Robin Hastings
Missouri River Regional Library

An Introduction to LibraryThing

LibraryThing (www.librarything.com) burst onto the internet in March 2006 (www.librarything.com/about). The idea behind Library Thing was that regular people might want to catalog their personal libraries and make them available to share and discuss with others— and they did, in droves! As of June 2009, more than 40 million books have been entered, cataloged, classified, tagged, and used to start conversations. In the beginning, the social aspects of the site set LibraryThing apart from other similar services. People who use the service can see the libraries of other members, start conversations about books—or just about anything else—and indulge their love of reading with other book lovers. Librarians have taken to LibraryThing as well; one of the largest groups on the site is the "Librarians Who LibraryThing" group, with more than 6,000 members who discuss everything from literature to what interesting things they have found returned with books at their workplaces (www.librarything.com/groups).

LibraryThing gets its information from various sources that provide book information on the web, including libraries, Amazon (www.amazon.com), and the users of the site. Books can be added by just entering an ISBN—the rest of the information is automatically populated. Books are bundled into units called *works*; different editions of the same book are linked together so that people can both be specific about the edition (paperback, hardback, etc.) that they own and see all of the information added about that particular work, regardless of the particular edition of the work for which the information was included. This is made possible by giving each work a unique *work ID* that will become very important as we start to work with LibraryThing data.

The information that LibraryThing collects about each book is pretty extensive. Some information is pulled from online sources, and some is added by members. Each work record in LibraryThing includes the number of members who have the book in their libraries, reviews, popularity and rating scales, conversations that cite the book (in the groups section of the site), members who have recently added the book, tags added by members, recommendations for similar books, "common knowledge" about the book, member-contributed descriptions of the book, and descriptions of the book culled from other sources.

LibraryThing's Common Knowledge database (www.library thing.com/commonknowledge) is a member-populated database of information about a book, most of which would not be found at a book retailer or most other online sources. It consists of series information; bibliographic information, such as title and publication date; important people and places, as well as characters in the book; awards and honors; epigraphic information; the content of the book's dedication; first and last words of the book; quotes; and information about who wrote the blurbs on the cover of the book. All of this information is available to anyone—provided you get an application programming interface (API) key (also known on the site as a *Developer's key*) first. You can pick up a key at www.librarything.com/services/keys.php, and, with that text-based token, get access to much of the data that LibraryThing collects. You can also get a JSON (JavaScript Object Notation) key that will work to get just your information out of the system. Some of the data provided by LibraryThing, though, doesn't require any sort of key at all for you to use it.

The LibraryThing API Explained

Linking APIs

One thing you will need the LibraryThing API key for is getting book covers from the LibraryThing service. (Note, though, that Library Thing covers are not comprehensive—according to the site, there are more than a million usable covers available—and the larger sized covers can be a bit blurry, depending on the original upload's size.) The only other thing you need to get these book covers is a properly formatted URL (Uniform Resource Locator). Tim Spalding (the creator of

LibraryThing; see Chapter 10) wrote a blog post at www.library thing.com/blog/2008/08/million-free-covers-from-librarything.php that gives all the details. Just create a URL in the form *www.library thing.com/devkey/YourDevKey#/medium/isbn/ISBN#*. Replace the *ISBN#* in the URL with the actual ISBN of the book to get the data. You can also customize the size of the cover that is returned by changing the word *medium* in that URL to either *small* or *large*. LibraryThing has a limit of 1,000 requests per day; you can contact it to get permission to exceed that number if necessary. The speed of requests is also limited; if you have an automated script that makes requests of the LibraryThing servers, you will need to make sure that this script doesn't hit its servers more than once per second. As long as you stay within those limits, 1,000 requests per day and no more than one hit per second, you will have no problems. Of course, if your application takes off and starts to get very popular, you may wish to contact LibraryThing and ask permission for increased access to their servers.

The linking API is equally simple to use. It lets you link to a LibraryThing work in a predictable way, which means you can pull information from a database or an OPAC (Online Public Access Catalog) and create links automatically, without needing to hand code each link. The linking API takes either the ISBN number or a title—with underscores, + signs, or spaces—in its URL. The structure is either *www.librarything.com/isbn/ISBN#* or *www.librarything.com/ title/TITLE*. Replace *ISBN#* or *TITLE* in the example URLs with the actual ISBN or title of the book. This makes automating links to LibraryThing works in a catalog very easy. This method gives you a link for every record in your OPAC or database—if you want to conditionally link to a LibraryThing work, use the JSON Works API, described later in this chapter.

The other APIs that LibraryThing offers are a bit more complicated to use. Instead of just offering links to LibraryThing data, they return data to your webpage or application; you can then work with that data in many different ways. The following APIs all return data in either serialized JSON format or in an XML (eXtensible Markup Language) data structure.

JSON Works API

The first API mentioned on the LibraryThing website is the JSON Works API. This gives you a way to put a conditional LibraryThing link into a book record without knowing in advance whether LibraryThing actually has a "work" record for that book. To use this API, you put a script call in your page to the URL *athena.library thing.com/api/json/workinfo.js?ids=ISBN#*. Replace *ISBN#* in the ids value with a real ISBN. This will check to see if there is a work record for that ISBN and, if there is, put a "see on LT" link inside of an element with the ID LT_xxx (where xxx is one of your identifiers). All you have to do is call the script, create an element (DIV, SPAN, P, whatever) with that ID, and the script will either add a link or not, depending on the availability of the data. You can do other things with the data that the script returns (a simple JavaScript hash of data about the work) by creating a JavaScript callback function and adding it to the end of the URL (*ids=ISBN#&callback=function_name()*). The data in that hash will then be fed to whatever function is the callback value.

The Thing APIs

The first of the "Thing" APIs is the ThingISBN API, which takes an ISBN and returns a list of related ISBNs from the same "work." It too is URL-based—the structure for that call is *www.librarything. com/api/thing/ISBN#*. ThingISBN returns an XML data structure consisting of the list of ISBNs. ThingLang also takes an ISBN, but it returns the language of the book. The URL to call this data is *www.librarything.com/api/thinglang?isbn=ISBN#*. It returns the results, by default, as a three-letter MARC (MAchine-Readable Cataloging) language code, but you can add *&display=name* to the end of the URL and get the language name decoded for you. The ISBN Check service takes an ISBN and validates it, returning both the 10- and 13-number forms of the ISBN to you in an XML data structure. The URL for that is *www.librarything.com/isbncheck.php?isbn= ISBN#*. ThingTitle is similar to ThingISBN, but it takes a book title and returns a list of ISBNs and a link to the work page on LibraryThing. It also can be called through the URL *www.librarything.com/api/thing Title/The+Title* (and the title can use underscores, plus signs (+), or spaces, just like the easy linking API) and returns an XML data structure with the title, link, and list of ISBNs as the data.

The other big JavaScript API that LibraryThing provides is a way to easily code a widget to display books from your account on your webpages. The JSON Books API looks on your webpage for a DIV with the ID LT_Widget. The script code is added below that DIV, and the information is then pulled into the page and displayed. For the script call, you need to have the name of the user and the JSON key (not the developer's key) that you can get from LibraryThing at www.librarything.com/api/json.php (if you are logged into the service). The code that you add to your webpage, below the LT_Widget DIV, is *<script type="text/javascript" src=http://www.librarything.com/api/json_books.php?userid=USER&key=KEY></script>*. There are other parameters that you can control, all listed at www.library thing.com/wiki/index.php/LibraryThing_JSON_Books_API, which change the data you receive. Some of the options allow you to include reviews and other information from your account, sort and limit the data returned, and change the dimensions of the book covers that are displayed. Figure 18.1 shows an example of a widget pulling Tim Spalding's books from his account.

LibraryThing's Web Service

Finally, LibraryThing offers a web service, using REST (REpresentational State Transfer), which takes a specially formatted URL and returns data from the common knowledge database about a particular work. The URL is constructed as *www.librarything.com/services/rest/VERSION/?METHOD&ARGUMENTS&apikey=KEY*. The version targets a specific version of the API. As of June 2009, the only version available is version 1.0. Two methods are available—either Librarything.ck.getwork or Librarything.ck.getauthor. The getwork method returns all data available from the common knowledge database, and the getauthor method returns the name, education, places of residence, nationality, occupations, awards, birthday, and gender of the author. The arguments that you can use in the API are listed on the individual methods' pages and are expressed as key=value pairs. For the getwork method, all you can add is the id of the work in the id=work# format. The API key is your developer's key. All this data is returned in an XML data structure, and it is up to you to parse that XML and display it or use it however you want.

Doing Something With the LibraryThing API

Now that you know what the API can offer, what should you do with it? One option is to use the Covers API to replace a paid subscription to a commercial cover provider service. As more and more covers are added to the LibraryThing works pages, this will become more and

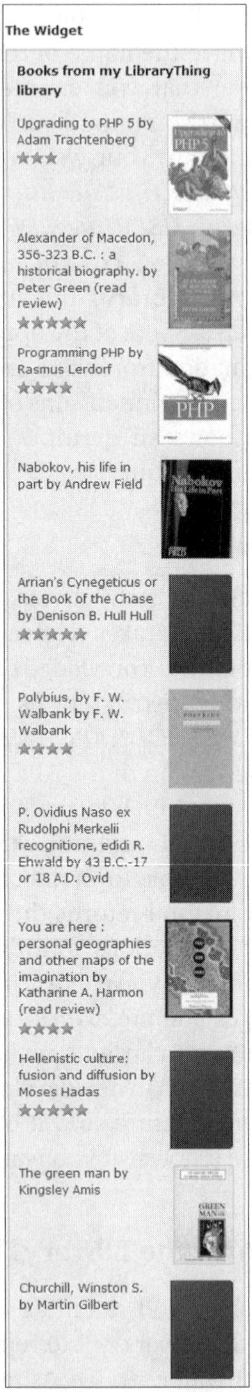

The Widget

Books from my LibraryThing library

Upgrading to PHP 5 by Adam Trachtenberg
★★★

Alexander of Macedon, 356-323 B.C. : a historical biography. by Peter Green (read review)
★★★★★

Programming PHP by Rasmus Lerdorf
★★★★

Nabokov, his life in part by Andrew Field

Arrian's Cynegeticus or the Book of the Chase by Denison B. Hull Hull
★★★★★

Polybius, by F. W. Walbank by F. W. Walbank
★★★★

P. Ovidius Naso ex Rudolphi Merkelii recognitione, edidi R. Ehwald by 43 B.C.-17 or 18 A.D. Ovid

You are here : personal geographies and other maps of the imagination by Katharine A. Harmon (read review)
★★★★

Hellenistic culture: fusion and diffusion by Moses Hadas
★★★★★

The green man by Kingsley Amis

Churchill, Winston S. by Martin Gilbert

Figure 18.1 LibraryThing widget pulling Tim Spalding's books from his account

more feasible—and because they are offered for free, this is a cost-effective option. The Basic or Easy Linking API can be used to conditionally add links from your catalog records or any other automatically created list of books to more information on the LibraryThing website. This gives your site's visitors easy access to reviews, common knowledge database information, and more!

The JSON Books API can easily be used by those smaller libraries that have chosen to use LibraryThing as their automation solution. If the books are being entered into the system, you can then pull them back out via a widget to display the newest books or display your books in either title or author order. This widget will let you show the book information (including the cover image if one is available), as well as the reviews that you enter into the LibraryThing system and the tags that you have entered for the book. This is limited, however, only to books in your account, so you would have to enter the books into your library's account to be able to get anything out of LibraryThing using this API.

The Web Services API can be used to get all the Common Knowledge information for a particular work. This could be useful additional information about a book being discussed in a library book club or featured in some other way. Once you have a handle on dealing with the XML that is returned, you can do just about anything with the information contained in that database!

Uses in Libraries

Currently, there are just a few examples of the use of the LibraryThing API in the wild. Because the API is so new, only a few libraries have jumped in and started using it. One example available now is the Library Labs (www.nla.gov.au/library-labs) of the National Library of Australia. This is a beta version of a search that includes information from LibraryThing in the search results. A quick look at the search results for the term *enigma* (Figure 18.2) shows what information the library is displaying from the LibraryThing API.

The number of copies owned by LibraryThing members, the number of reviews for that particular work, and the rating for the work are all included in the search results. All this information is linked to the work page for the given title. This gives patrons an easy way to get to far more information about the book than most library catalogs offer.

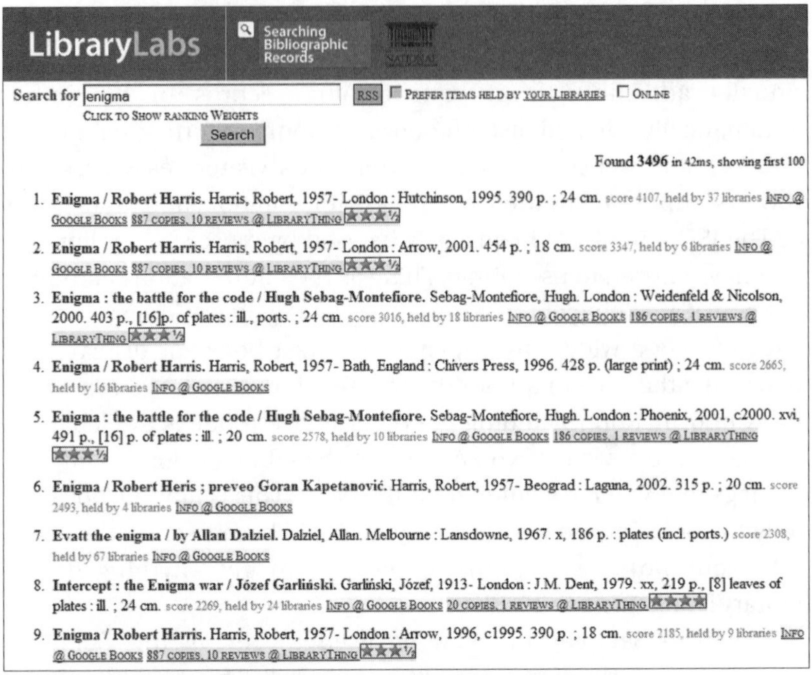

Figure 18.2   A quick look at the search results for the term *enigma* shows what information the library is displaying from the LibraryThing API.

Karen Coombs, the head of web services at the University of Houston Libraries, has created a widget that can be installed into a WordPress blog and takes information from the LibraryThing API (as well as the WorldCat API, Google Books API, OpenLibrary API, and Amazon Web Services see Chapter 13) and creates a book information sidebar for a blog. She explains the process that she went through to create the widget with links to all the APIs listed previously and a link to the prototype code that she's using at www.library webchic.net/wordpress/218/worldcat-wordpress-widget. You can download the code and use it today to bring together a bunch of information about a particular book and display it on a blog.

Eric Lease Morgan has created a prototype service called *Send it to me*, which takes an ISBN and searches the OPAC for an exact match. If no match is found, then it uses the ThingISBN service to find related ISBNs (same work, different edition) and does a search on the ISBNs that are returned. If no books are found with any of the ISBNs, the catalog supplies other options—Interlibrary Loan, a request for the library to purchase the book, a link to buy the book from Amazon, and a search for similar books. This extends the usefulness of the library OPAC considerably, using LibraryThing and other services to provide information to library users directly from the catalog. This implementation is still in beta form, but the source code is available (dewey.library.nd.edu/hacks/send) and can be tweaked to work with your library system.

Other mashups that have been created from the LibraryThing API can give libraries some ideas for ways in which they can use the API themselves. The folks at ProgrammableWeb (www.programmable web.com) collect information on APIs and have links to any mashups that have been created (and submitted to the site). They list two non-library uses of the LibraryThing API that might be useful for libraries to explore. The first is called Books Most Wanted at Bookmooch, which seems to still be in development. The second is CodexMap (codexmap.com/codexmap.php), which places books on a map in all of the geographical locations mentioned in the book, then provides links to more information about the book, including a link to the works page at LibraryThing (Figure 18.3).

LibraryThing in Libraries

LibraryThing allows regular people to discover the joys of cataloging books. Millions of books have been entered into the system, and that data is waiting there for anyone to use. If you follow the LibraryThing

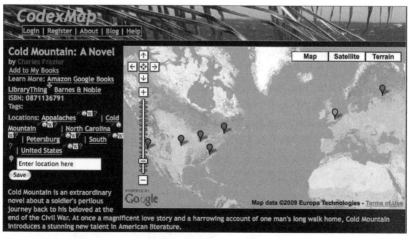

Figure 18.3   CodexMap for *Cold Mountain*

terms of service (TOS), you can have access to all of that data in your own library's catalogs, book group pages, and special book collection pages. LibraryThing offers a fee-based service, LibraryThing for Libraries (www.librarything.com/forlibraries), which gives you easy access to reviews and tags for any book that has been added to LibraryThing. However, if you want to use any of the information in the Common Knowledge database or to any of the books in your own account, all you have to do is use the APIs that have been provided to access that information and use it in any way you would like.

The LibraryThing API is as of this writing very new and still in the process of being put out there for people to use. For more information about the various APIs, be sure to check the LibraryThing blog (www.librarything.com/blog) for announcements of new features added to the APIs. You can also use the API reference pages to find specific information about each API and what kind of information a particular request will return.

For even more information about the APIs, consult the LibraryThing wiki. This is a great source of information about LibraryThing in general, but it is also a way to get into the code behind at least one of the APIs (JSON Books API) being used right now. This code is displayed on a wiki page (www.librarything. com/wiki/index.php/LibraryThing_JSON_Books_API), and you can view it, grab it for your own use, or edit it. If the edits are particularly useful, they will be added into the standard JSON Books API and will be available to everyone who uses the API. Even if you don't contribute code, however, just being able to read through what each function does will give you an understanding of how best to use the API for your needs.

Tim Spalding and the folks at LibraryThing have made an excellent start at opening up their data and sharing their resources with the world. With just a few lines of code, or in some cases just a well-formatted URL, you can get data from LibraryThing, massage it into a useful format for you, and display it to your patrons. Combining that data with other web services and other APIs will extend the usefulness of your webpages and catalogs even more.

CHAPTER 19

ZACK Bookmaps

Wolfram Schneider
Berlin, Germany

Introducing ZACK

ZACK (opus.tu-bs.de/zack) was developed as part of my diploma thesis in 1999, and I continue to maintain it, both as a hobby and to improve my programming skills. ZACK is a federated search engine that mashes up data from Google Maps (maps.google.com), Z39.50 Search Targets (z3950.intute.ac.uk), Geo Databases, and Amazon (www.amazon.com) to graphically show the location of library books in your area. The distributed search by means of ZACK is carried out in several databases in parallel. Duplicates are recognized, and a short list of matches without double entries is offered. The library locations are then shown on a Google map.

With ZACK you can search 130 million records worldwide and up to 50 databases simultaneously. Rare books are often available in only two or three libraries around the globe, and users don't know which ones. ZACK shows the book cover, customer reviews, and location of the library on a map so that the user can find the item in the nearest library. In addition, you get information about hours, phone numbers, addresses, and a link to the local catalog so that you can order the book or find out the loan status.

Originally this site was relatively static, but due to the ever-increasing amount of information being made accessible online, the mashup aspects of the system were added after the initial release.

History of ZACK

ZACK has been online since 1999. It was developed to assist in copy cataloging for librarians in the Cooperative Library Network

Berlin-Brandenburg (KOBV) at the Zuse Institute Berlin, a research institute for applied mathematics and computer science.

The architecture of ZACK is a simple client server model based on the Z39.50 protocol, a client-server protocol for searching and retrieving information. Z39.50 is an established standard from 1988.

ZACK's basic features are the following:

- It supports asynchronous search and duplication check.

- It supports multiple bibliographic formats: USMARC, UNIMARC, and MAB2.

- It supports multiple character sets: ISO 8859–1, ANSEL, IS0 5426, and CP850.

- It provides Boolean search capabilities: author and title.

- Its response time averages 3 to 5 seconds, more than sufficient for most users.

How It Works

A mashup is a web application that combines data from more than one source into a single integrated tool. ZACK does not have its own database and uses only remote data, acting as a gateway that combines data from multiple sources. For that reason, ZACK depends on the following web services:

- Z39.50 servers

  - The main source for bibliographic data

- Book search services (AbeBooks)

  - Modern web services use XML over HTTP instead of Z39.50.

  - Implemented with a Z39.50 proxy, which transforms the Z39.50 queries to a web service query and converts the resulting XML to USMARC.

- Web catalogs (Pica, Aleph500)

  - Not all libraries offer a Z39.50 server or give free access.

  - Implemented with a Z39.50 proxy, which transforms the Z39.50 queries to a web catalog, starts a session, runs

the query, downloads HTML pages and extracts bibliographic information, and converts the information to
USMARC.

- Amazon

    - Amazon has book covers for most books published dur-
      ing the past 20 years.

    - A search query can be started with ISBN number on
      Amazon, and the URL (Uniform Resource Locator) of
      the book cover and customer reviews can be extracted.

- MARC (MAchine-Readable Cataloging) record data for
  enhanced content

    - Many library records contain references to full text or
      table of contents in the 856 field in USMARC.

- xISBN/thingISBN related ISBN services

    - These web services return a list of related ISBN num-
      bers for a search.

- Google Maps

    - This is used to show the libraries on a map.

- *Directory of Library Codes* databases

    - Every library has a unique ID that can be found in
      USMARC field 851, 900, or 901.

    - A query on the library ID makes it possible to extract
      addresses, opening hours, and homepages.

- Geographic databases

    - Using the ZIP code/postcode from the library address,
      we get the Global Positioning System (GPS) coordinates
      from a geographic database.

    - Another option is to extract the homepage information
      to get the IP (Internet Protocol) address for reverse
      domain name system (DNS) lookup. With this infor-
      mation, you can make a request from the GeoIP data-
      base and get the GPS coordinated to the IP address.
      This option provides only the address of the owner of

the domain name, which may be an external hosting service.

- Bookmaps API (opus.tu-bs.de/zack/bookmaps.html)

  - Bookmaps API provides the location of books within specified boundaries (e.g., public libraries only, specified geographical areas, etc.).

Technical Details

In addition to a dependence on web services, ZACK makes use of free and open source software such as Perl and YAZ (www.indexdata.dk/yaz) to power searching of 130 million worldwide records in up to 50 databases simultaneously.

Because ZACK was developed to support copy cataloging, it offers a way to export records so that they can be imported into your own system (Figure 19.1).

The ZACK service, which is hosted at the University of Technology at Braunschweig, Germany, gets up to 10,000 search requests on an average weekday. Our statistics show that it is used

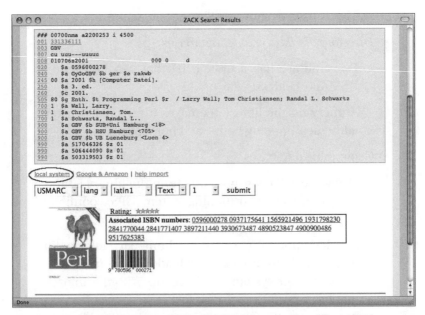

Figure 19.1 After clicking on a library link from the search results, you'll be offered options for exporting the record.

by 100 to 150 professional librarians (mainly from Germany and Austria) for copy cataloging. Even with all of this, maintenance costs only about half an hour a week for log analysis and email support requests.

Searching ZACK

Say that a patron wishes to search for published works by Larry Wall. Figure 19.2 shows this simple author search.

The search options allow the user to choose from any number of libraries, the maximum results to return per library, a timeout period (so that if a server is down, it doesn't interrupt the search process), and a duplication check. To make it easier for the user to edit a search once results are returned, ZACK retains the search menu at the top of the results page.

The results page is divided into two other parts (in addition to the search form). In the middle of the page (Figure 19.3), you will find information on your search, such as the fact that it took 6 seconds to

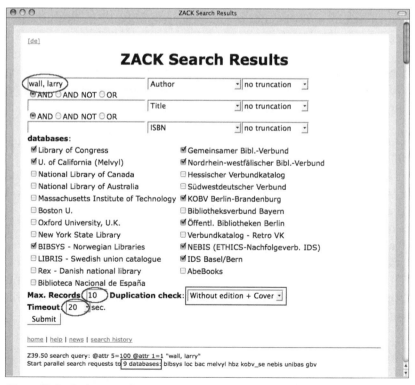

Figure 19.2   Author search on nine different libraries in ZACK

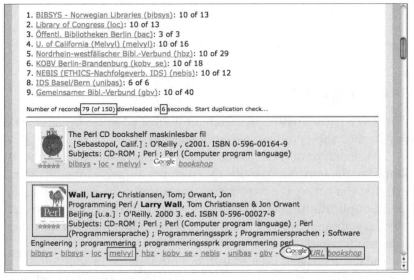

Figure 19.3   ZACK search results

return results and that all nine libraries responded successfully. Your search terms will be highlighted, and covers from Amazon will appear as available. Below each result, the page lists the different libraries where the book was found, along with a link to a Google map showing where each library is located. Last, you have the option of purchasing the title from any number of sites or linking directly to the full text.

Below your search results, you'll have a summary of the search, links to facets, and the ability to rerun the search on other sites (Figure 19.4).

You can easily see that the duplication check narrowed the results from 79 to 28 and that the 62 records found were narrowed to 11. You also have a timeline of books that match your results. The list of authors in the results shows that, from a search for the author Larry Wall, Randal Schwartz also published eight books together with Larry Wall. Clicking on an author will run a new search for just that author. The subjects are printed in a tag cloud, sorted alphabetically, and popular subjects are printed in larger fonts. Clicking these links will run a search solely for that subject.

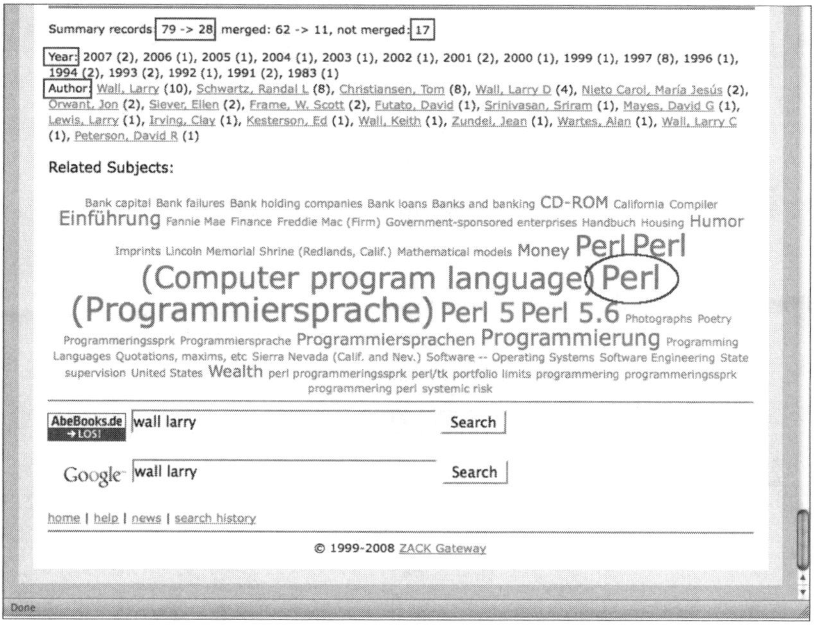

Summary records [79 -> 28] merged: 62 -> 11, not merged: [17]

Year: 2007 (2), 2006 (1), 2005 (1), 2004 (1), 2003 (1), 2002 (1), 2001 (2), 2000 (1), 1999 (1), 1997 (8), 1996 (1), 1994 (2), 1993 (2), 1992 (1), 1991 (2), 1983 (1)

Author: Wall, Larry (10), Schwartz, Randal L (8), Christiansen, Tom (8), Wall, Larry D (4), Nieto Carol, María Jesús (2), Orwant, Jon (2), Siever, Ellen (2), Frame, W. Scott (2), Futato, David (1), Srinivasan, Sriram (1), Mayes, David G (1), Lewis, Larry (1), Irving, Clay (1), Kesterson, Ed (1), Wall, Keith (1), Zundel, Jean (1), Wartes, Alan (1), Wall, Larry C (1), Peterson, David R (1)

Related Subjects:

Bank capital Bank failures Bank holding companies Bank loans Banks and banking CD-ROM California Compiler Einführung Fannie Mae Finance Freddie Mac (Firm) Government-sponsored enterprises Handbuch Housing Humor Imprints Lincoln Memorial Shrine (Redlands, Calif.) Mathematical models Money Perl Perl (Computer program language) Perl (Programmiersprache) Perl 5 Perl 5.6 Photographs Poetry Programmeringssprk Programmiersprache Programmiersprachen Programmierung Programming Languages Quotations, maxims, etc Sierra Nevada (Calif. and Nev.) Software -- Operating Systems Software Engineering State supervision United States Wealth perl programmeringssprk perl/tk portfolio limits programmering programmeringssprk programmering perl systemic risk

AbeBooks.de →LOSI | wall larry   Search

Google | wall larry   Search

home | help | news | search history

© 1999-2008 ZACK Gateway

Done

Figure 19.4   Additional options for narrowing your search on ZACK

ZACK Bookmaps

Each result has a link to a Google map that includes data from your search results. Clicking on the Google Maps icon under the result will bring up a map with markers for each library where your book was found. Figure 19.5 shows a zoomed-in view of Europe showing locations holding *Programming Perl,* by Larry Wall. The top left contains information from Amazon, including the book jacket and reviews. The map identifies the libraries by markers of different colors to make it easy to identify library types. Clicking on the marker for a library (such as the Technical Information Library/Hanover University Library in Figure 19.5) shows you the address, phone number, opening hours, and size of the library, as well as other information.

Other ZACK Tools

In addition to the cataloging and mapping tools, ZACK has additional features to make your searching experience just a little bit better. One of those features is spell checker for authors and book titles.

Figure 19.5 Zoomed-in view of Europe for *Programming Perl*, by Larry Wall

The database for spell-checking author names contains more than 2 million records. So if you misspell the author "Dalitz" as "Dality," ZACK will still be able to find the right author (Figure 19.6). If a search for an author returns zero hits because of too many spelling errors, the spell checker will automatically offer a *Did you mean* search, as found on many popular search engines.

ZACK also has a live search available (opus.tu-bs.de/zack/cgi/livesearch). From here you can see the latest search queries in ZACK, including the covers (Figure 19.7). You can limit this results list to either show all searches on the site or just one user's searches.

Last, ZACK can be added to your browser's search engine list by means of the OpenSearch plug-in (opus.tu-bs.de/zack/opensearch. html) for Firefox and Internet Explorer. This plug-in supports searching ZACK by author, title, and ISBN right from your browser's toolbar (Figure 19.8).

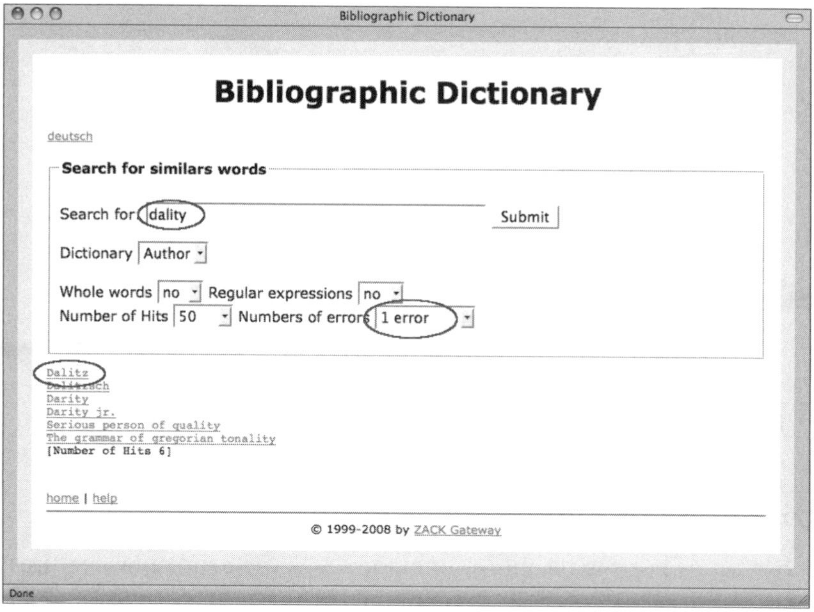

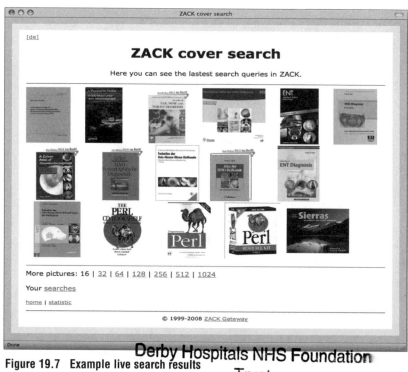

Figure 19.6   If you misspell the author "Dalitz" as "Dality," ZACK will find the right author.

Figure 19.7   Example live search results

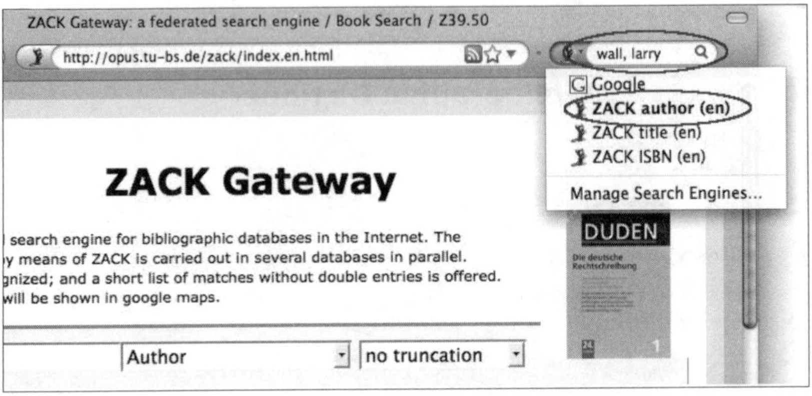

Figure 19.8 Searching ZACK from the browser

Future Wish List

Over time I hope to be able to upgrade ZACK to include new features, tools, and sources of data. Some of the items on this wish list include

- Addition of more large book databases such as Google Book Search (books.google.com)

- Additional APIs, such as Google Book Search for covers

- A format converter for USMARC, UNIMARC, and MAB2

- UTF-8 support

- Semantic searching to better understand what the user wants

- Log file analysis to clarify what the users search for, what they find, and what they really want to find

- Data mining; for example, search for "Larry Wall" -> Author of Perl/Computer Language -> search in a University of Technology library

I'd also like to offer certain ZACK features as web services to promote further mashups. One possible service would be a ZackTOC, a web service for finding books' tables of contents.

Summary

ZACK produces a distributed search that makes it easier to find rare books and saves the user time and effort. By taking advantage of copy cataloging, one can find up to 70 to 80 percent of bibliographic records needed.

The mashups improve the usability and design and make it easier to get the relevant information on a result page, while allowing for a more user-friendly visual representation (e.g., book covers). Mashups also give additional pieces of information about the books (cover, table of contents, full text), as well as information about related books (editions, translations).

An online catalog should be easy to use, just like a search engine. Keep in mind that searching is the core feature of an online catalog. Ninety percent of users just want to search; additional features are used by less than 10 percent of users. This is common knowledge and not a cause for concern. Don't stop thinking about adding new features—even if they are helpful only to a minority.

Credits

I'd like to give credit to:

- University of Technology at Braunschweig for hosting ZACK
- Index Data for the Z39.50 toolkit YAZ
- All libraries that allow access to their Z39.50 server

CHAPTER 20

Federated Database
Search Mashup

Stephen Hedges, Laura Solomon, and Karl Jendretzky
Ohio Public Library Information Network

Libraries spend a considerable amount of money each year on subscriptions to proprietary databases of online information, such as newspaper and magazine articles, authoritative encyclopedias, and reference resources. The current *Gale Directory of Databases* lists more than 20,000 information databases and related products that libraries can purchase, including, of course, the *Gale Directory of Databases*. These databases are so strongly associated with the libraries that purchase them that they are often simply called *library databases*; they allow libraries to gather and provide information that is not normally available on the World Wide Web.

Although the vendors that sell this information devote a great deal of time and effort to making their search interfaces smooth and efficient, many libraries that serve the general public try to offer a single "federated" search interface that pulls information from a variety of library databases simultaneously, saving the user from having to visit each individual database's interface and repeat the search. A handful of commercial vendors offer federated search tools, and the market for such tools has been growing over the past 5 years.[1] Ideally, such an interface provides the library's users with a simple but effective "Google-like" search for accessing the library's entire collection of online resources. As Roy Tennant has written, at their best these tools are "the correct solution for unifying access to a variety of information resources."[2]

If a federated searching tool is desirable for a single public library, consider how much more important it would be for a network of more than 250 public library systems. Such is the case for the Ohio Public Library Information Network (OPLIN).

Since 1996, OPLIN has provided a basic collection of online databases to Ohio public libraries. Currently purchased in cooperation with the Ohio academic library information network (OhioLINK) and the school library network (INFOhio), with additional funds from an Institute of Museum and Library Services LSTA grant awarded by the State Library of Ohio, the total cost of this extensive collection tops $4 million annually. In 2004, the network partners began referring to this communal collection of databases as the *Ohio Web Library*.

The Problem

Although a federated search of these valuable resources may not be as critical in an education environment, where students are often instructed to use a particular database, for public libraries the lack of a good federated search interface results in low use of the databases and a high cost per search. Public library users are uncomfortable with being forced to select which database to search, often with no idea of what type of information a database provides, and with the need to repeat their search in each individual database search interface. Confronted with this task, they simply turn to Google or some other web search engine to find online information and never get access to the information that libraries purchase and provide.

OPLIN began offering a federated search interface to the Ohio Web Library in 2004, when a WebFeat Search Prism was installed. This search tool was based primarily on the search functions included in the Z39.50 information retrieval protocol (ISO 23950), which is the protocol most commonly used by federated search tools. The Library of Congress is the maintenance agency and registration authority for the Z39.50 standard, which specifies a client/server-based protocol for searching and retrieving information from remote databases. Z39.50 is a large standard, with lots of functionality, but usually an implementation does not support the complete standard. Instead, a subset of functions, called a "profile," is commonly used to meet specific requirements. A profile provides a specification for vendors to use when setting up their servers so that search applications can interoperate. For example, the author, title, and subject (ATS) profile defines a basic subset of services for Z39.50 support of public access library catalogs. The ATS profile is quite simple, requiring support for only three search attributes (ATS), and mandates support for MARC (MAchine-Readable Cataloging) record data transfer. Other profiles are more complex to fit more complex needs.[3]

Although the WebFeat Search Prism provided a federated search using Z39.50, the return of search results from a database collection the size of the Ohio Web Library was slow, and results were presented in groupings by source rather than in order of relevance. Nevertheless, it was judged by OPLIN to be the best federated search tool available at the time. By 2007, however, Ohio public librarians were voicing dissatisfaction with these limitations. In focus groups they repeatedly expressed a desire for a search that was "more like Google." OPLIN, for its part, had not made any significant changes to the federated search interface since it had been installed. Clearly it was time for a change.

The Possibilities

In late 2007, OPLIN began the search for a new search. We first con-tacted WebFeat, the existing vendor, to explore newer versions of their product. WebFeat demonstrated WebFeat Express, its newest offering, which had significant improvements over the WebFeat product in use by OPLIN, including control over search results ranking. Ultimately, however, OPLIN rejected this possibility because it still did not allow us enough control over the product to be able to make rapid, incre-mental changes in response to user feedback, which we felt would be an important feature of any new search interface.

Next we investigated Google Custom Search Engine (CSE; www.google.com/coop/cse); after all, librarians had told us they wanted something "more like Google." CSE allows you to create your own Google search against a list of websites you specify. Once you have defined your search targets, Google gives you a simple piece of code for a search box to place on your site. Any search done through this search box starts a Google search, but the search is limited to the sites you have specified. At the time we looked at CSE, there was no way to tailor the ranking of search results; the results that ranked highest in Google's standard algorithm always came to the top. Google staff told us at the time that they were planning to release CSE with the capability for the host site to tailor rankings to reflect the host's preferences or area of expertise, and indeed, this capability was added a few months later.

The biggest shortfall of the Google CSE technology was the fact that the only sources that it could hit were the ones that were already indexed by Google. Although this worked well for open content such as Wikipedia (www.wikipedia.org), proprietary sources such as EBSCO, which require user authentication to access, had no presence. We went through several iterations trying to devise a way to integrate proprietary content. These ranged from possibly using MARC records from EBSCO to build our own open website with the article descriptions and links in it for the Google bot to crawl, to having talks with Google to see if there was any way of making the data available. In the end we found that the CSE just was not well suited for accessing the type of data we provided, and we moved on.

About this time, Index Data announced a demonstration of its MasterKey federated search. OPLIN staff members were impressed by the speed and ease of this product. It had the additional advantage of being built around the Z39.50 protocol, which we knew would work with most of the databases we purchased. Initial discussions with Index Data indicated, however, that the MasterKey hosted search solution was not the best fit for our needs. Rather, Index Data suggested we build a search around its open source pazpar2 metasearching middleware, which is the engine within MasterKey (indexdata.com/pazpar2).

The pazpar2 software is a web-oriented Z39.50 client that can search a lot of targets in parallel and provides on-the-fly integration of the results. It works particularly well with Ajax (Asynchronous JavaScript and XML) for building a dynamic page displaying search results. It provides record merging, relevance ranking, record sorting, and faceted results. This was the option that seemed to offer the functionality we needed, the features we wanted, and the critical ability to make rapid changes. We identified some features of the MasterKey hosted service which we felt could be improved, looked closely at the pazpar2 code, and came to an agreement with Index Data to install a slightly customized version of pazpar2 on one of our servers to be the engine for our federated search.

First Feedback

Although we knew that neither Google CSE nor a hosted MasterKey web service would be our eventual federated search tool, we decided to use these two searches for some early user testing to guide our future decisions.

We built a Google Custom Search and targeted some open websites that had good content, such as NetWellness (www.netwellness. org), Wikipedia, HowStuffWorks (www.howstuffworks.com), and Project Gutenberg (www.gutenberg.org). We took that and the MasterKey demo to the ScanPath Usability Lab at the Kent State University School of Library and Information Science in November 2007 to observe how users reacted to the two searches. ScanPath uses high-tech software to measure and record a user's eye movements while using a website, tracking how often the eye travels to certain areas of a page, how long it lingers, etc. ScanPath staff members also interview users while they are using a page to get them to verbalize their experience.

Our observations stunned us. Until that time, we had not appreciated how thoroughly Google has defined the online searching behavior of most people. Users expected results lists that looked like Google, down to the colors of the components of a search result. They were adept at judging the reliability of search results based on the URL (Uniform Resource Locator); for example, URLs ending in .org were judged to be generally trustworthy, while URLs containing the word "blog" might contain interesting, but not necessarily reliable, information. They expected the links in search results to take them to another website, not directly to an article. Clearly the librarians were right; to meet user expectations, libraries needed a federated search that was "more like Google."

The Mashup

With this user feedback in hand, we now started putting the pieces of the new search together. First, we contracted with Index Data to do the custom install of their pazpar2 and JavaScript software on our server. OPLIN owned the www.ohioweblibrary.org domain name from a previous promotional campaign, and with the agreement of the other library organizations that contribute funds to purchasing the Ohio Web Library database collection, we decided to repurpose this domain as the site of our new federated search. On the server for this site, Index Data installed pazpar2 configuration files for our list of database Z39.50 targets, as well as a custom version of the JavaScript that writes the search results to the page.

This custom JavaScript wrote page content to three divisions: one containing the results; one containing a list of sources; and one containing a list of subjects. We also asked that the search results be modified so that they showed the title of the article (which was also a link to the article), the name of the database containing the article, the date of the article if available, and a brief description of the article.

While Index Data was working on their installation, OPLIN contracted with a local Ohio web design company, 361 Studios, to redesign the www.ohiowebilibrary.org site. We specified a very simple, clean layout dominated by one search box. As much as possible, the design was to rely on a CSS (Cascading Style Sheet) for the page look, and the entire design had to be compliant with accessibility standards. We also specified that the initial page load had to be less than 100 KB. Other than that, 361 Studios had a free hand in designing the graphics and navigation for the page.

Once we had the pazpar2 configuration files, the custom JavaScript, and the CSS, we started working on fitting the pieces together. The pazpar2 software uses one configuration file for each Z39.50 target to be searched. We set up a basic Z39.50 client to test the pazpar2 configuration files against our targets and see the raw data the target Z39.50 server was returning in response to our queries. This was not something we had to do, but we wanted to understand as much as possible about the processes going on in the background during a search. Because we wanted to be able to make fast changes to the search interface, it was important to know how each part of the configuration files affected the search results.

We also looked a little at the JavaScript, again wanting to be able to understand how we might make changes. In this case, however, the complexity of the script led us to decide to try *not* to make changes. If at some point in the future we felt something in the JavaScript needed to be changed, we decided our best option was to contact Index Data and make arrangements for it to make the changes. After our initial investigation, however, it seemed likely that most changes we wanted could be accomplished by changing the pazpar2 configuration files and the CSS.

It did not take very long for us to get a basic federated search against a few targets up and running for testing. Now we began to work on turning the basic search into something good enough for production. We set a production launch date of July 1, 2008.

Z39.50 Translators

One weakness of using Z39.50 as the protocol for retrieving information from commercial databases is the fact that not all database vendors operate Z39.50 servers. In 2000, Sebastian Hammer, cofounder of Index Data, wrote that "most major library-systems vendors now support Z39.50 to some extent."[4] It was the words "most" and "to some extent" that would cause problems for OPLIN.

Several of the vendors supplying databases to the Ohio Web Library collection do not support Z39.50, including a couple of well-known vendors such as *World Book* and *Facts on File*. How could we get their databases included in our federated search? The answer came indirectly from our previous federated search vendor, WebFeat. WebFeat received a patent in late 2004 on a method for managing the authentication and communication necessary to perform a search against a licensed database and convert the results into Z39.50, XML (eXtensible Markup Language), or HTTP format. In other words, WebFeat created a tool that could access unstructured data and deliver it in a structured format. It called this access tool a *translator* and built thousands of translators for databases that do not support structured data. These translators are prominently used in the WebFeat federated search products.

OPLIN now needed to find a way to get translators from the very vendor whose search product we were abandoning. Fortunately, someone else had anticipated this problem. CARE Affiliates had developed a partnership with both WebFeat and Index Data to market OpenTranslators, WebFeat translators that are hosted on Index Data servers for a fee to allow a federated search tool to get to unstructured databases, including open sites on the World Wide Web.[5] OPLIN provided CARE Affiliates with a list of database and open web targets for which we wanted translators, and CARE Affiliates took care of having the translators built, hosted, and made available as targets for pazpar2 configuration files. Once these were all in place, we were able to do a federated search across all the Ohio Web Library databases, as well as some open sites, such as Wikipedia, NetWellness, and OAIster (www.oaister.org).

Making It User Friendly

Now we went back to the results of our early usability testing, included some feedback from test users of our new prototype, and started adding some amenities based on what our users might expect.

For one thing, we knew that users would try to do advanced "Google" searches, meaning using quotes around phrases, plus signs to make some words mandatory, etc. Most users seemed to assume that if Google search uses these conventions, every search uses them. While Z39.50 can handle some complex searching behavior, it does not use the Google notation conventions. Moreover, although many library information vendors may support Z39.50 "to some extent," quite a few do not support complex Z39.50 queries. We learned that including quotes and other Google notations in the search term often caused our search software to crash, so one of the first things we did was set up a parsing routine to strip these problem characters from users' search terms before passing the terms to pazpar2. We hope someday to find a work-around that will allow pseudo-phrase searching when terms are enclosed in quotes, but for now the quotes are ignored.

Another amenity was actually specified in our instructions to Index Data for customizing the JavaScript. The default pazpar2 JavaScript behavior was to search against either all targets or one target; we asked that this be modified so that we could pass a string of specific targets to pazpar2. This allowed us to group several related databases into one "category" search, such as Health, Careers, or Business. We built a drop-down box on the search page containing these groupings of sources so that the user could limit a search to targets with a specific kind of information.

We also added a "Searching …" progress bar to the page. This is *not* needed to show the user that the search has started, because the JavaScript starts writing results to the page as soon as the user launches the search. Rather, it is needed to let the user know when the search is finished, because the results list is continuously rewritten by the JavaScript until the search is complete. Without the progress bar, the user sees the page "jumping" as results appear and disappear, and this could be disconcerting. The progress bar distracts from this effect and provides the user with a little more information about what is happening to the page.

The heavy use of JavaScript on the page also places the browser in a very insignificant role. Unlike a standard webpage that is sent from the server and loaded a single time on the user's browser, the search's use of Ajax makes the page act much more like a running application. The browser and the server are constantly communicating back and forth, updating the current view of the page, and reacting to new events created by the user. Although this has the advantage of making the search work in any browser that has JavaScript enabled, it can confuse users who are not used to sites that make such heavy use of JavaScript and try to navigate to a previous search by using the browser's navigation buttons. To try to avoid this confusion, we added a small "do not use back button" note in the upper left corner of the screen. We hope to be able to remove this as users become more accustomed to Ajax pages.

We also added a spell checker, to suggest spellings for search terms that seemed to be misspelled. The problem with trying to implement search suggestion functionality is that for it to actually make good suggestions, it needs a large bank of data to draw from. We looked into just using dictionary files, but that type of setup would not automatically change with trends and we would have to manually update the dictionary. Next we took a look at the application programming interface (API) made available by Google. Though this is something that Google used to offer, it had changed what the API exposed, and search suggestions were not available at that time. The same path that led us to Google brought us to Yahoo! next. Yahoo! also offers an API, and using a simple JSON (JavaScript Object Notation) call, we were able to retrieve search suggestions from Yahoo! These suggestions tend to be more accurate than anything we could construct in-house, because they have a large database of search query information to pull from.

The display of the search results received a lot of attention as we developed the interface. The pazpar2 middleware does a good job of ranking results by relevancy, so that was not a problem. It also includes an option to rank results by date, although the effectiveness of this ranking is limited somewhat by the fact that not all vendors have their Z39.50 servers configured to return date information. But other than the ranking, there was the question of what information to display in the search results. We decided to display four items of information for each individual search result: the title, the source(s), the date, and a brief description. Not all Z39.50 servers returned all of this information, but at a minimum the search result displays title and source. In all cases, the title is a link to the article (Figure 20.1).

In most cases, the search results link to full-text articles, but some of the EBSCO databases included in the Ohio Web Library also contain just citations to articles, not the full text of the articles. In these cases, we found that in the Z39.50 data EBSCO makes available, no

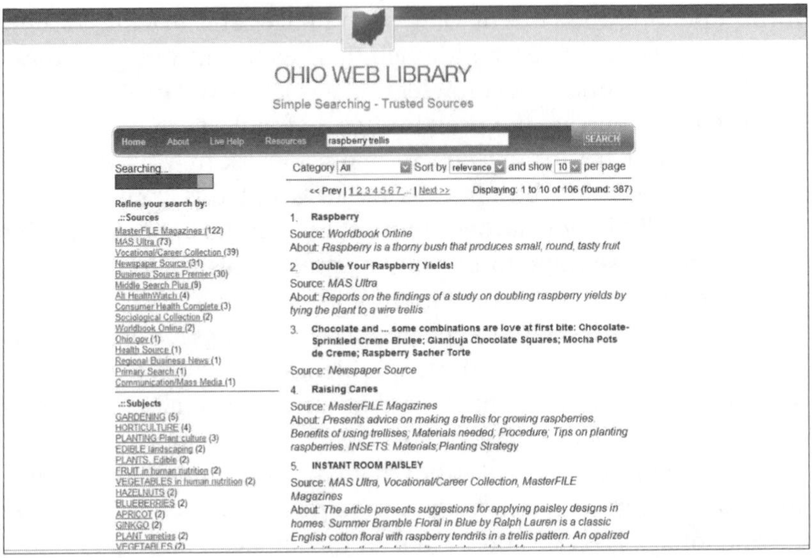

Figure 20.1   Each title in the search results links to the article in question.

URL to the article is returned if only a citation exists. By parsing the returned data before it was displayed on the search results page, we were able to test for the presence of a URL. If the search result failed this test, we appended "(Citation only)" to the title of the article to warn the user.

Once a user finds an article of interest and clicks on the title, then the process of authenticating the article begins. If the link points to an "open" article from the Open Archives Initiative, Wikipedia, NetWellness, etc., then no authentication is necessary, but if the source of the article is a proprietary database, then we have to check to make sure the user is covered by our license agreement with the vendor. OPLIN has used EZproxy for several years to handle this task and still uses that system to handle Ohio Web Library user authentication. We acquired EZproxy before it was purchased by OCLC. Like pazpar2, EZproxy is middleware; it authenticates users against our local authentication system and provides remote access to our licensed content based on the user's authorization. In OPLIN's case, we use the IP (Internet Protocol) addresses assigned to libraries as the basic test to authenticate a session. Traffic coming from within a library passes through the authentication with no interruption. Users accessing the system from outside a library can give their public library card number (or a username and password if they are associated with a K–12 school) to authenticate their session. Once they have been authenticated, they can access as many articles as they want without any further interruptions; the system remembers them until they close their browser.

Finally, we included a "Live Help" link to the Ohio KnowItNow 24/7 reference service (www.knowitnow.org). If users find the whole searching process to be too difficult or unproductive, they have instant recourse to a live reference librarian to assist them. KnowItNow is a live online information service provided free of charge for the citizens of Ohio by the State Library of Ohio and local public libraries. Professional librarians are available 24 hours a day, 7 days a week to answer reference questions and assist Ohioans in finding information (Figure 20.2).

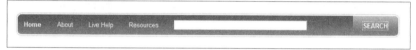

Figure 20.2   A link to "Live Help" is prominently placed in the header of our website.

Launching, Relaunching, Relaunching ...

Not all these changes were implemented on July 1, 2008, when the www.ohioweblibrary.org page was launched, nor do we ever expect to have *all* our changes implemented. Whenever we introduce the site to librarians, we emphasize that the open source code that runs the site allows us to incorporate their suggestions to make the site better. Several of the changes mentioned above came about because of suggestions from librarians using the site. In most cases, we were able to make the changes within hours.

As mentioned earlier, our goal is to continually be making small, incremental changes to the search interface based on user feedback. Because so much of the code that runs the site is open source, we have exceptional ability to do just that. The www.ohioweblibrary.org search interface will never be "finished" until the day we take the site down. We intend to just keep mashing cool things into it as we find them.

To recap, these are the components of our mashup (so far):

- Pazpar2 (with customizations)
- OpenTranslators

- Yahoo! spell-checker API

- EZproxy

- Custom page design

- Custom scripting

We're proud of what we have built, and we invite you to check it out at www.ohioweblibrary.org (Figure 20.03).

Figure 20.3 www.ohioweblibrary.org

Endnotes

1. Alexis Linoski and Tine Walczyk, "Federated Search 101," *Library Journal Net Connect* 133 (Summer 2008): 2.

2. Roy Tennant, "The Right Solution: Federated Search Tools," *Library Journal* 128:11 (June 15, 2003): 28.

3. For a good general discussion of Z39.50 and profiles, see Mark Hinnebusch and Charles B. Lowry, "Z39.50 at Ten Years: How Stands the Standard?" *Journal of Academic Librarianship* 23:3 (May 1997): 217.

4. Sebastian Hammer, "Dr. Metadata, or: How I Learned to Stop Worrying and Love Z39.50," *American Libraries* 31:9 (Oct. 2000): 54.

5. At the end of July 2008, LibLime acquired this division of CARE Affiliates.

CHAPTER 21

Electronic Dissertation Mashups Using SRU

Michael C. Witt
Purdue University Libraries

Leveraging Electronic Theses and Dissertations

Most, if not all, academic libraries collect the doctoral dissertations and master's theses written by their institutions' students. In some cases, the library may administer the thesis office that manages the process of accepting, producing, and publishing theses. (Both doctoral dissertations and master's theses can be referred to as *theses*.) From a collection development perspective, theses represent one of the most unique and scholarly collections in an academic library. Their subject matter is highly specialized and refined as a product of students earning advanced degrees. In the case of dissertations, these are typically a doctorate or other terminal degree.

Faculty who are the foremost experts in their fields advise these students; the research methods and findings are deemed original and are thoroughly reviewed by faculty before a degree is granted. In this way, theses represent an important part of the record of the knowledge that is created by an institution of higher education, and preserving and providing access to its theses is closely aligned to the scholarly mission of an academic library.

With the emergence of digital libraries in the past 15 years, it is no surprise that many librarians have viewed their collections of theses as "low-hanging fruit" to be picked for digitization and inclusion in online institutional repositories. Apart from their scholarly value, theses may be particularly appealing to librarians because there is a great deal of local control and standardization in the document submission and production processes that can result in high-quality descriptive metadata and uniformity in description and format across the body of work. Students are given strict guidelines to follow in preparing their documents, and they are self-motivated to provide thorough and accurate information to avoid having their submissions rejected. They are typically required to fill out a form containing mandatory fields such as the title, author, advisers, committee members, degree granted, date of publication, abstract, department, and subject codes. Entries can be controlled; for example, the university's personnel directory may be used as a name authority. For many years now, theses have been created using word processing software and are submitted in an electronic format. These electronic theses and dissertations (ETDs, as they are commonly called) are easily captured as "born digital" content by simply adding a step to the end of the thesis-processing workflow to deposit them into a digital library or online repository.

This was the case at the Purdue University Libraries in 2006 when it launched its Purdue e-Pubs (docs.lib.purdue.edu) digital document repository, with the majority of its original content consisting of electronic dissertations. Full-text document downloads and complete, qualified Dublin Core[1] metadata records are available in the Purdue e-Pubs repository for all dissertations awarded by the University since 1997. After its first 2 years of operation, the repository grew to include 6,719 electronic dissertations that have registered more than 100,000 full-text downloads (Figure 21.1).

As awareness of the electronic dissertation collection grew, we took advantage of opportunities to interact with our campus to better understand how our users perceived and used the collection. We heard from the Graduate School Admissions Office, who wanted to use the dissertations to help recruit new, prospective graduate students to the university. We heard from departmental faculty who wanted to include dynamic links to the dissertations they advised in their faculty profile webpages. And we heard from the vice president for research, who was interested in building a search engine to help people locate faculty researchers by indexing the dissertations for which our faculty served as advisers. Although the general perception of making the collection available online in Purdue e-Pubs was very positive and usage statistics were good, it became clear that additional value and new points of access could be created by making the collection available to be integrated with systems from other units on campus and beyond. In other words, we needed the ability to mashup our dissertations!

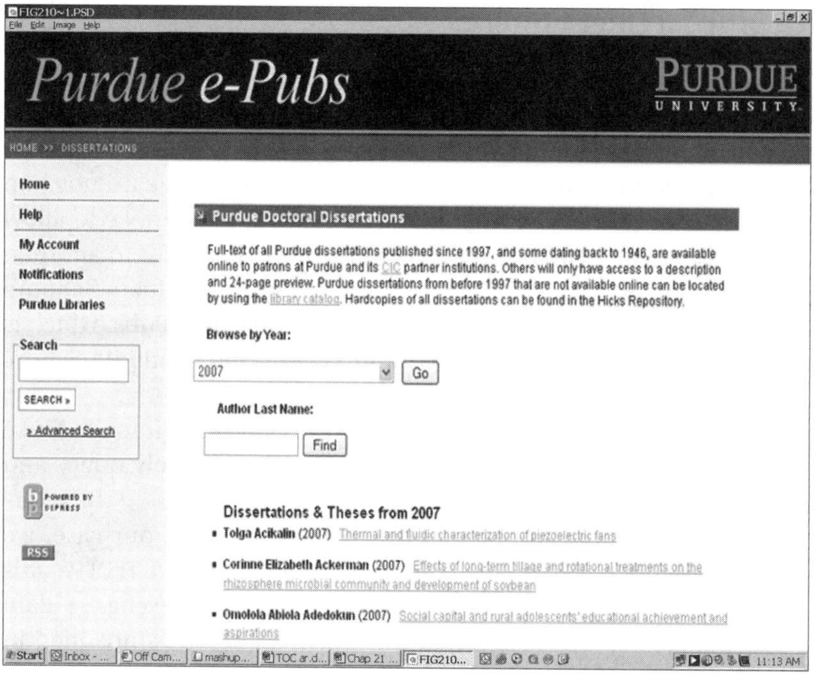

Figure 21.1   Purdue e-Pubs doctoral dissertations (docs.lib.purdue.edu/ dissertations)

To set the stage for creating these mashups, we put four key ingredients in place:

- Unique digital content of high scholarly value housed together in one place

- Well-structured and highly descriptive metadata records

- Needs that were stated loudly and clearly by our users for new ways of accessing the content

- Support from our administration to experiment with new ways of adding value to our services by representing our content outside a library context

All that we needed to do was develop an appropriate interface for exposing the collection and then begin mashing up our dissertations.

Creating a Query Interface

Our selection of an interface was guided primarily by the functionalities that were required by our users but also by a desire to adhere to adopted, open standards and to not reinvent the wheel. As opposed to a *user* interface such as the one presented by Purdue e-Pubs in a web browser, we needed to implement a *machine* interface to allow communication from a program running on one system to another. For example, we wanted to let a user visiting the Graduate School's website search and locate dissertations from Purdue e-Pubs (which is located on a different server) without leaving the Graduate School website.

Because all these machines present a web interface, it made sense to employ a *web service* to provide a means to remotely query and return dissertation information. In fact, many mashups on the internet are built on top of one or more web services. In our case, we implemented a "RESTful" web service that uses the same HTTP commands that web browsers use to communicate and exchange data with web servers.[2] To enable our mashups, a query is embedded in the URL (Uniform Resource Locator) provided by a client, but instead of returning a webpage from the server, the web service returns encoded dissertation metadata records from the repository.

The Search and Retrieve URL (SRU) protocol maintained by the Library of Congress was a perfect fit for us. SRU defines a standard mechanism and format for querying remote databases over the internet and for the structure of their responses.[3] It is an open standard that has evolved from the popular Z39.50 protocol, which has been widely adopted by libraries and supported by software such as citation managers and federated search engines. Implementations of SRU and related tools have been developed on a number of different platforms and in familiar programming languages, such as Perl and Java. Most important, SRU provides the functionality we needed in a web service.

SRU supports three operations: Explain, Scan, and searchRetrieve. Invoking the Explain operation returns a record that contains information about the server, such as the version of the protocol it is running, a description of the database and its location, and what functions are supported by the interface. The purpose of the Scan operation is to request a range of search terms from the database's index and the number of hits that match them. So a client would "scan" the remote database's index, much as a reader would scan the index at the back of a book to see what topics are covered in it. The third operation, searchRetrieve, provides the meat and potatoes for our mashups: a means for the client to submit a search and then retrieve matching records from the remote database.[4]

SRU's searchRetrieve operation uses the CQL (Contextual Query Language), a simple but powerful language for expressing queries. CQL supports searching with free text, Boolean and relative operators, nesting, proximity, and modifiers, although a given SRU interface may provide only some of these functions.[5] For example, to retrieve metadata records from our repository with the term "foo" in any field, a client would construct a URL that looks like

```
http://sru.lib.purdue.edu/dir/sru?operation
=searchRetrieve&recordSchema=dc&query=foo
```

The result is that an XML (eXtensible Markup Language) document is returned to the client that contains matching records in a qualified Dublin Core schema. The records can be displayed or otherwise used by the client application in a mashup.

Putting a New Skin on an Old Drum

XML is a markup language for expressing and transporting structured data, and as its name implies, it is extensible in that users can define their own elements. Where the purpose of HTML is to format and display information for human beings to read as webpages in a web browser, XML is intended for machine processing.[6] It is widely adopted and commonly used for data interchange on the internet. XML documents are self-descriptive, and they can be validated by means of schemas that are published on the World Wide Web.

We modeled our schema after the Open Archives Initiative (OAI) XML Schema for Dublin Core[7] (DC) because its generic nature lends itself well to interoperability, and its simple set of elements mapped easily to metadata we already had for the dissertations. The schema was also familiar to us from metadata-harvesting applications that we had used in other digital library projects. The mapping from our metadata to DC elements was straightforward: The dissertation's author became dc.creator, the title became dc.title, the dissertation abstract became dc.description, the date of publication became dc.date, and the URL to a dissertation in the repository became dc.identifier. We chose to represent the dissertation advisers as a repeating, qualified element called dc.adviser. Records constituted from these metadata elements provided the underlying data needed for representing the dissertations in our mashups.

One powerful feature of XML is its ability to convert a document from one format to another on the fly using XSLT (XML Stylesheet Language Transformation).[8] A stylesheet acts as a template for processing the data from one document and reconstituting it into another. For example, an XML document that consists of DC metadata records could be transformed by a stylesheet into XHTML and presented as a list of records on a webpage. This processing can be done by a client such as a web browser—the newest versions of Mozilla Firefox, Microsoft Internet Explorer, Opera, and Apple Safari all support XSLT—or the document can be rendered by the server. In fact, the SRU specification allows the client to provide a link to a stylesheet with a query so that the results can be transformed and returned in another format.

A Tale of Three Mashups

Although all of this may sound complex and technical, it is intelligible once you can decode the acronyms! To summarize how these technologies work together: A client constructs a URL that contains a CQL query and a link to a stylesheet and sends it to an SRU interface, which is running as a web service on a server. The server executes the query and uses the stylesheet to format and return the matching results from the database to the client. Now that we understand how the interface works, let's take a look at three examples of mashups that were built using it.

Graduate School

The Graduate School Admissions Office used the electronic dissertations in the process of recruiting new graduate students to the University. The dissertations serve as advertisements of the quality and quantity of research being done by our students. Admissions counselors consult with students one on one to help them identify faculty who share their same research interests and areas of specialization by searching the dissertations in the repository. The students can then contact the faculty to be their potential advisers.

Originally, the Admissions Office contacted the library to ask about linking to the repository from the Admissions Office website.

The Admissions Office wanted prospective students to be able to search and browse dissertations in advance of applying to the university, but it was concerned about redirecting students to the Purdue e-Pubs website because it had a different look and feel and did not link back to the Graduate School website. It was critical that their users "stick" to the Graduate School website so that, after learning more about the university, they could easily click a link to complete an online application.

This was easily accomplished by embedding a "Search Dissertations" box as an HTML form in the Graduate School webpages (Figure 21.2). A snippet of JavaScript accepts the form input, constructs a simple CQL query and URL, and sends it to the SRU interface of the repository. We used Stylus Studio Pro (www.stylus studio.com) to take a snapshot of the Graduate School website and create an XSLT stylesheet from it. The SRU interface parses the URL to execute the query and uses the stylesheet to return a list of dissertations in a webpage that has the same look and feel as the Graduate School's website (Figure 21.3). The stylesheet uses the dc.identifier to

Figure 21.2   The "Search Dissertations" box allows potential students to search e-Pubs without leaving the Graduate School's website.

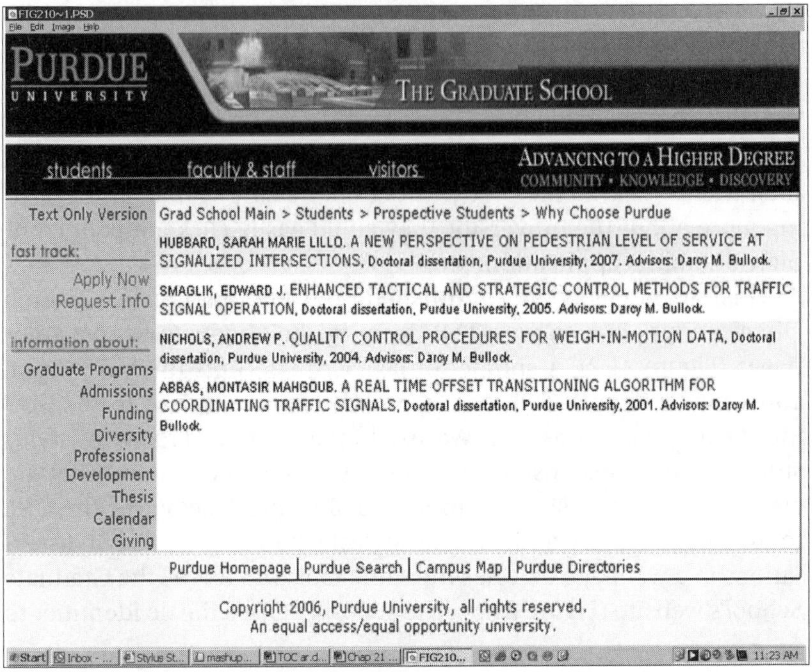

Figure 21.3   A list of dissertations returned from e-Pubs that has the same look and feel as the Graduate School's website

anchor a link to the dissertation so that a user can click on the title of the dissertation to view its full text from the repository.

Faculty Profiles

After presenting the mashup to the Graduate Council, we were approached by a faculty member from the Department of Civil Engineering who wanted to know if he could use the same interface to list the dissertations of students he advised on his faculty profile webpage. His department used a content management system (CMS) to generate webpages for its faculty members that listed common information about them such as their contact information, degrees, research interests, classes taught, and publications. Because the faculty had to manually update much of their own information on the webpages, keeping the content current was a major challenge. By capturing the faculty member's first and last names from variables that were provided by the CMS, it was easy to add a "Doctoral Dissertations" link to every faculty member's profile (Figure 21.4) that dynamically queried the SRU interface on the dc.adviser field of the

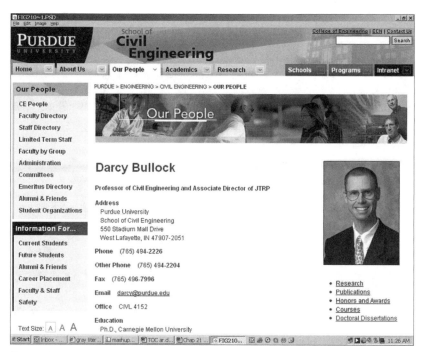

Figure 21.4   A Doctoral Dissertations link can be found under faculty members'
photos on their profile page

dissertation index. As new dissertations are added to the repository, the index is updated so that the links always display current information. We originally created a stylesheet that matched the design of the faculty profiles; interestingly, though, the faculty felt that if the dissertations were coming from the library, then the webpage should look like the library's webpages and not their department's (Figure 21.5). Unlike the Graduate School, they desired that users "wander" from the dissertations to their other content in the repository such as their technical papers and other gray literature.

Indiana Directory of University Research Expertise

The third mashup example is a component of the Indiana Database of University Research Expertise (INDURE; www.indure.org), a project that originated as a collaboration between Purdue's Department of Computer Science and the Indiana Economic Development Corporation. INDURE is a statewide directory of university researchers and a search engine of their research interests, patents,

Figure 21.5   List of dissertations for which the faculty member was an adviser

grants, and collaborators (Figure 21.6). The purpose of INDURE is to help researchers and businesses in the state of Indiana identify new opportunities to collaborate as well as to aid research administration and to promote the commercialization of research outputs.

Data is fed into INDURE from the personnel and sponsored programs systems from Purdue, Indiana, and Ball State Universities and the University of Notre Dame. Researchers and administrators can also manually add and update information such as keywords to describe their areas of research. Using the SRU interface to the electronic dissertations, a dynamic data feed was created to pull DC metadata records from the repository into the back end database for INDURE. In this case, the SRU client is a program that downloads records directly into INDURE and not a web browser, so a stylesheet was not needed to format the records for display in a webpage. A list of dissertations is presented for each researcher in INDURE (Figure 21.7), and the records are indexed to improve the precision of the INDURE search engine. The computer scientists working on the project had a great appreciation for the descriptive, structured metadata that the repository provided to them—and, by extension, to our

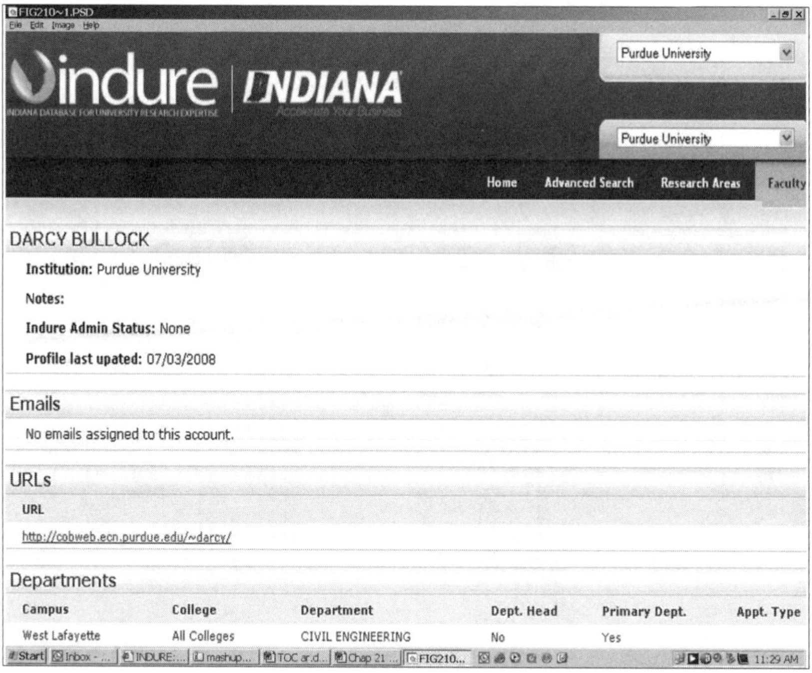

Figure 21.6   Page for a Purdue faculty member on INDURE

librarians. In many cases, the metadata describing the dissertations of the faculty's students was richer and more accurate than the information that the faculty members themselves provided to INDURE.

Wrapping Up

The technology that enabled these mashups is interesting—and, I'll admit, even seductive—but this work was driven by the core principles of librarianship and not done for the sake of the technology itself. We are utilizing metadata to create new points of access to a collection, helping our users locate and use this information in a convenient and purposeful manner, and promoting further scholarship. At the same time, we are increasing the visibility and value of the library to the university by exposing our collections to be used outside a library context for other purposes, such as recruiting new students, helping faculty members maintain their vitae, and facilitating new research collaborations in our state. As librarians approach changes in scholarly communication and a rapidly evolving information environment,

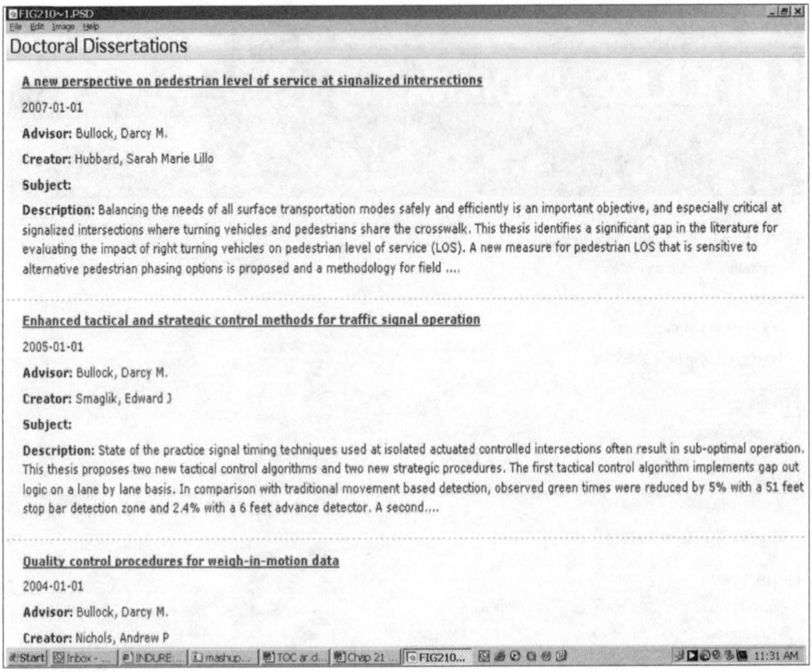

Figure 21.7 Dissertation listing from e-Pubs printed on INDURE

mashups can be one tool to better meet the information needs of our users and create new value in our services. What is even more exciting than the mashups that we have created are the possibilities of mashups that others may now create for themselves using the interface. Herein lies the promise of using open standards to expose library collections to creative and unintended uses.

Endnotes

1. Dublin Core Metadata Initiative, "DCMI Metadata Terms," dublincore.org/documents/dcmi-terms.

2. Ryan Tomako, "How I Explained REST to My Wife," tomayko.com/writings/rest-to-my-wife.

3. Search/Retrieve Via URL Editorial Board, "SRU Version 1.2 Specifications," Library of Congress, www.loc.gov/standards/sru/specs.

4. Eric Lease Morgan, "An Introduction to the Search/Retrieve URL Service (SRU)," *Ariadne* no. 40 (July 2004), www.ariadne.ac.uk/issue40/morgan.

5. Search/Retrieve Via URL Editorial Board, "CQL: Contextual Query Language (SRU Version 1.2 Specifications)," Library of Congress, www.loc.gov/standards/sru/specs/cql.html.

6. W3Schools, "XML Tutorial," www.w3schools.com/xml/default.asp.

7. Pete Johnson, "XML Schema for Dublin Core," Open Archives Initiative, www.openarchives.org/OAI/2.0/oai_dc.xsd.

8. World Wide Web Consortium, "XSL Transformations (XSLT) Version 1.0)," www.w3.org/TR/xslt.

Afterword

Nicole C. Engard

Is your head spinning yet—or are you ready to jump right in? Let's go back to the beginning: *A mashup is a web application that uses content from more than one source to create a single new service displayed in a single graphical interface.* Put simply, a mashup takes data from two or more web services and mashes them together to create something the original developers never thought of. To create a mashup, you must first look to see if the site you would like to pull data from has a public application programming interface (API). If the site offers you the ability to mash up its data with someone else's, then you're all set to create your first mashup.

While this is a very simplified way to summarize mashups, it is the basic gist of what the authors in the first section of this book taught you. Once you find the API for the service that interests you, you just need to read the instructions and the terms thoroughly before moving on.

So, where do you start? When talking with librarians, I always recommend starting small and building up to the bigger, grander mashups. Start by creating a simple pipe on Yahoo! Pipes (pipes.yahoo.com) to mash up feeds for area libraries or local news sources. Then try using some of the tools that offer graphical interfaces for their mashups, such as Delicious (delicious.com). Sometimes it even helps if you just start with a mashup for your own personal use. You can also copy examples from this book: That's why we shared screenshots and code snippets from working projects.

The key to learning new technologies is taking time to play without fear. Once you free yourself from worrying about breaking things, you'll be surprised at what you can achieve.

Don't get caught up in trying to remember all the terminology. You can always refer to the book, the companion website (mashups.web2 learning.net), or your favorite reference resource to refresh your memory. The most important thing to take away from this guide is the knowledge that librarians can, and are, using mashups to improve on their services—and there is just a little bit of learning separating you from them.

I hope that you have taken away at least one mashup that will improve the way you provide services to your patrons via the web. Should you want to share your success stories with others, feel free to contact me at nengard@gmail.com, and I will post your *Library Mashups* story to the book's blog.

Websites

Websites are listed in alphabetical order by chapter. All of these links can be found online at mashups.web2learning.net, where they will be kept up-to-date.

Chapter 1: What Is a Mashup?

The Ad Generator, theadgenerator.org
Amazon, www.amazon.com
Amazon Web Services, aws.amazon.com
Ann Arbor District Library Catalog, www.aadl.org/catalog
Book Burro: The Book Browsing Companion, www.bookburro.org
Bookr, www.pimpampum.net/bookr
Cambridge Libraries and Galleries, Library Locations & Hours,
    cambridgelibraries.ca/library.cfm?subsection=locations
Colr Pickr, Color Fields, krazydad.com/colrpickr
Data Mining 101: Finding Subversives with Amazon Wishlists,
    Applefritter, www.applefritter.com/bannedbooks
EVDB, eventful.com
Flickr, www.flickr.com
Four Obsessions: Reading, Writing, Cooking and Crafting,
    4obsessions.blogspot.com
Google, www.google.com
Google Maps, maps.google.com
Google Street View, maps.google.com/help/maps/streetview
Google Video, video.google.com
Hillsborough County Public Library Cooperative, Full Service
    Library Locations, www.hcplc.org/hcplc/liblocales
Hillsborough County Public Library Cooperative, Map of All
    Locations, www.hcplc.org/hcplc/liblocales/locationsallmap.html
Information Environment Service Registry, iesr.ac.uk

LazyLibrary, www.lazylibrary.com

Library Application Program Interfaces (APIs), TechEssence.info, techessence.info/apis

LibraryThing, www.librarything.com

Microsoft Popfly, www.popfly.com

MySpace, www.myspace.com

ProgrammableWeb, www.programmableweb.com

Superpatron: Edward Vielmetti Is Mobilizing the Friends of the Library for the Blind, vielmetti.typepad.com/superpatron

Technorati, technorati.com

Viral Video Chart, viralvideochart.unrulymedia.com

Yahoo!, www.yahoo.com

Yahoo! People Search, people.yahoo.com

Yahoo! Pipes, pipes.yahoo.com

YouTube, www.youtube.com

Chapter 2: Behind the Scenes: Some Technical Details on Mashups

Ajax: A New Approach to Web Applications, www.adaptivepath.com/ideas/essays/archives/000385.php

Amazon, www.amazon.com

The Beauty of REST, www.xml.com/pub/a/2004/03/17/udell.html

cURL and libcurl, curl.haxx.se

Dapper, www.dapper.net

Feedreader.com, www.feedreader.com

Flickr, www.flickr.com

Google, www.google.com

Google Code, APIs and Developer Tools, code.google.com/more

How to Add an API to Your Web Service, particletree.com/features/how-to-add-an-api-to-your-web-service

How to Create a REST Protocol, www.xml.com/pub/a/2004/12/01/restful-web.html

How to Design a Good API and Why It Matters, www.slideshare.net/guestbe92f4/how-to-design-a-good-a-p-i-and-why-it-matters-g-o-o-g-l-e

HTML URL Encoding Reference, W3 Schools, www.w3schools.com/TAGS/ref_urlencode.asp

Information Environment Service Registry, iesr.ac.uk

Implementing REST Web Services: Best Practices and Guidelines, www.xml.com/pub/a/2004/08/11/rest.html

Intel Mash Maker, mashmaker.intel.com/web/index.php

JackBe.com: Presto, www.jackbe.com/products

JSON and the Dynamic Script Tag: Easy, XML-less Web Services for JavaScript, www.xml.com/pub/a/2005/12/21/json-dynamic-script-tag.html

Library Application Program Interfaces (APIs), TechEssence.info, techessence.info/apis

Library Software Manifesto, TechEssence.info, techessence.info/manifesto

LibraryThing, www.librarything.com

Mashed Library (sponsored by UKOLN), mashedlibrary.ning.com

Mashup Camp, www.mashupcamp.com

Mashup Feed, ProgrammableWeb, www.mashupfeed.com

Mashup Guide: A Blog about Raymond Yee's Book *Pro Web 2.0 Mashups: Remixing Data and Web Services*, blog.mashupguide.net

Mashup the Library: A Workshop on Mashup Technology and the Art of Remixing Library and Information Resources, carl-acrl.org/ig/carlitn/archives.html

Mashup University 4: Intro to Mashups, www.slideshare.net/jhherren/mashup-university-4-intro-to-mashups

Microsoft Popfly, www.popfly.com

Microsoft Silverlight, silverlight.net

OASIS SOA Reference Model TC, www.oasis-open.org/committees/tc_home.php?wg_abbrev=soa-rm

openkapow, openkapow.com

"Percent-encoding," Wikipedia, en.wikipedia.org/wiki/Percent-encoding

Poster :: Firefox Add-ons, addons.mozilla.org/en-US/firefox/addon/2691

ProgrammableWeb, www.programmableweb.com

The REST Dialogues, duncan-cragg.org/blog/tag/dialogue

REST Wiki, www.markbaker.ca/restwiki [**ED: URL doesn't work.**]

Scraping with Style: scrAPI toolkit for Ruby, blog.labnotes.org/2006/07/11/scraping-with-style-scrapi-toolkit-for-ruby

Semantic Search the US Library of Congress, blog.programmableweb.com/2008/04/29/semantic-search-the-us-library-of-congress

Serena Business Mashups, www.serena.com/mashups

The Social OPAC, www.thesocialopac.net

STREST (Service-Trampled REST) Will Break Web 2.0, duncan-cragg.
org/blog/post/strest-service-trampled-rest-will-break-web-20

Technorati, www.technorati.com

W3 Schools SOAP Tutorial, www.w3schools.com/soap

Web 2.0 & Mashups: How People Can Tap into the "Grid" for Fun &
Profit, www.slideshare.net/wuzziwug/web-20-mashups-how-
people-can-tap-into-the-grid-for-fun-profit-20924

Web Services + JSON = Dump Your Proxy, www.theurer.cc/blog/
2005/12/15/web-services-json-dump-your-proxy

World Wide Web Consortium (W3C): What Is a Web Service?,
www.w3.org/TR/ws-arch/#whatis

Yahoo!, www.yahoo.com

Yahoo! Answers, answers.yahoo.com

Yahoo! APIs Terms of Use, info.yahoo.com/legal/us/yahoo/api/api-
2140.html

Yahoo! Developer Network, developer.yahoo.com

Yahoo! Developer Network, Creating a REST Request,
developer.yahoo.com/search/rest.html

Yahoo! Developer Network, Developer Registration,
developer.yahoo.com/wsregapp

Yahoo! Developer Network, Yahoo! Answers,
developer.yahoo.com/answers

Yahoo! Developer Network, Yahoo! Answers: Search for Questions,
developer.yahoo.com/answers/V1/questionSearch.html

Yahoo! Developer Network, SDK Software Agreements,
developer.yahoo.com/download/download.html

Yahoo! Pipes, pipes.yahoo.com

Yahoo! Terms of Service, info.yahoo.com/legal/us/yahoo/utos/utos-
173.html

YouTube, www.youtube.com

Chapter 3: Making Your Data Available to Be Mashed Up

Dbpedia, dbpedia.org

Drupal, www.drupal.org

lcsh.info, lcsh.info

Library of Congress Authorities and Vocabularies, id.loc.gov

LibX, libx.org
OpenURL Referrer, openly.oclc.org/openurlref
Operator :: Firefox Add-ons, addons.mozilla.org/en-US/firefox/addon/4106
Wikipedia, www.wikipedia.org
Yahoo! Pipes, pipes.yahoo.com

Chapter 4: Mashing Up With Librarian Knowledge

Biblioteksvar, biblioteksvar.no
Biblioteksvar: English Version, biblioteksvar.no/en
Google, www.google.com
Google Earth, earth.google.com
Knol: A Unit of Knowledge, knol.google.com
Whichbook, www.whichbook.net
Wikipedia, www.wikipedia.org
ønskebok.no, www.onskebok.no

Chapter 5: Information in Context

BookLetters, www.bookletters.com
Delicious, delicious.com
Delicious Registration, secure.delicious.com/register
Delicious, Styling Linkrolls, delicious.com/help/linkrolls
Embeddable Google Books, googlesystem.blogspot.com/2008/09/embeddable-google-books.html
Every Flash Game, www.everyflashgame.com
Feed2JS, www.feed2js.org
flexiPoll, www.flexipoll.com
Flickr, www.flickr.com
Google Book Search, books.google.com
LibraryThing, www.librarything.com
Meebo Me!, www.meebome.com
The Weather Channel, www.weather.com
YouTube, www.youtube.com

Chapter 6: Mashing Up the Library Website

"365 Library Days" Project on Flickr, www.flickr.com/groups/365libs

FeedBurner, www.feedburner.com
Flickr, www.flickr.com
Google Calendar, calendar.google.com
Manchester City (NH) Library, www.manchesterlibrary.org
Manchester City Library's Photostream on Flickr,
    www.flickr.com/photos/manchesterlibrary
New Year's Party & Day One on Flickr, www.flickr.com/photos/
    manchesterlibrary/2159938682
Paul Newman: He Was Part of Our Times,
    manchesterlibrary.org/read/523
WordPress, wordpress.com

Chapter 7: Piping Out Library Data

Cambridge Libraries & Galleries, www.cambridgelibraries.ca
Cambridge Libraries GeoResults, Yahoo! Pipes,
    pipes.yahoo.com/pipes/pipe.info?_id=SrPHCrkv3BGClBN9
    mLokhQ
Flickr, www.flickr.com
LibLime, www.liblime.com
LibLime News, Yahoo! Pipes, pipes.yahoo.com/liblime/news
Library Literature Journals, Yahoo! Pipes,
    pipes.yahoo.com/madinkbeard/NlG6cYgE3BG6qtZJmLokhQ
Library Science in Kansas, Yahoo! Pipes,
    pipes.yahoo.com/nengard/libsciks
NEKLS Search/LibraryThing Covers, Yahoo! Pipes,
    pipes.yahoo.com/nengard/neklscovers
Northeast Kansas Library System NExpress Shared Catalog,
    nekls.kohalibrary.com
Southeast Kansas Library System SEKnFIND Catalog,
    seknfind.kohalibrary.com
The Ultimate Yahoo! Pipes Creations List, ReadWriteWeb, www.read
    writeweb.com/archives/the_ultimate_yahoo_pipes_list.php
Wakefield Library News, Yahoo! Pipes,
    pipes.yahoo.com/pipes/pipe.info?_id=VCj4DCfZ2xGLhaUFE
    pPZnA
Yahoo! Local, local.yahoo.com
Yahoo! Pipes, pipes.yahoo.com
Yahoo! Pipes, About Pipes, blog.pipes.yahoo.net/about-pipes

Chapter 8: Mashups @ Libraries Interact

Aggregate and Share Your Citations, techxplorer.com/projects/
citation-aggregator

Aussie Library Blogs, Libraries Interact, librariesinteract.info/
australian-library-blogs

Blogger, www.blogger.com

Connotea, www.connotea.org

Create a Group Tag Cloud, techxplorer.com/projects/diverse-group-
tag-cloud

Delicious, delicious.com

Google Custom Search, www.google.com/coop/cse

Google Custom Search, Google Linked Custom Search Engines,
www.google.com/coop/docs/cse/cref.html

Libraries Interact, librariesinteract.info

SimplePie, simplepie.org

Turn your Blogroll into a Google CSE,
techxplorer.com/projects/blogroll-google-cse

"whatcha talking 'bout?" version 4!,
www.daveyp.com/blog/archives/146

WordPress, wordpress.org

WordPress Plugin Directory, wordpress.org/extend/plugins

Yahoo! Pipes, pipes.yahoo.com

YouTube, www.youtube.com

Chapter 9: Library Catalog Mashup:
Using Blacklight to Expose Collections

Apache License, Version 2.0, www.apache.org/licenses/LICENSE-
2.0.html

Apache Solr, lucene.apache.org/solr

Blacklight: Project Info, rubyforge.org/projects/blacklight

Encoded Archival Description Version 2002 Official Site,
www.loc.gov/ead

Endeca, www.endeca.com

Facebook, www.facebook.com

Fedora Commons, www.fedora-commons.org

Flickr, www.flickr.com

Google, www.google.com

Google Book Search, books.google.com

Lucene, lucene.apache.org

Netflix, www.netflix.com
NINES, nines.org
Ruby on Rails, www.rubyonrails.org
Solr: Indexing XML with Lucene and REST,
    www.xml.com/pub/a/2006/08/09/solr-indexing-xml-with-
    lucene-andrest.html
Syndetics, www.syndetics.com
Twitter, www.twitter.com
University of Virginia Art Museum Numismatic Collection,
    coins.lib.virginia.edu
University of Virginia Library Subject Guides, guides.lib.virginia.edu
Yahoo! Music, new.music.yahoo.com
Yahoo! Pipes, pipes.yahoo.com

Chapter 10: Breaking Into the OPAC

AquaBrowser, www.aquabrowser.com
Amazon, www.amazon.com
Facebook, www.facebook.com
Google Book Search, books.google.com
Greasemonkey :: Firefox Add-ons, addons.mozilla.org/en-US/
    firefox/addon/748
Library Lookup Project, jonudell.net/librarylookupgenerator.html
LibraryThing, www.librarything.com
LibraryThing for Libraries, www.librarything.com/forlibraries
MySpace, www.myspace.com
The Social OPAC, www.thesocialopac.net
Syndetics, www.syndetics.com
Userscripts.org: Download Greasemonkey Scripts, userscripts.org
Wikipedia, www.wikipedia.org

Chapter 11: Mashing Up Open Data
With ‡biblios.net Web Services

Announcing ‡biblios.net, the World's Largest Database of Freely
    Licensed Library Records, liblime.com/news-items/press-
    releases/announcing-biblios-net-the-worlds-largest-database-
    of-freely-licensed-library-records
"Authority control," Wikipedia,
    en.wikipedia.org/wiki/Authority_control

‡biblios: An Open Source Cataloging Editor, The Code4Lib Journal, journal.code4lib.org/articles/657

‡biblios.net Cataloging Productivity Suite, biblios.net

‡biblios.net Forum, biblios.net/forum

‡biblios.net: Harvesting with OAI-PMH, bws.biblios.net/doku.php/harvesting_with_oai-pmh

‡biblios.net Web Services, bws.biblios.net

‡biblios.org, biblios.org

Example ‡biblios Mashup Code, kados.org/stuff/aggregate_biblios.net_changes.pl

Ext JS, extjs.com

Gmail, www.gmail.com

GNU General Public License, www.gnu.org/copyleft/gpl.html

Google Gears, gears.google.com

Google Maps, maps.google.com

Google Summer of Code, code.google.com/soc

Internet Archive, www.archive.org

LibLime, www.liblime.com

Library of Congress LCCN Permalink, lccn.loc.gov

Open Archives Initiative, www.openarchives.org

Open Data Commons, www.opendatacommons.org

Open Library, openlibrary.org

Talis, www.talis.com

Yahoo! User Interface Library (YUI), developer.yahoo.com/yui

Chapter 12: SOPAC 2.0:
The Thrashable, Mashable Catalog

AADL.org Goes Social, www.blyberg.net/2007/01/21/aadlorg-goes-social

Ann Arbor District Library, www.aadl.org

Ann Arbor District Library Catalog, www.aadl.org/catalog

Drupal, www.drupal.org

Google Book Search, books.google.com

PHP: cURL Library, us3.php.net/curl

PHP: Hypertext Preprocessor, www.php.net

The Social OPAC, www.thesocialopac.net

Sphinx, www.sphinxsearch.com

Chapter 13: Mashups With the WorldCat Affiliate Services

Chapter 14: Flickr and Digital Image Collections

Design Beyond the Interface,
blogs.lib.berkeley.edu/shimenawa.php/2008/04/17/ah_screw_the
_interface

Flickr, www.flickr.com

Flickr API Discussion Group, www.flickr.com/groups/api

Flickr: The Commons, www.flickr.com/commons

Flickr: Machine Tags, www.flickr.com/groups/api/
discuss/72157594497877875

Flickr Services: API Documentation, www.flickr.com/services/api

Ghost in the Machine Tags, adactio.com/journal/1274

jQuery, jquery.com

Machine Tags, last.fm and Rock 'n' Roll,
code.flickr.com/blog/2008/08/28/machine-tags-lastfm-and-
rocknroll

Omeka, www.omeka.org

Playing Catch in the Dark on Flickr, www.flickr.com/
photos/25205574@N03/2557247936

Re-ingesting Flickr Tags from the Commons Back into Our
Collection OPAC,
www.powerhousemuseum.com/dmsblog/index.php/2008/07/25
/re-ingesting-flickr-tags-from-the-commons-back-into-our-
collection-opac

Chapter 15: blip.tv and Digital Video Collections in the Library

blip.tv, blip.tv

blip.tv for Developers, blip.tv/about/api

Codes and Files, Jason A. Clark,
www.lib.montana.edu/~jason/files.php

Google Reader, google.com/reader

iTunes, www.apple.com/itunes

"Lazy Sunday," Wikipedia, en.wikipedia.org/wiki/Lazy_Sunday

Raw XML from blip.tv for TERRApod, www.blip.tv/post/?user=
terrapoduser&pagelen=20&file_type=blu&skin=rss

TERRApod, www.terrapodcast.com

terrapod on blip.tv, terrapod.blip.tv

Yahoo!, www.yahoo.com

YouTube, www.youtube.com

Chapter 16: "Where's the Nearest Computer Lab?" Mapping Up Campus

craigslist, www.craigslist.org
Exhibit 2.0, simile.mit.edu/wiki/Exhibit
Exhibit 2.0: Creating, Importing, and Managing Data,
    simile.mit.edu/wiki/Exhibit/Creating%2C_Importing%2C_and_
    Managing_Data
Exhibit 2.0: Map View, simile.mit.edu/wiki/Exhibit/2.0/Map_View
Firebug, getfirebug.com
geocoder.us, geocoder.us
Google Maps, maps.google.com
Google Maps API, code.google.com/apis/maps
HousingMaps, www.housingmaps.com
SIMILE, simile.mit.edu
SIMILE: Babel, simile.mit.edu/babel
SIMILE: Exhibit, simile.mit.edu/exhibit
Yelp, www.yelp.com

Chapter 17: The Repository Mashup Map

Amazon.com, www.amazon.com
Bing, www.bing.com
Bing Maps, microsoft.com/maps
Example OAI-PMH response from CADAIR #1,
    cadair.aber.ac.uk/dspace-oai/request?verb=Identify
Example OAI-PMH response from CADAIR #2,
    cadair.aber.ac.uk/dspace-oai/request?verb=ListSets
Example OAI-PMH response from CADAIR #3,
    cadair.aber.ac.uk/dspace-oai/request?verb=ListMetadataFormats
Example OAI-PMH response from CADAIR #4,
    cadair.aber.ac.uk/dspace-oai/request?verb=ListRecords&
    metadataPrefix=oai_dc
Google Chart API: Developer's Guide, code.google.com/apis/chart
Google Maps, maps.google.com
Google Maps API, code.google.com/apis/maps
Google Scholar, scholar.google.com
Hostip.info, www.hostip.info
Intute Repository Search, www.intute.ac.uk/irs
"Logarithmic scale," Wikipedia,
    en.wikipedia.org/wiki/Logarithmic_scale

OAIster, www.oaister.org

OpenDOAR (Directory of Open Access Repositories), www.open
doar.org

OpenDOAR: Application Programmers' Interface (API), www.open
doar.org/tools/api.html

OpenDOAR: Download All, www.opendoar.org/api.php?all=y

OpenDOAR: New Zealand Search,
www.opendoar.org/api.php?co=nz

Repository Maps, maps.repository66.org

ROAR (Registry of Open Access Repositories), roar.eprints.org

ROAR: Complete List, roar.eprints.org/index.php?action=rawlist

ROAR: OAI-PMH Response, roar.eprints.org/oai.php?
verb=ListRecords&metadataPrefix=oai_dc

SHERPA, www.sherpa.ac.uk

SHERPA: JULIET, www.sherpa.ac.uk/juliet

"Venn diagram," Wikipedia, en.wikipedia.org/wiki/Venn_diagram

WordPress, wordpress.org

Yahoo! Maps Web Services, developer.yahoo.com/maps

Chapter 18: The LibraryThing API and Libraries

Amazon, www.amazon.com

CodexMap, codexmap.com/codexmap.php

Library Labs, www.nla.gov.au/library-labs

LibraryThing, www.librarything.com

LibraryThing: About LibraryThing, www.librarything.com/about

LibraryThing: Common Knowledge, www.librarything.com/
commonknowledge

LibraryThing: Developer Profile,
www.librarything.com/services/keys.php

LibraryThing: Groups, www.librarything.com/groups

LibraryThing: JSON API, www.librarything.com/api/json.php

LibraryThing: JSON Books API, www.librarything.com/wiki/
index.php/LibraryThing_JSON_Books_API

LibraryThing Blog, www.librarything.com/blog

LibraryThing Blog: A Million Free Covers from LibraryThing,
www.librarything.com/blog/2008/08/million-free-covers-from-
librarything.php

LibraryThing for Libraries, www.librarything.com/forlibraries

ProgrammableWeb, www.programmableweb.com

Send It to Me, dewey.library.nd.edu/hacks/send
WorldCat Wordpress Widget, www.librarywebchic.net/
   wordpress/218/worldcat-wordpress-widget

Chapter 19: ZACK Bookmaps

Amazon, www.amazon.com
Google Book Search, books.google.com
Google Custom Search Engine, www.google.com/coop/cse
Google Maps, maps.google.com
YAZ, www.indexdata.dk/yaz
Z39.50 Search Targets, z3950.intute.ac.uk
ZACK, opus.tu-bs.de/zack
ZACK Bookmaps, opus.tu-bs.de/zack/bookmaps.html
ZACK Live Search, opus.tu-bs.de/zack/cgi/livesearch
ZACK Search Plug-ins for Firefox and IE7, opus.tu-
   bs.de/zack/opensearch.html

Chapter 20: Federated Database Search Mashup

HowStuffWorks, www.howstuffworks.com
Index Data: pazpar2, indexdata.com/pazpar2
KnowItNow, www.knowitnow.org
NetWellness, www.netwellness.org
OAIster, www.oaister.org
Project Gutenberg, www.gutenberg.org
Wikipedia, www.wikipedia.org

Chapter 21: Electronic Dissertation
Mashups Using SRU

CQL: Contextual Query Language,
   www.loc.gov/standards/sru/specs/cql.html
DCMI Metadata Terms, dublincore.org/documents/dcmi-terms
How I Explained REST to My Wife, tomayko.com/writings/rest-to-
   my-wife
INDURE, www.indure.org
An Introduction to the Search/Retrieve URL Service (SRU), www.
   ariadne.ac.uk/issue40/morgan
Purdue e-Pubs, docs.lib.purdue.edu

Purdue e-Pubs Doctoral Dissertations, docs.lib.purdue.edu/
dissertations
Search/Retrieve Via URL Editorial Board,
www.loc.gov/standards/sru/specs
Stylus Studio, www.stylusstudio.com
XML Schema for Dublin Core,
www.openarchives.org/OAI/2.0/oai_dc.xsd
XML Tutorial, www.w3schools.com/xml/default.asp
XSL Transformations (XSLT), www.w3.org/TR/xslt

Glossary

Ajax. Asynchronous JavaScript and XML. Programming language comprised of JavaScript and XML that is used for creating dynamic web applications.

API. Application Programming Interface. Spells out how to formulate a query for the data from a web service.

ATS. Author, title, and subject. Defines a basic subset of services for Z39.50 support of public access library catalogs. The ATS requires support for only three search attributes—author, title, and subject—and mandates support for MARC record data transfer.

badge. A term used by some services that refers to a snippet of code that pulls data from one site for you to include on another. With Flickr, this is a way to add your images to your website, and with Yahoo! Pipes, it's a way to add your pipe content to your site.

bookmarklet. A JavaScript function or set of functions saved to the browser as bookmarks or favorites.

browser-side programming. *see* client-side programming.

client-side programming. Computer programs that are executed client-side, by the web browser. Also known as browser-side programming.

cloud computing. *see* internet cloud.

CMS. Content Management System. A software package used to manage an entire website.

COinS. Context Objects in Spans. Developed as a way to incorporate citation information inside HTML pages to send to a user's OpenURL link resolver without prior knowledge of the user's institutional affiliation.

CQL. Contextual Query Language. A standard language for representing queries in a human readable format to information retrieval systems such as search engines and library catalogs. CQL was known as Common Query Language in past versions of SRU.

CSS. Cascading Style Sheets. Used to define the look and feel for HTML elements.

CSV. Comma Separated Values. A text file in which each value is separated by a comma. Can also be used to refer to other text delimited files.

cURL. Client URL Library. A library of functions that can be used within PHP and allows you to connect and communicate with many types of servers with many types of protocols.

DOM. Document Object Model. An API for HTML and XML documents that defines a logical structure of documents and rules for accessing and manipulating those files.

Dublin Core. A metadata schema made up of 15 elements that offer expanded cataloging information. Dublin Core was created out of a cooperative venture involving academic institutions.

eRDF. Embedded RDF. The syntax for writing HTML so that the information in the document can be extracted into RDF.

ETDs. Electronic theses and dissertations.

geocoding. Converting an address (typically a street address, city name, or ZIP code or postcode) to map coordinates.

Greasemonky scripts. Work like bookmarklets, but without the clicking. Instead, JavaScript can work its magic on every page by default, without any special action on the user's part. To use these scripts, you must first have a plug-in installed into the Firefox browser and then the script enabled.

hAtom. Microformat that provides a means to embed the Atom Syndication Protocol into HTML pages.

hCalendar. Microformat for sharing calendar data.

hCard. Microformat based on the internet standard for contact information, vCard.

hResume. Microformat for sharing resume data.

HTML. HyperText Markup Language. A programming language used to format and display information for human beings, to be read as web pages in a web browser.

HTTP. HyperText Transfer Protocol. The protocol used to transfer information and retrieve information over the web.

iCal. A file format that allows users to send meeting requests and tasks via email or by sharing files with an .ics extension.

IFRAME. Inline Frame. Allows a page to set aside a part of itself—a rectangle—and load a separate page within that area. If the "parent" page and the IFRAME page have the same background color, the effect can be seamless.

internet cloud. Also referred to as cloud computing. Refers to computations that take place over the network, usually the internet. An example of cloud computing would be Google Apps, in which all the editing and storing of data occur over the internet.

IP. Internet Protocol. The protocol that allows for transferring information between networks.

JSON. JavaScript Object Notation. A text-based, human-readable format use for representing simple data structures and arrays. Many web services make their data available in JSON format.

MARC. MAchine-Readable Cataloging. The standard used by catalogers to represent bibliographic and related information in machine-readable form.

mashup. A web application that uses content from more than one source to create a single new service displayed in a single graphical interface. The term originally comes from pop music, in which people seamlessly combine music from one song with the vocal track from another, thereby mashing them together to create something new.

metadata. Data that describes data.

microformats. Abbreviated as mF or uF. A set of simple, open data formats built on existing and widely adopted standards that allow expression of semantics in HTML (or XHTML).

NISO. National Information Standards Organization. Provides information standards that libraries, publishers, and developers can use to easily share data and communicate with each other.

OAI-PMH. Open Archives Initiative Protocol for Metadata Harvesting. A protocol used to gather metadata from records in an archive.

OPAC. Online Public Access Catalog. Common name for a library's catalog as it is viewed on the web.

OpenURL. A type of web address used to create web-transportable parcels of metadata about an object. It was designed to support linking from journal databases to library cataloging systems.

percent encoding. Also known as URL encoding. A technique used to convert special characters in a URL to a valid format. For example, the space between words in compound terms like "solar energy" should be encoded as %20 ("solar%20energy").

PHP. An open source programming language.

pipes. A term used by the Yahoo! Pipes mashup builder that refers to the linking together of multiple web services or RSS feeds to create a new output.

plug-in. A snippet of code that can be plugged into an existing application to add additional features and functionality that the original developers didn't include.

POSH. Plain Old Semantic HTML.

RDF. Resource Description Framework. A means to model information on the web by assigning resources unique identifiers (generally by use of a URI) and describing the relationships between that resource and other resources via a structure known as *triples*.

RDFa. Resource Description Framework Attributes. The addition of nonstandard attributes to HTML tags to help define the RDF triples.

REST. REpresentational State Transfer. The simplest, and thus by far the most used, protocol in the creation of mashups. A series of principles that explain how resources are defined and addressed.

RESTafarians. Fans of REST.

RSS. Really Simple Syndication. A way of delivering website updates in XML.

screen scraper. Uses a page's HTML and CSS tags as hooks to identify the desired information resources to return for processing by some other program.

screen scraping. Extracting information intended exclusively for human consumption from the web page and sending it as input to a computer program known as a screen scraper. This method can be used to gather information from sites that do not provide readily available APIs to their data.

server-side programming. A technology in which scripts are run directly on the web server in order to generate dynamic web pages.

service consumer. Someone who makes use of the information or the services provided via a web service.

service provider. Application that makes certain information available or that provides the capability to perform certain operations.

shortcode. Similar to an HTML tag. Used to integrate a plug-in with the generation of a page or post in the WordPress system. When a shortcode is encountered, the plug-in associated with that shortcode is activated, and the results of the plug-in's execution will replace the shortcode in the page or post.

SOAP. Originally stood for Simple Object Access Protocol, a definition that is no longer used. Relies on international standards and protocols and has been adopted primarily in the enterprise world. SOAP uses HTTP as the transport protocol for exchanging information, but it requires that both the requests sent by the service consumer and the answers returned by the service provider be wrapped in an XML envelope.

SOPAC. The Social OPAC. An open source social discovery platform for bibliographic data.

SQL. Structured Query Language. A language used to query data found in databases.

SRU. Search and Retrieve URL Service. An XML-focused search protocol for internet search queries. SRU is an open standard that has evolved from the popular Z39.50 protocol that has been widely adopted by libraries and supported by software such as citation managers and federated search engines.

SRW. Search and Retrieve Web Service. Provides a SOAP interface to queries, to augment the URL interface provided by its companion protocol SRU.

TOS. Terms of Service.

triples. Maps to the mental picture of a subject, predicate, and object phrase, where the subject is the URI of the resource in question, the predicate is an attribute defined in a controlled RDF vocabulary, and the object is either another URI (therefore establishing the relationship between two unique resources) or what is called a literal (such as a string or number, which defines the actual value of a property associated with a given resource).

tweet. A message sent via Twitter.

unAPI. A specification to enable cut and paste of metadata on the web.

URI. Uniform Resource Identifier. A string of letters, numbers, and symbols used to identify or name a resource on the internet. A URL is an example of a URI.

URL. Uniform Resource Locator. The address of a page on the internet.

URL encoding. *see* percent encoding.

vCard. The internet standard for contact information commonly seen in people's email signature files, attached with a .vcf extension.

web service. A technology that enables information and communication exchange between different applications. Web services are based on a conceptual model that has a *service provider*, which is an application that makes certain information available or that provides the capability to perform certain operations, and a *service consumer*, which will make use of the information or the services.

WYSIWYG. What You See Is What You Get. A graphical editor that makes editing web pages easy by removing the need to know HTML.

XML. eXtensible Markup Language. A markup language for expressing and transporting structured data, and as its name implies, is extensible in that users can define their own elements.

XSLT. XML Stylesheet Language Transformation. Acts as a template for processing the data from one document and reconstituting it into another.

Z39.50. An established client-server protocol for searching and retrieving information.

About the Contributors

Derik A. Badman is the digital services librarian at Temple University in Philadelphia, Pennsylvania. He was an American Library Association Emerging Leader for 2008 and has been working in libraries nonstop since he was 16. His comics criticism and webcomic can be found at madinkbeard.com. Email Derik at dbadman@temple.edu.

Bonaria Biancu works for the Library of the University of Milano-Bicocca, in Milan (Italy), managing the website, the digital library, and the university's open archive. She is the author of the blog The Geek Librarian and the social network Biblioteca 2.0. She holds courses on Web 2.0 and Library 2.0 and has attended numerous conferences and seminars. Email Bonaria at bonariabiancu@gmail.com.

John Blyberg is the assistant director for innovation and user experience at the Darien Library in Connecticut. John was named a *Library Journal* Mover and Shaker and took first prize in Talis' Mashing-Up the Library competition. He is an open source software advocate and considers unfettered collaboration and participation the primary intent of information technology. To that end, he has authored a number of open source projects, including SOPAC. Email John at john@blyberg.net.

Thomas Brevik is head librarian at the Royal Norwegian Naval Academy and former president of the Norwegian Library Association Special Interest Group for Information and Communication Technology (SIKT). He is the father of two, blogger, twitterer, enthusiast for all things shiny and new but also very fond of library history and learning from the past. Email Thomas at thomas.brevik@gmail.com.

Jason A. Clark builds digital library applications and sets digital content strategies for Montana State University Libraries. When he's not thinking about APIs, Jason likes to hike the mountains of Montana with his wife, Jennifer, his daughter, Piper, and his dog, Oakley. You can follow his occasional thoughts about library digital stuff at diginit.wordpress.com. Email Jason at jaclark@montana.edu.

Karen A. Coombs serves as the head of web services at the University of Houston Libraries. Karen has presented at many national conferences and written numerous articles. With Jason Griffey, she is the coauthor of the book *Library Blogging*. She is the author of the Library Web Chic weblog. Email Karen at librarywebchic@gmail.com.

Mark Dahl is associate director for digital initiatives and collection management at Watzek Library, Lewis & Clark College, in Portland, Oregon. He lives in Portland with his wife, son, and dog, Charlie. Email Mark at dahl@lclark.edu.

Joshua Ferraro is the founding CEO of LibLime. He has been promoting open source in libraries since 2001, when he oversaw implementation of Koha at the first library system in the U.S. to adopt an open source integrated library system. In 2008, he was recognized in *Library Journal* as a Mover and Shaker for his work promoting open source in libraries. Email Joshua at jmf@liblime.com.

Darlene Fichter is the data librarian and adviser on emerging technologies at the University of Saskatchewan Library. Darlene is interested in new media, social software, human computer interaction, and experience design. She is a consultant, project manager, writer, and speaker about new and emerging technologies and libraries. Email Darlene at darlene.fichter@usask.ca.

Joseph Gilbert is the scholars' lab coordinator for the University of Virginia Library. Joseph collaborates with teaching faculty and graduate students on digital projects in the humanities and social sciences and coordinates various outreach events as well as the library's graduate fellowship program in digital humanities. Email Joseph at joegilbert@virginia.edu.

Robin Hastings, the information technology manager at the Missouri River Regional Library, frequently presents at conferences all over the world and writes about Web 2.0 technologies, mashups, and the upcoming Web 3.0 possibilities. Email Robin at robin.hastings@gmail.com.

Stephen Hedges has served as executive director of the Ohio Public Library Information Network since April 2006. He came to OPLIN from the Nelsonville Public Library system in Athens County, Ohio, where he had served as director since 1997. Stephen is the coauthor of the book *Best in the Nation: The First Two Hundred Years of Ohio Libraries.* Email Stephen at hedgesst@oplin.org.

Brian Herzog started out part-time in a library in Maine and then earned his MLIS from Kent State University. He is currently the head of reference at the Chelmsford Public Library in Massachusetts. He has been known to read a lot, knit, bike, hike, and kayak. Find Brian at www.swissarmylibrarian.net.

Karl Jendretzky has been with OPLIN since January 2006. Originally hired as a support tech, he was fresh out of DeVry University, where he obtained a BS in computer information systems. He has now moved into the position of technology project manager and oversees all things technical at OPLIN. Email Karl at jendreka@oplin.org.

Stuart Lewis is a developer at the University of Auckland Library (he formerly worked at Aberystwyth University), a committer with the open source DSpace repository platform, and the creator of the maps.repository66.org mashup site. He is married to Lauren and has two fun young kids, Jacob and Lily. Email Stuart at stuart@stuart lewis.com.

Jeremy McWilliams is the digital services coordinator at Watzek Library, Lewis & Clark College, in Portland, Oregon. He lives in Lake Oswego, Oregon, with his wife, two sons, and dog, Stella. Email Jeremy at jeremy2443@gmail.com.

Matt Mitchell is a part of the research and development team at the University of Virginia Library, where he works as a web application developer and systems programmer. While Matt strives daily to become a professional Ruby ninja, some of his personal interests include music synthesis and recording. Email Matt at mwm4n@ virginia.edu.

Lichen Rancourt is the head of technology at Manchester City Library, Manchester, New Hampshire; the author of remaining relevant.net, a library-focused blog; and contributor to Scriblio, an open source tool for online library collections. She believes that librarians have an essential role to play in the information age by providing context and expertise to the wild information frontier of the internet. Email Lichen at lichentherelevant@gmail.com.

Bess Sadler is the research and development librarian at the University of Virginia Library. In addition to her core duties assisting university faculty with programming support for their research, she conducts research in the areas of interface design, knowledge representation, information behavior, and usability. She is a passionate supporter of open source software, open access publishing, open data, and community developed technology solutions. Email Bess at bess@virginia.edu.

Wolfram Schneider is a software developer in Berlin, Germany. He studied computer science at the Berlin University of Technology and specializes in search engines, catalog enrichment, and data mining. Wolfram is also a developer at the FreeBSD Project, a Unix-like free operating system. He enjoys traveling and long bicycle tours. Find Wolfram at wolfram.schneider.org or email him at wosch@freebsd.org.

Ross Singer is interoperability and open standards champion for Talis. Previously, he has worked as an application developer for the Georgia Tech Library, Emory University Libraries, and the University of Tennessee Libraries. Ross is currently based in Chattanooga, Tennessee. His blog is dilettantes.code4lib.org. Email Ross at rossfsinger@gmail.com.

Laura Solomon has been the library services manager for OPLIN since February 2008 and is the former web applications manager for Cleveland Public Library. She has been doing web development and design for more than 10 years, both in libraries and as an independent consultant. Email Laura at laura@oplin.org.

Tim Spalding is the founder of LibraryThing.com, a social networking and "social cataloging" site for booklovers. Since 2005, LibraryThing's 600,000 registered members have added more than 36 million books. Before LibraryThing, Tim worked for the publisher Houghton Mifflin in Boston. He lives in Portland, Maine. Email Tim at tim@librarything.com.

Corey Wallis currently works in the Office of Research at Flinders University as a project manager. His role also involves web development and managing the university's WordPress MU installations. He has held a variety of positions in libraries and has been part of the Libraries Interact group since mid-2006. Email Corey at corey@tech xplorer.com.

Michael C. Witt is the interdisciplinary research librarian and an assistant professor of library science at the Purdue University Libraries and its Distributed Data Curation Center (D2C2). His research interests lie at the intersection of computer science and library science in the development and application of new technologies to preserve and improve access to information. Email Michael at mwitt@purdue.edu.

About the Editor

Nicole C. Engard is the Open Source Evangelist at LibLime, where she directs the company's open source education endeavors. In addition to her daily responsibilities, Nicole has been published in several library journals and keeps the library community up to date on web technologies via her website "What I Learned Today …" (www.web2learning.net).

Nicole's interest in library technology started at the Jenkins Law Library in Philadelphia, where she worked as the Web Manager. In addition to her web development experiences, Nicole has worked as a Metadata Librarian and librarian trainer. For her innovative uses of technology in libraries, Nicole was named one of *Library Journal's* Movers & Shakers in 2007.

Nicole received her BA in Literary Studies and Computer Programming from Juniata College in Huntingdon, Pennsylvania, and her MLIS from Drexel University in Philadelphia, Pennsylvania. She is also an active member of the Special Libraries Association (SLA) as the chair of the SLA-IT Blogging Section and the Webmaster for the Greater Philadelphia Law Library Association.

Some of Nicole's previous publications include articles in *Computers in Libraries, ONLINE Magazine,* and *Journal of Hospital Librarianship.* She has also written chapters for *Thinking Outside the Book: Essays for Innovative Librarians* and *Writing and Publishing: The Librarian's Handbook,* both edited by Carol Smallwood.

You can reach Nicole via email at nengard@gmail.com.

Index

Italicized page references indicate figures and illustrations. Tables are indicated using "t" following the page number.

Blacklight
additional services provided
with, 121–123, *122*
benefits of, 115–116
description, 113–114
digital objects and searchability,
117
digital scholarship access,
118–120, *120*
goals, 116
music library records using,
125–126
as a OPAC mashup, 114–115
record examples, *127*
usage example, 123–125
blip.tv, 195–203
blocks, 161–162
Blogroll to Google Custom Search
Engine, 99–103, *101*
blogs
cooperative librarian (*see*
Libraries Interact)
on LibraryThing key instructions,
244–245
for LibraryThings, 252
for library websites, *82*, 82–84
lists for Australian library, 99–100
platforms for, 82, 98–99
for repository maps, 238
Blyberg, John, 24, 132
Book Burro, 14, *14*
book covers
carousels for, 10
OPAC break ins and adding,
134–135
search services for, 121
sources for, 172
walls for, 11, *12*, 13, *13*
ZACK search options for, 260, *261*
BookLetters, 60–61, *61*
bookmaps, 259, *260*
Bookmaps API, 256
bookmarklets, 41
bookmark plug-ins, 103–106, *106*
Bookr, 6
Books Most Wanted, 251
book suggestion services, 60–61, *61*
book talks, digital, 52

Brantley, Peter, 193
browser buttons, 67–68, *68*
browser (client) filtering, 231
browser-side programming, 133–134
Bumgardner, Jim, 4
BWS, 146, 150

C

calendars, 84–86, *85*
Cambridge Libraries, 94
CARE Affiliates, 271
catalogs. *See also* ábiblios.net;
OPACs; SOPAC; WorldCat
Search API
authority control and, 147
availability and holdings, 121
book cover search services, 121
as closed systems, 129
digital scholarship accessibility,
117–120, *120*
hidden collection accessibility,
116–117
mashup benefits to, 115–116
mashups enhancing, 9–10, *10*
music libraries and, 125–126
open, user-driven interfaces,
importance of, 126–127
open source data and improvements to, 114–115
RSS of filtered search, *122*,
122–123
short book searches, 11, *12*
URIs for items and searches, 121
user tags, 122
censorship of objectionable content, 70
charting services, 236–237
Citation Aggregator, 103–106, *106*
client (browser) filtering, 231
Client URL Library (cURL), 153–154
CMSs (content management systems), 44
Code4Lib Journal, The, 145
CodexMap, 251, *251*
COinS (Context Objects in Spans),
45–46, *46*, 47, 172
Collex, 114–115
Colr Pickr, 4, 6

commercial licensing, 7, 20
Computers in Libraries (Fagan), 87
confidentiality, 15–16
Connotea, 104
consumers, 8
CONTENTdm, 181
content management systems
(CMSs), 44
context, information in *vs.* out of,
60–61
Context Objects in Spans (COinS),
45–46, *46*, 47, 172
Contextual Query Language (CQL),
281
Cooliris, 189
Coombs, Karen, 250
Cooperative Library Network Berlin-
Brandenburg, 253–254
copyright, 14, 20
CQL (Contextual Query Language),
281
Creative Commons License, 188
creators, 8
credibility issues, 16
CSEs (Custom Search Engines),
100–103, *102*, 267–269
cURL (Client URL Library), 153–154

D
Dapper, 31
data source authority, 229, *230*
DBpedia, 43–44
DC (Dublin Core), 281
Delicious, 64–70, *66*, *67*, *68*, 104
digital objects, 116–117, *118*
digital scholarship, 117–120, *120*
Directory of Open Access
Repositories (DOAR), Open,
222–223, 224, 228
disclosure issues, 15–16
dissertation mashups
collection development, 280–282
overview of importance, 277–279
types and uses of, 282–287, *283*,
284, *285*, *286*, *287*
Diverse Group Tag Cloud, 107–109,
108
document object models (DOMs),
136–137

dots for map locations, 233–234,
234, *235*
Drupal, 49, 153, 161–162
Dublin Core (DC), 281

E
EBSCO, 268, 273
editors, 30–31. *See also* ábiblios.net
educational applications, 191–194
email notifications, 85
embedded content
digital audio, 117
drawbacks of, 70–71
ideas for, overview, 65t
photographs, 63, *77*, 77–79, *78*, *79*
RSS feeds for streaming, 63
subject guides, 64–70, *66*, *67*, *68*
subscription-based services,
60–62, *61*
text of books, 64
videos, *62*, 62–63, 117
Endeca system, 114
eRDF (Embedded RDF), 42
EVDB, 6
Exhibit, 207
EZproxy, 274

F
faculty profiles, 284–285, *285*
Fagan, Jody Condit, 87
FCKEditor, 170–171
federated search mashups
development and alterations,
267–276, *274*, *275*, *276*
functions of, 265–266
problems addressed, 266–267
Fedora objects, 115
FeedBurner, 82–83
Feedreader, 27
feeds
blogs using, 82–83
as embedded content type, 63,
65t
mashup technology using, 7, 11,
13, 26–27, 30
merging, using pipes, 88–89, *89*,
90, *91*